An **AB**e**C**e**D**arian of Animal Spirit Guides

Spiritual Growth through Reflections on Creatures

Mark G. Boyer

WIPF & STOCK · Eugene, Oregon

AN ABECEDARIAN OF ANIMAL SPIRIT GUIDES
Spiritual Growth through Reflections on Creatures

Copyright © 2016 Mark G. Boyer. All rights reserved. Except for brief quotations in critical publications or reviews, no part of this book may be reproduced in any manner without prior written permission from the publisher. Write: Permissions, Wipf and Stock Publishers, 199 W. 8th Ave., Suite 3, Eugene, OR 97401.

Wipf & Stock
An Imprint of Wipf and Stock Publishers
199 W. 8th Ave., Suite 3
Eugene, OR 97401

www.wipfandstock.com

PAPERBACK ISBN 13: 978-1-4982-3792-5
HARDCOVER ISBN 13: 978-1-4982-3794-9

Manufactured in the U.S.A.   03/01/2016

An **AB**e**C**e**D**arian
of Animal Spirit Guides

Dedicated to the Kosslers:
John, Amy, Ethan, Jacob

"Praise the LORD from the earth,
You sea monsters and all deeps....
Wild animals and all cattle,
Creeping things and flying birds!
Let them praise the name of the LORD,
For his name alone is exalted;
His glory is above earth and heaven."

(Ps 148:7, 10, 13)

"... [A]sk the animals, and they will teach you;
the birds of the air, and they will tell you;
... and the fish of the sea will declare to you.
Who among all these does not know
that the hand of the LORD has done this?
In his hand is the life of every living thing
and the breath of every human being."

(Job 12:7, 8b–10)

"Ever since the creation of the world
[God's] eternal power and divine nature, invisible though they are,
have been understood and seen through the things he has made."

(Rom 1:20)

"The Master said,...
[T]he songs... will widen your acquaintance
with the names of birds, beasts, plants, and trees."

(*Analects* 17:9)

"Commendable is the taming
Of mind, which is hard to hold down,
Nimble, alighting wherever it wants.
Mind subdued brings ease."

(*Dhp* 3:35)

"There is not a creature that moves on the earth
whose nourishment is not provided by God,
whose place of sojourning and depositing
is not known to him.
All things conform to a manifest law."

(*Quran* 11:6)

"[The dawn], stirring up the world, has shown us riches;
dawn has awakened every living creature.
Rich dawn, she sets afoot the coiled-up sleeper,
One for enjoyment, one for wealth or worship.
Those who saw little for extended vision.
All living creatures has the dawn awakened.
One to high sway, one to exalted glory,
one to pursue his gain, and one his labor;
all to regard their different vocations,
all moving creatures has the dawn awakened."

(*RV* 1:113:4b–6)

Contents

Abbreviations | xi
Notes on Sacred Texts | xv
Introduction | xix

Ass (Donkey) | 1
Bear | 6
Bee | 10
Camel | 16
Dog | 20
Dove (Turtledove) | 29
Eagle | 33
Elephant | 39
Fox | 44
Goat | 50
Hedgehog | 58
Ibex | 63
Jackal | 65
Kudu (Antelope) | 68
Leviathan (Behemoth, Rahab, Dragon) | 70
Lion | 81
Mule Deer | 91
Nighthawk | 97
Owl | 100
Partridge | 104
Quarter Horse | 107
Raven | 122

Rooster (Cock) | 132
Serpent (Snake) | 138
Sheep (Ram, Ewe, Lamb) | 152
Tadpole (Frog) | 169
Turtle (Tortoise) | 178
Unicorn | 184
Vulture | 188
Wolf | 191
Yak (Ox) | 209
Zebu (Cattle, Bull, Cow, Steer, Heifer, Calf) | 221

Bibliography | 247
Other Books by Mark G. Boyer | 251

Abbreviations

Aesop = *Aesop's Fables*
Analects = *The Analects of Confucius*

CB (NT) = Christian Bible (New Testament)
1 Cor = First Letter of Paul to the Corinthians
2 Cor = Second Letter of Paul to the Corinthians
Heb = Letter to the Hebrews
John = John's Gospel
Luke = Luke's Gospel
Mark = Mark's Gospel
Matt = Matthew's Gospel
1 Pet = First Letter of Peter
2 Pet = Second Letter of Peter
Phil = Letter of Paul to the Philippians
Rev = Revelation
Rom = Letter of Paul to the Romans
2 Tim = Second Letter of Paul to Timothy

Dhp = *The Dhammapada*
D&C = *The Book of Doctrine and Covenants*
Grimm = *Grimm's Complete Fairy Tales*

HB (OT) = Hebrew Bible (Old Testament)
Amos = Amos
1 Chr = First Book of Chronicles

2 Chr = Second Book of Chronicles
Dan = Daniel
Deut = Deuteronomy
Eccl = Ecclesiastes
Esth = Esther
Exod = Exodus
Ezek = Ezekiel
Ezra = Ezra
Gen = Genesis
Hab = Habakkuk
Hos = Hosea
Isa = Isaiah
Jer = Jeremiah
Job = Job
Joel = Joel
Jonah = Jonah
Josh = Joshua
Judg = Judges
1 Kgs = First Book of Kings
2 Kgs = Second Book of Kings
Lam = Lamentations
Lev = Leviticus
Mal = Malachi
Mic = Micah
Nah = Nahum
Neh = Nehemiah
Num = Numbers
Obad = Obadiah
Prov = Proverbs
Ps = Psalm
1 Sam = First Book of Samuel
2 Sam = Second Book of Samuel
Zech = Zechariah
Zeph = Zephaniah

Mormon = **The Book of Mormon**
Alma = Alma
Enos = Enos
Ether = Ether
Hel = Helman
Mosiah = Mosiah
Morm = Mormon
1 Ne = First Book of Nephi
2 Ne = Second Book of Nephi
3 Ne = Third Book of Nephi

OT (A) = Old Testament (Apocrypha)
Bar = Baruch
Jdt = Judith
1 Macc = First Book of Maccabees
2 Macc = Second Book of Maccabees
4 Macc = Fourth Book of Maccabees
Sir = Sirach (Ecclesiasticus)
Tob = Book of Tobit
Wis = Wisdom (of Solomon)

Quran = *The Quran*
RV = *The Rig Veda*

Notes on Sacred Texts

The Analects of Confucius

The Analects of Confucius contains twenty numbered books. In notating texts from this book, abbreviated *Analects*, the first number refers to the book, and the second number refers to the paragraph within the book. Thus, *Analects* 13:19 means that the quotation comes from book 13, paragraph 19.

The Bible

The Bible is divided into two parts: The Hebrew Bible (Old Testament) and the Christian Bible (New Testament). The Hebrew Bible consists of thirty-nine named books accepted by Jews and Protestants as Holy Scripture. The Old Testament also contains those thirty-nine books plus seven to fifteen more named books or parts of books called the Apocrypha or the Deutero-canonical Books; the Old Testament is accepted by Catholics and several other Christian denominations as Holy Scripture. The Christian Bible, consisting of twenty-seven named books, is also called the New Testament; it is accepted by Christians as Holy Scripture. Thus, in this work:

— Hebrew Bible (Old Testament), abbreviated HB (OT), indicates that a book is found both in the Hebrew Bible and the Old Testament;

— Old Testament (Apocrypha), abbreviated OT (A), indicates that a book is found only in the Old Testament Apocrypha and not in the Hebrew Bible;

— and Christian Bible (New Testament), abbreviated CB (NT), indicates that a book is found only in the Christian Bible or New Testament.

Unless otherwise noted, the *New Revised Standard Version* (NRSV) of the Bible is used throughout this work.

In notating biblical texts, the first number refers to the chapter in the book, and the second number refers to the verse within the chapter. Thus, HB (OT) Isa 7:11 means that the quotation comes from Isaiah, chapter 7, verse 11. OT (A) Sirach 39:30 means that the quotation comes from Sirach, chapter 39, verse 30. CB (NT) Mark 6:2 means that the quotation comes from Mark's Gospel, chapter 6, verse 2.

Book of Doctrine and Covenants

The *Book of Doctrine and Covenants* contains 140 numbered and named sections, each of which is subdivided into numbered paragraphs. In notating texts from this book, abbreviated *D&C*, the first number refers to the section in the book, and the second number refers to the paragraph within the section. Thus, *D&C* 12:1 means that the quotation comes from the *Book of Doctrine and Covenants*, section 12, paragraph 1.

The Book of Mormon

The Book of Mormon contains fifteen named books. In notating texts from this book, abbreviated *Mormon*, the first number refers to the chapter in the named book, and the second number refers to the verse within the chapter. Thus, 1 Ne 6:9 means that the quotation comes from the First Book of Nephi, chapter 6, verse 9.

The Dhammapada

The Dhammapada contains twenty-six named chapters, each of which is subdivided into 423 continuously numbered paragraphs. In notating texts from this book, abbreviated *Dhp*, the first number refers to the chapter, and the second number refers to the paragraph within the chapter. Thus, 26:383 means that the quotation comes from chapter 26, paragraph 383.

The Quran

The Quran contains 114 numbered and named books. In notating texts from this book, abbreviated *Quran*, the first number refers to the book, and the second number refers to the verse within the book. Thus, 23:34 means that the quotation comes from book 23, verse 34.

The Rig Veda

The Rig Veda contains ten numbered books, each of which is subdivided into numbered hymns, and each hymn is subdivided into numbered verses. In notating texts from this book, abbreviated *RV*, the first number refers to the book, the second number refers to the hymn within the book, and the third number refers to the verse within the hymn. Thus, 3:30:4 means that the quotation comes from book 3, hymn 30, verse 4.

Introduction

Title of Book

This book is titled *An Abecedarian of Animal Spirit Guides: Spiritual Growth through Reflections on Creatures*. As we look at each part of the title, keep in mind that this book is designed to foster the spiritual growth of people through reflections on thirty-two animals arranged in alphabetical order.

Abecedarian

An abecedarian, as its onomatopoetic sound (a, b, c, d) suggests, is a book whose contents are in alphabetical order. For our purposes here, animals are chosen to coincide with the letters of the alphabet. Thus, the first entry begins with a, the second with b, the third with c, etc. While there are only twenty-six letters in the alphabet, there are thirty-two entries in this tome; this means that some letters get more than one entry, and x has no entry.

Animal

The word "animal" is being used in its broadest understanding as a living organism that is distinguished from plants by independent movement and responsive sense organs. I take the same position as that of Thomas Berry, namely, "[t]he universe is composed of subjects to be communed with, not of objects to be exploited."[1] Thus, "the universe as a whole and in each of its individual components has an intangible inner form as well as a tangible physical structure."[2] More will be said about this below, but suffice it to be

1. Berry, "Prologue," 8.
2. Ibid.

said now that humans are connected to animals in an intimacy that is beyond description.

Spirit

Animals have religious significance in most, if not all, cultures. If it is not the animal itself that is honored, then it is an aspect of the animal that is applied to the human. A human may run like a deer; this implies that humans and deer have something in common. A human may be as strong as a bull; this implies that humans and bulls have something in common. A human may be as wise as an owl; this implies that humans and owls have something in common. Thus, knowing animals, and in some sense being known by them, fosters self-knowledge and social cohesion in the universal context of life, especially the spiritual movement in the broader cosmos. The author of the longer ending of Mark's Gospel in the CB (NT) seems to have understood this when he portrays the risen Jesus telling the eleven apostles, "Go into all the world and proclaim the good news to the whole creation" (Mark 16:15; cf. Col 1:23). The good news of the death and resurrection of Jesus is to be proclaimed universally; this implies that animals, too, need to hear this good news, and humans need to listen as animals proclaim it to them, too.

The best example of a human who understood the religious aspect of animals is St. Francis of Assisi. This famous twelfth- to the thirteenth-century saint is often depicted standing in a birdbath and using his arms as a perch for several flying creatures. In some depictions, a wolf stands near his feet. He is the patron saint of animals and the environment. Many stories about him preaching the good news to animals and listening as they reply surround the life of the poor man of Assisi. The second line of his "Canticle of the Sun," praises the Lord God "with all his creatures."

Francis understood that animals tell us about ourselves and about the divine. God's spirit is in all things; God's finger prints can be seen on every creature. The intangible inner form that Berry mentions above is the universal divine—no matter what name one gives to him, her, or it—and how all things spirit are both connected to and flow from the one pervading source. This is what the epigrams that open this book are about. The HB (OT) Psalm 148 calls upon every living thing to praise the name of its creator. Job, too, knows that the animals have a lot to teach humans, since both share the breath of life, another way to speak about spirit. Even the fiery St. Paul knows that the invisible power and divine nature of God are invisible, but they can be seen in the animals he made.

Introduction

Confucius, the master teacher, exhorts his pupils to sing songs in order to learn the names of birds and beasts, among other things. Hinduism compares the mind to a wild animal that needs to be tamed, held down, subdued. Moslems are reminded that every creature on earth is nourished by God. And, as *The Rig Veda* makes clear, the dawn awakens every living creature to his or her appointed task, that is, to his or her vocation.

According to *The Quran*, all animals worship God. "Creation of the heavens and the earth . . . and the scattering of beasts of all kinds upon it are surely signs for the wise," states Allah in Islam's Holy Book (*Quran* 2:164). Another verse asks the reader, "Do you see how all things in heaven and the earth, the . . . beasts, and men in abundance, pay homage to God?" (*Quran* 22:19) "He . . . dispersed on it all varieties of creatures . . ." (*Quran* 31:10). ". . . [A]ll the moving things (on earth) are signs for people firm in faith" (*Quran* 45:4).

In other words, the word "spirit" indicates that there is spirituality to animal and human dialogue. Sheldrake writes "that spirituality concerns a fully integrated approach to life (holism), involves a quest for the 'sacred,' underpins a desire for meaning, and implies some understanding of human identity, purpose, and thriving."[3] He adds that "spirituality points to a desire for ultimate values and invokes the intentional pursuit of a principled rather than purely pragmatic way of life."[4] Because we share the planet with creatures, they are not objects to be exploited, as Berry states above; they have the ability to help us reach (w)holeness if we learn their wisdom and integrate it into our lives. Spirituality demands that the intangible God be made tangible in some way; this quest for the sacred can be somewhat satisfied by entering into dialogue with some animals through the use of this book. The human desire for meaning which requires an understanding of self, that is, an identity which is both distinct from others and similar to other humans and animals, also involves having a purpose for the years we inhabit the third rock from the sun with creatures of all shapes and sizes. Hopefully, we thrive together, but this takes intentionality grounded in a disciplined way of life. This means that we have to spend time with our fellow creatures, either face to face at the zoo, in our back yard, on the farm, or in the woods.

Guide

Once we are focused on learning from animals, then we begin to realize that they can serve as guides, leading us deeper and deeper into the divine

3. Sheldrake, *Spirituality*, 22–23.
4. Ibid., 23.

life we share with them. "All creatures are interconnected through the Creator, through creation, through the breath of life, and through our shared purpose as Adam's helpmates in serving God," states Kemmerer.[5] The stories and animal images that abound reveal the close connection between humans and creatures, the dialogue that has taken place between them. Sometimes referred to as totems, "the mystic bond between the spirit, the place, and the people,"[6] many native peoples narrate stories about receiving help or guidance from an animal.

Thus, an animal spirit guide is one who is more in touch with the spiritual than most people are. The animal discloses something, such as essence, being, spirit, about its creator in a degree that is less than human, but nevertheless divine. In the HB (OT), the psalmist declares that human beings are a little lower than God (cf. Ps 8:5) in whose image they are created and have dominion over all creatures. The CB (NT) Letter to the Colossians declares that Jesus Christ "is the image of the invisible God" (Col 1:15). "He himself is before all things, and in him all things hold together" (Col 1:17). This means that Christ is all and in all (cf. Col 3:11). This same idea is captured in Eucharistic Prayer III in *The Roman Missal*: ". . . O Lord, . . . you give life to all things and make them holy . . . ."[7] ". . . Father most holy, . . . you have fashioned all your works in wisdom and in love. . . . [Y]our Only Begotten Son . . . sent the Holy Spirit from you, Father, . . . so that . . . he might sanctify creation to the full."[8]

Christ sent the Holy Spirit to sanctify creation to the full after becoming human and dying on the cross. Jesus Christ was simultaneously human and divine and a sacrificial animal whose carcass on the cross awaited the re-enlivening Spirit of God. As God incarnate, Jesus' corporeality is a given; St. Paul states that he "once knew Christ from a human point of view" (2 Cor 5:16). *The New American Bible Revised Edition* translates that verse as knowing "Christ according to the flesh." His animal, human, body received an enlivening substance, like blood, that contained life's very force—what we identify as spirit or divinity. The Spirit that enlivened the animal body of Jesus has also sanctified creation—all animals—to the full. Animals are not just meat, leather, or horn; they are bearers of the spirit, just like people are. God became a human animal to show human animals how to embrace spirit. Because humans share this spiritual connection with each other and with the other creatures on the planet, the animals can teach them spirituality.

5. Kemmerer, *Animals*, 230.
6. *Spirit*, 65.
7. *Roman Missal*, par. 108.
8. Ibid., par. 117.

Introduction

In other words, animals are beckoned by and carriers of the Spirit, manifestations of the God who created them. Some spiritual writers refer to this as concrescence, the experience of the world through prehension, total perception by the senses. If this concept is applied to God, then he—in terms of spirit or divinity—becomes the concrescent subject, in whom everywhere at once the many of the universe are perceived as being one. Thus, an animal can be a revelation; it attracts a person and speaks to him or her about spirit, participating in God's own truth and inexhaustibility. In other words, a person sees an animal as an expression of grace.

Because divinity is disguised by the skin of various creatures, a spirit guide is needed to get under that skin. A spirit guide helps us to experience transcendence through immanence. The spirit guide leads us to the divine. While the sacred is often defined in opposition to the profane—such as "the recognition of something that is wholly other, something basically and totally different that appears to our conscious awareness"[9]—it is better to think of it as "an act of manifestation" that is, a hierophany, to use Eliade's word.[10] Consolmagno says that we find "the unexpected hidden among the mudane" which "is the pattern of how we experience God in the real world."[11] A spirit guide leads a person to see a connection between the mundane human and the unexpected divine. "What appears in the world as immanent is at the same time a representation of what we take to be the transcendent."[12] In other words, ". . . [W]e recognize God when the story is true. That truth is God's presence; God is truth."[13]

Spiritual Growth through Reflections on Creatures

People visit zoos and maintain them in order to experience the divine; they want to see the animals they are. They want to experience the union between themselves and the divine that comes through the spirit guide animal. We see how important this was to ancient Greek and Roman cultures. In their attempt to get at this idea, there developed the half-animal, half-human creatures, such as the satyr and centaur (half man, half horse), minotaur (half man, half bull), faun (half man, half goat), and mermaid (half woman, half fish). Thus, there was a fusion of human and animal, of human spirit and animal spirit. For many native peoples this was accomplished by dressing in

9. Eicher-Catt, "Signs," 231.
10. Ibid.
11. Consolmagno, "Sci-fy Guy," 36.
12. Eicher-Catt, "Signs," 231.
13. Consolmagno, "Sci-fy Guy," 36.

the skin of the animal and/or wearing a mask shaped into the face of the animal and/or carving a totem of the animal. About all that survives today of this concept are the animal names given to sports teams. There has to be some connection between the human and the animal to begin to see the manifestation of the divine in each.

In order for humans to see animals as manifestations, hierophanies, of spirit, they have to stop looking at them as items to be consumed with the eyes, mouth, or emotions. That for what we look is what we find. Being present, mindful of the here and now, resting in awareness, enables one to see the ants moving in procession one behind the other over the sidewalk as individuals submitting themselves to a community, working together for the common good of the anthill. Instead of sweeping them away or spraying them with insect killer, the ants serve as spiritual guides, spiritual teachers, just like many other animals can. Contacting this deeper understanding or plumbing the depths of the universal spirit is referred to as blood in the HB (OT) Book of Leviticus. The Hebrew LORD forbids the eating of blood "for the life of the flesh is in the blood; and [he] has given it . . ." (Lev 17:11). An animal or bird that is killed for food must have its blood poured into the earth, that is, given back to the source from which all was made. For every creature its blood is its life. The life of every creature is its blood (cf. Lev 17:14). All blood, life, spirit is sacred. An animal spirit guide can facilitate our viewing of this manifestation of divinity.

In the eternal dialogue between the human and the animal, the animal spirit guide assists the human to hear the divine. In the HB (OT) only a snake and a donkey speak, but in other texts other animals have a lot to say, especially in the fables and tales narrated by Aesop and Grimm. By our attentiveness, the animals' wisdom can be heard and come through to people in silence. The prophet Isaiah, as we will see, presents animals and humans in harmony in the new world order. As we saw above, the Letter to the Colossians refers to this as being all in all. Paul's letters to the Corinthians and the Letter to the Ephesians capture this in terms of the one body of Christ. In the Book of Revelation, John of Patmos sees a new Jerusalem descending from heaven to the earth with its new creation.

Organization of this Book

A five-part exercise is offered for every one of the thirty-two entries.
1. The name of an animal indicates the focus of the chapter. As indicated above, the entries are arranged in abecedarian format. For several

Introduction

entries the name of the animal is followed by a parenthesis indicating other names for the animal, such as Turtle (Tortoise).

2. A few verses or sentences from a text are provided. The text may be from the Bible (Hebrew Bible [Old Testament], Old Testament [Apocrypha], Christian Bible [New Testament]), from a world religion (*The Book of Mormon, The Quran, The Dhammapada, The Rig Veda, The Analects of Confucius*), from a fable, a tale, a legend, or a story (Aesop, Grimm), or from some other source that illustrates a truth about the animal under consideration.

3. A reflective study follows the text. The reflection presents some of the context for the text, attempting to surface its meaning. It also presents other references to the animal in other sources. The reflective study is not be understood as exhaustive of the presence of the animal in biblical, world religions, fables, tales, legends, stories, or other texts. The study is a sampling, a sketch of the animal spirit guide across religions and cultures. It is designed to get the reader to stop and consider the wondrous works of God (cf. Job 37:14). Some entries go into more detail than others. Thus, some reflective studies are longer than others, and some are shorter than others.

4. The reflection is followed by a question for journaling and/or personal meditation. The question functions as a guide for personal appropriation of the message of the reflective study, thus leading the reader into journaling and/or personal prayer. The journal/meditation question is designed to foster a process of actively applying the reflection to one's life. The question gets one started; where the journal/meditation goes cannot be predetermined. It may be a single statement or an idea with which one lingers for a few minutes, a few hours, or a few days. The process has no end; the reader decides when he or she has finished exploring the topic because he or she needs to attend to other things.

5. A prayer concludes the exercise and summarizes the original theme announced in the title, which was studied and explored in the reflection and which served as the foundation for the meditation.

Using This Book

This book can be used at any time a person desires to develop further his or her spiritual life. It can be used in one's home as a daily exercise for a month, or the parts of each entry may be spread over several days or a week. A reader may take it to the zoo and, while sitting on a bench watching an animal, read the entry and reflect upon the spiritual truths learned from the creature. In warmer climates, one can sit in the back yard while listening to the sounds made by animals and read an entry, or a reader may choose to go to a farm, observe some of the animals there, and read the entry in this book about the animals in which one has an interest. This book can also be used during a retreat or on days set aside for reflection. Small groups of people might use it, reading its entries, sharing their reflections, and closing with its concluding prayer.

The book is designed to help the reader grow in spirituality using animals as spirit guides. The creatures on the earth, those which fly through the air, and those in the sea reveal the divine to us if we but open our eyes to see. Some of our human ancestors have recorded the truths learned from animals, and we are enriched by what they have left us. May our reflections further this spiritual journey and process for our descendants.

Mark G. Boyer
October 4, 2015
St. Francis of Assisi

Ass (Donkey)

Text: "... [T]he LORD opened the mouth of [Balaam's] donkey, and it said to Balaam, 'What have I done to you, that you have struck me these three times?' Balaam said to the donkey, 'Because you have made a fool of me!' But the donkey said to Balaam, 'Am I not your donkey, which you have ridden all your life to this day? Have I been in the habit of treating you this way?' And he said, 'No.'" (Num 22:28–29a, 30)

Reflection: Until a few years ago, biblical translators rendered the name of the horse-like animal with long ears as ass. With the developing negative connotations of that word in common parlance, translations in English became donkey, ignoring the biblical connotation of ass as a wild animal and donkey as the domesticated form.

In the Hebrew Bible's (Old Testament) Book of Numbers, Balaam was summoned by Balak, King of Moab, to curse the Israelites, who were preparing for war against the Moabites. However, God says to Balaam, "You shall not go . . . ; you shall not curse the people, for they are blessed" (Num 22:12). It is important to note the meaning of the word "curse." In contemporary understanding, "curse" refers to vulgar language. In biblical understanding, however, "curse" means to wish evil or destruction. Ancient people thought that if a prophet, like Balaam, wished evil upon the Israelites, Balak would easily defeat them.

Ultimately, Balaam sets out on the way to King Balak, but along the road God has sent an angel to serve as Balaam's adversary. His ass can see the angel, but he cannot. When his donkey veers off the road to avoid the angel, Balaam strikes the ass three times. The three times serves to alert the reader that a theophany is about to occur, that is, God is about to manifest himself to Balaam, and so he does when the ass begins to speak to the prophet. Ultimately, Balaam learns from his donkey that God's angel was going to strike him, but the ass has saved his life. Once Balaam arrives at King Balak's camp and sees the Israelites camped in the distance, he opens his mouth to curse the Israelites, but blessings come out instead! The ass saves Balaam from death, and God stops Balaam from cursing his chosen people. In the CB (NT), the author of the Second Letter of Peter refers to Balaam as one who "was rebuked [by] a speechless donkey [which] spoke with a human voice and restrained the prophet's madness" (2 Pet 2:16).

The wild ass's stubbornness, as presented in the above story, is used by the angel who appears to Hagar to describe Ishmael: "He shall be a wild ass of a man," states the angel, "with his hand against everyone, and everyone's hand against him; and he shall live at odds with all his kin" (Gen 16:12). Likewise, before he dies Jacob declares that his son Issachar is a strong donkey (cf. Gen 49:14a). Samson demonstrates his strength against the Philistines by taking "a fresh jawbone of a donkey" and using it to kill one thousand men (Judg15:15).

The prophet Zechariah employs the donkey as an animal representing humility. "Rejoice greatly, O daughter Zion!" he writes. "Shout aloud, O daughter Jerusalem! Lo, your king comes to you; triumphant and victorious is he, humble and riding on a donkey, on a colt, the foal of a donkey" (Zech 9:9). The king does not arrive on a horse, the animal of war, but on a humble beast of burden. In the CB (NT), a few days before his crucifixion Jesus is presented riding into Jerusalem in peace on a donkey by all four gospel writers (cf. Mark 11:1–11; Matt 21:1–11; Luke 19:28–38; John 12:12–18). Jesus enters the city in humility where he will be humiliated even more when he is nailed to the cross.

An ass was considered an asset to ancient people. That is why the last commandment of the Decalogue declares that a person shall not covet, that is, yearn or strongly desire, his neighbor's donkey (cf. Exod 20:17; Mosiah 13:24). This is also why on the seventh day (Sabbath) not only are people to rest, but the donkey may have relief, too (cf. Exod 23:12). The donkey is so important that if an Israelite were to see his enemy's donkey going astray, he is obligated to bring it back (cf. Exod 23:4), or if he were to see an overburdened donkey, he is obligated to set it free (cf. Exod 23:5).

Mormon understands the ass or donkey as being useful to people (cf. Ether 9:19; 1 Ne 18:25). It also echoes the Decalogue's prohibition against coveting a neighbor's ass (cf. Mosiah 13:24; 5:14). However, this book sees the donkey as dumb. Because of the people's iniquities, the Lord will punish them. ". . . [T]hey shall have burdens lashed upon their backs; and they shall be driven before like a dumb ass" (Mosiah 12:5; 21:3). *The Quran*, too, declares that people who refuse to listen to the truth are like frightened asses fleeing a lion (cf. *Quran* 74:50). While God created "donkeys for riding and for splendor" (*Quran* 16:8), *The Quran* states, "The likeness of those who were charged with (the law of) Torah, which they did not observe, is that of a donkey who carries a load of books (oblivious of what they contain)" (*Quran* 62:5).

In *The Rig Veda*, the ass or donkey is seen as being lower than a horse. In one hymn, Indra, the chief Hindu god, is asked to "destroy this ass . . . who in tones discordant brays to him" (*RV* 1:29:5) and to give horses and cattle to the petitioner. The verse of another hymn states that one should never "lead an ass before a charger" (*RV* 3:53:23). And yet in the Hindu world, a "mighty ass" (*RV* 1:34:9; cf. 1:116:2; 8:74:7) draws the chariot of the Asvins, the Hindu gods of sunrise and sunset, even though "to the ass's pole is yoked the charger" (*RV* 1:162:21).

Grimm's Complete Fairy Tales elevates the donkey. In "The Table, the Ass, and the Stick," the second of three sons, who are driven away from home by their tailor father, binds himself to a miller. After completing his training, the miller gives him a remarkable ass, which draws no cart and carries no sack. Instead, "[h]e spews forth gold," states the miller. "If you put a cloth before him and say, 'Bricklebrit,' out come gold pieces from back and front."[1] On the way home, this son spends the night in an inn. The innkeeper spies on him getting gold from the ass, and, while he sleeps, switches the donkey for another one. Unbeknown to the son, the next day he heads home to his father, where, after calling all the neighbors to witness the shower of gold from the ass, which, of course, does not happen, the second son of the tailor is shamed. Thus, the second son would spend his life as a miller. The donkey represents wealth that the tailor's second son lost.

"The Donkey" is another tale about a rich king and queen who have no children. "At last God gave [the queen] her wish, but when the child came into the world, it did not look like a human child, but was a little donkey."[2] The queen recommends drowning the donkey, but the king decides to keep it and make it his heir. After the donkey grows, he learns to play the lute. He leaves home and travels to another king's castle, where he so entertains the king that he promises him anything he requests. He marries the king's daughter. On the first night of the honeymoon, the king instructs a servant to spy on the newlyweds, and the servant observes the donkey removing his

---

1. Grimm, 172.
2. Ibid., 481.

skin and revealing a handsome, royal, young man. The next night, the king spies on the newlyweds, observes the same procedure as did the servant, and steals the donkey skin. The next morning after the young man wakes, he cannot find his disguise and is revealed to the king, who gives him half his kingdom. Within the year the old king dies and the donkey-turned-young-man inherits both this kingdom and his father's kingdom to spend the rest of his life in magnificence. Thus, like the other Grimm story, the donkey represents wealth.

Over twenty of Aesop's Fables feature donkeys; so, only a few can be highlighted here. Echoing the dumb ass of *Mormon*, "The Ass and the Lap Dog" tells the story about a dumb donkey which breaks out of his master's stable, enters the house, and proceeds to act like the lap dog he has observed. The dumb ass frolics around the house, destroying furniture, and, when he attempts to jump into his master's lap, the servants beat him off and send him back to the stable, where the ass bemoans his stupidity.[3]

Other fables feature the smartness of the ass. In "The Ass and His Burdens," a peddler loaded large bags of salt on his donkey, which stumbled into a stream. The water dissolved most of the salt and made the ass's burden lighter. After returning to the town, the peddler loaded the ass again with salt; this time the ass lay down in the water, which dissolved the salt and made its burden lighter. A third time the peddler put bags of salt on his ass, but this time he also put sponges under them. When the ass lay down in the water, the sponges soaked up the water; the ass had a heavier burden to bear. The moral is that one "may play a good card once too often."[4]

Many of *Aesop's Fables* feature other animals along with an ass, such as a cock, a wolf, or a dog. One animal, however, that is often a part of many stories about asses is the lion. The lion, portrayed as smart and cunning, serves as the foil for the dumb donkey. In "The Ass, the Fox, and the Lion," the lion outwits both the ass and the fox, which betrayed the ass into the lion's paws.[5] In "The Lion and the Wild Ass," the donkey hunts with the lion, only to have the lion claim the whole of the hunt.[6] In "The Lion and the Ass," both creatures partner to hunt wild goats in a cave; again the lion outwits the ass.[7] In "The Ass, the Cock, and the Lion," the starving king of beasts attacks the ass, which convinced the cock to scare away the lion with

---

3. Cf. Aesop, 27–28.
4. Ibid., 41.
5. Cf. Ibid., 15–16.
6. Cf. Ibid., 85.
7. Cf. Ibid., 103.

his crowing.[8] A lion, fox, and ass go hunting together in "The Lion, the Fox, and the Ass." After dividing the spoils into three equal portions, the lion falls upon the donkey and eats him. The fox quickly learns the lesson and gives all the booty to the lion before leaving the scene.[9]

The ass or donkey becomes a paradox in literature. On one hand, the animal represents wildness, and on the other hand it represents domesticity. It is both smart and dumb; it is both stubborn and cooperative; it is both strong and weak; it both speaks its own will and God's word; it is both proud and humble. And so it becomes a vehicle for divine revelation.

Journal/Meditation: What do you learn about God from the stories about asses or donkeys in literature? What do you learn about yourself from the stories about asses or donkeys in literature?

Prayer: O LORD, you opened the mouth of Balaam's ass to reveal your word to your prophet about blessing the Israelites. Help me to hear your word through all your creatures. I pray in the name of the eternal Word, Jesus Christ. Amen.

---

8. Cf. Ibid., 127–28.
9. Cf. Ibid., 196–97.

Bear

Text: "Urging his waning strength to one last effort, the Ah-wah-nee-chee raised his club high above his head and brought it down with a heavy, well-aimed stroke that crushed the grizzly's skull and sent him rolling among the boulders, dead. That night as the Ah-wah-nee-chees feasted themselves on bear meat, the story of the young chief's bravery was told and told again; and from that hour he was known as Yo-sem-i-te, the Large Grizzly Bear."[1]

Reflection: The above selection comes from "Yosemite: Large Grizzly Bear" by Bertha H. Smith, found in Conron's *American Folktales, Myths, Legends*. The rest of the six-page story explains why the boy ends up battling the bear. However, the end of the story reveals how the famous U.S. Park became known as Yosemite. In other words, the Native American's battle with a grizzly bear is the mythology behind the name of Yosemite National Park. It answers the question: Why was the park named Yosemite?

When most people see the word "bear," they think of the grizzly bear, the black bear, or the polar bear. No matter which bear comes to mind, it is a large, strong, thick-furred, omnivorous, four-legged mammal with sharp claws. In most literature, the bear represents strength, introspection, and self-knowledge. The teddy bear represents the tamed or domesticated version of the bruin.

In biblical literature, the bear represents enraged strength. Before he goes to do battle with Goliath, David tells King Saul that the LORD has saved him from the bear's paw (cf. 1 Sam 17:37). Likewise, as Absalom

---

1. Smith, "Yosemite," 27–28.

attempts to take his father David's throne, he is told that his father and his men are warriors, and "they are enraged, like a bear robbed of her cubs in the field" (2 Sam 17:8). The phrase, like "a she-bear robbed of its cubs" occurs several other times in the Bible (Prov 17:12; Hos 13:8). Also, in biblical literature the bear is known for its charging (cf. Prov 28:15) and lying in wait (cf. Lam 3:10) characteristics.

The HB (OT) Book of Daniel presents the account of a vision of four great beasts emerging from the sea. The second beast to appear looked like a bear. According to Daniel, "It was raised up on one side, had three tusks in its mouth among its teeth and was told, 'Arise, devour many bodies!'" (Dan 7:5) In Daniel's vision the bear represents the Media Empire which followed the Babylonian Empire. From a Jewish perspective, any empire other than that of David was considered to be a strong persecutor of the Jews.

Daniel's vision forms the basis for the apocalyptic material in the CB (NT) Book of Revelation. Instead of several beasts, only one arises out of the sea; its feet were like a bear's (cf. Rev 13:2). The beast with bear-like feet, mythologically representing evil, prepares to do battle with the lamb and his army of saints, mythologically representing good.

Mevlana Jalaluddin Rumi, Islam's thirteenth-century Sufi mystic, compares God's grace to a bear. In *Rumi*, Schimmel narrates the mystic's story "of the poor schoolmaster who, shivering in extreme hardship and cold, sees a bear in the stream." She continues,

> The schoolchildren call out to him to seize the fur coat which they take the bear to be. And the desperate teacher indeed jumps into the water where the bear grapples him. The appalled children call out to him to let go [of] the fur coat. But he cries: "I am well and truly letting go of the fur coat, but the fur coat is not letting go of me!"[2]

Schimmel adds, "How indeed could God's grace let us go?"[3]

"The Story of the Three Bears," first recorded in 1837, features three bears who live together in a house of their own in the woods. After fixing their porridge for breakfast, they set it on their table to cool while they go for a walk. "The door was not fastened, because the bears were good bears, which did nobody any harm, and never suspected that anybody would harm them," states the story in *The Annotated Classic Fairy Tales*, edited by Tatar.[4] In other words, the bears have earned a good housekeeping seal of approval! A little girl named Goldilocks enters their home, eats all the porridge of the

---

2. Schimmel, *Rumi*, 100.

3. Ibid.

4. Tatar, *Annotated Fairy Tales*, 247.

smallest bear after tasting the porridge of the other two bears and finding it too hot or too cold, sits in the smallest chair and breaks it after trying the other two chairs and finding them either too hard or too soft, and goes upstairs and, after trying two of the three beds, discovers that the smallest one is just right and falls asleep on it.

Once they come home, the bears retrace Goldilocks's journey through their home, discovering the eaten porridge, the broken chair, and Goldilocks asleep on the smallest bed. Once the young lady awakens and sees the three bears standing by the bed, she notices that "the window was open, because the bears, like good, tidy bears, as they were, always opened their bedchamber window when they got up in the morning."[5] Goldilocks jumped through the window and ran away as fast as she could, and the three good bears never saw her again.

In "'Caught with Ourselves in the Net of Life and Time': Traditional Views of Animals in Religion," Patton narrates how a Native American Sioux named Bear with White Paw in the early twentieth century stated, "The bear has a soul like ours, and his soul talks to mine in my sleep and tells me what to do."[6] Patton continues to write about the earliest time, "when both people and animals lived on earth [and] a person could become an animal if he wanted to and an animal could become a human being." She adds: "Sometimes they were people and sometimes animals, and there was no difference. All spoke the same language."[7]

This is illustrated by "The Willow-Wren and the Bear" in *Grimm's Complete Fairy Tales*. After a bear insults the chicks of a pair of willow wrens, the birds gather an army of animals and declare war on the bear, which also gathered some forces. The bear put a fox in charge of his army; the signal to attack was to be the erect tail of the fox, while the signal to retreat was to be the tail hanging down. However, the wren sent a hornet to sting the fox's tail and cause it to fall down. Thus, the bear's forces retreated, and the wren won the battle. Later in the day, the bear crept to the wren's nest and apologized for his insult.[8]

A bear and a person speak the same language in Aesop's fable about a bear and two travelers. After seeing a bear on the road, one traveler climbs a tree and one pretends to be dead. The bear approaches the man on the ground, sniffs him, concludes that he is a corpse, and goes away. After the traveler in the tree climbs down, he asks the one on the ground what the

---

5. Ibid., 252.
6. Patton, "Traditional Views," 34.
7. Ibid.
8. Cf. Grimm, 152–53.

bear whispered to him. He replied, "He told me never again to travel with a friend who deserts you at the first sign of danger."[9]

Another fable features a bear bragging to a fox about his generous feelings and how refined he is in comparison to other animals. The fox tells him, "My friend, when you are hungry, I only wish you would confine your attention to the dead and leave the living alone." The moral of the tale is this: "A hypocrite deceives no one but himself."[10]

"The Lion, the Bear, and the Fox" is about a lion and bear fighting for possession of a young goat. The battle for the kid went on for a long time while the fox merely watched. After both animals were exhausted and too weak to move, the fox slipped in, seized the kid, and ran off with it. The lion said to the bear, "Here we've been mauling each other all this while, and no one is the better for it except the fox!"[11] Thus, both the strong lion and bear learn a lesson.

The bear discloses strength, especially in its paws, which Rumi compares to God's grace, which fosters personal, tidy housekeeping. For Native Americans, the bear is a sacred animal which discloses the divine, even serving as the name for a U.S. National Park: Yosemite, the Large Grizzly Bear.

Journal/Meditation: What characteristics of the bear do you discover within yourself? What characteristics of the bear do you apply to God? Explain.

Prayer: God of all strength, your grace is like a bear that will not let me go. Grant me the grace to know myself that I may serve you all the days of my life. I ask this through Christ, my Lord. Amen.

---

9. Aesop, 31.
10. Ibid., 78.
11. Ibid., 84.

Bee

Text: "A queen bee from Hymettus flew up to [Mount] Olympus with some fresh honey from the hive as a present to Jupiter, who was so pleased with the gift that he promised to give her anything she liked to ask for. She said she would be very grateful if he would give stings to the bees, to kill people who robbed them of their honey. Jupiter was greatly displeased with this request, for he loved [human]kind. But he had given his word, so he said that stings they should have. The stings he gave them, however, were of such a kind that whenever a bee stings a man [or a woman], the sting[er] is left in the wound, and the bee dies."[1]

Reflection: The above story, titled "The Bee and Jupiter," is a myth explaining why bees have stingers and what happens to them after they have stung anyone robbing their hive. Aesop attaches a moral to the story, namely, "Evil wishes, like fowls, come home to roost."[2] However, there is more meaning to the story than that. The fable also means that the bee should think carefully before stinging a hive-robber because such action will result in the bee's death. In other words, actions have consequences, sometime deadly consequences.

A similar story, titled "The Bee-Keeper," narrates how a thief found his way into an apiary while the bee-keeper was away and stole the honey. The bee-keeper arrives home before the bees, and the bees think that he has robbed the hives of their honey. So, they begin to sting him, which means that many of them die. The bee-keeper cries out, "You ungrateful

---

1. Aesop, 35.
2. Ibid.

scoundrels, you let the thief who stole my honey get off scot-free, and then you go and sting me who have always taken such good care of you!"³ The moral of the fable is this: "When you hit back, make sure you have got the right man."⁴ Another moral could be this: Do not sting the hand of the one who feeds you!

Mormon describes how bees got spread around the earth. The story picks up after the biblical narrative about the tower of Babel and how people were scattered because God created many languages out of the one language of humans, and they could not understand each other. In the Book of Ether, a man named Jared begins his journey to an unknown land. Along with his family and friends, they "carry with them deseret, which, by interpretation, is a honey bee; and thus did they carry with them swarms of bees . . ." (Ether 2:3).

Bees are known for their service to the hive, their incessant gathering of nectar which they turn into honey, and the community they form in the hive under a queen. These honey-making insects possess a furry body that buzzes with a stinger that inflicts harm on enemies, as seen in the story from *Aesop's Fables* above. All of these characteristics are illustrated in "The Queen Bee" in Grimm's *Complete Fairy Tales*. Two sons of a king are living a wild, reckless life when their younger brother finds them and urges them to return home. After stopping them from disturbing an ant hill and some ducks on a lake, they come to a beehive in a tree where "there was so much honey in it that it overflowed and ran down the trunk."⁵ The youngest brother stopped the other two from making a fire and using the smoke to stifle the bees and steal their honey.

After finding an enchanted castle, each of the brothers is given the same task to release the castle from its enchantment: They must find the one thousand pearls under the moss in the woods that belong to the princess of the castle or be turned into stone. The first brother finds only a hundred pearls and is turned into the stone. The second brother finds two hundred pearls and is turned into stone. However, the third brother enlists the help of the ants to find all the pearls and the ducks to find the key in the lake to the room of the three princesses. He is to choose the youngest princess. The bees help him determine the youngest princess, who had eaten a spoonful of honey before going to sleep.

> . . . [T]he queen-bee of those bees that [the youngest brother] had protected from the fire came at this moment, and trying

---

3. Ibid., 173.
4. Ibid.
5. Grimm, 239.

the lips of all three [princesses] settled on those of the one that had eaten honey, and so it was that the king's son knew which to choose. Then the spell was broken; every one awoke from stony sleep and took his right form again.⁶

Thus, the bee saved the day.

The Dhammapada, Buddhism's sacred writing, compares the gentleness of a wondering sage to a bee. The itinerant sage gathers alms from villagers, beginning with the first house and ending with the last, in order to support himself. "Even as a bee, having taken up nectar from a flower, flies away, not harming its color and fragrance, so may a sage wonder through a village," states *The Dhammapada* (*Dhp* 4:49). Just as the bee flies about from one flower to another without harming or destroying any of them, so does the itinerant sage—who may be a learner or one beyond learning—collect offerings from villagers without harming their faith, families, or livelihood. Just like the bee takes its nectar to the hive to be made into honey, so does the sage use his alms for his further growth in and development of wisdom.

Even though *The Quran* has a whole chapter (16) titled "The Bees," bees are mentioned only in two verses: "Your Lord predisposed the bees to make their hives in mountains, trees, and trellises, and suck from all fruits and flit about the unrestricted paths of their Lord. A drink of various hues comes out of their bellies which contains medicine for men. In this is a sign for those who reflect" (*Quran* 16:68–69). According to Kassam in "The Case of the Animals Versus Man: Toward an Ecology of Being," not "only humans have sciences and knowledge, thought and judgment, and the capacity to direct and govern," but "the bees in all these arenas [are] far more judicious and exacting."⁷ Then, commenting on the above quotation from *The Quran*, Kassam states that the bee has received "the gift of divine inspiration . . . , social organization, and the industriousness of swarming creatures . . . ."⁸ Kassam adds, "Further, the Lord has blessed bees with skill and knowledge of the geometrical arts, which they utilize in building their dwellings; the ability to take from every flower and fruit and to produce what is healing for humankind."⁹ In "From Cognition to Consciousness," Griffin attributes conscious thought to bees, declaring, "The waggle dances of honeybees . . . inform the dancer's sisters about important things they

---

6. Ibid., 240.
7. Kassam, "Animals Versus Man," 166.
8. Ibid.
9. Ibid.

cannot perceive directly."¹⁰ The lesson to be learned from the bee is that God creates and provides healing for people from everything that he has created.

The Rig Veda mentions the "milk . . . blended with the honey of the bee" (*RV* 8:4:8) and "the bee [that] bears . . . honey in her mouth" (*RV* 10:40:6). The HB (OT) mentions mixing curds, the ancient equivalent of modern cottage cheese, or milk with honey (e.g. 2 Sam 17:29; Job 20:17; Isa 7:15, 22). When the HB (OT) mentions bees, it is usually in the context of causing harm. The Amorites are compared to a swarm of bees (cf. Deut 1:44); the Assyrians are also compared to a swarm of bees (cf. Isa 7:18; 2 Ne 17:18). A mother's love for her child is like a swarm of "bees at the time for making honeycombs," according to the Fourth Book of Maccabees, because bees "defend themselves against intruders and, as though with an iron dart, sting those who approach their hive and defend it even to the death" (4 Macc 14:19). Psalm 118 captures this concept best; the singer declares that "nations surrounded [him] like bees," but he was able to stop them in the name of the LORD (Ps 118:12).

The HB (OT) seldom mentions bees, but uses repeatedly the phrase "land flowing with milk and honey," the product of the bee, to describe the promised land's abundance (cf. Exod 3:8; 3:17; 13:5; 33:3; Lev 20:24; Num 13:27; 14:8; 16:13, 14; Deut 6:3; 11:9; 26:9, 15; 27:3; 31:20; Josh 5:6; Jer 11:5; 32:22; Ezek 20:6, 15; Sir 46:8; Bar 1:20). The product of the bee was considered a delicacy by ancient people, and its sweetness was a measure for anything else that could be classified as sweet to the taste. For example, the manna with which God fed his people in the desert, is described as tasting "like wafers made with honey" (Exod 16:31). The prophet Ezekiel describes the taste of the scroll that God gives him to eat "as sweet as honey" (Ezek 3:3), and the author of the CB (NT) Book of Revelation, borrowing this event from the prophet Ezekiel, describes the little scroll which the angel gives him to eat as sweet as honey (cf. Rev. 10:9). Psalm 119 describes that the Lord's words are sweeter than honey: "How sweet are your words to my taste, sweeter than honey to my mouth!" (Ps 119:103) The Book of Proverbs declares that wisdom is to the soul as "the drippings of the honeycomb are sweet to [the] taste" (Prov 24:13). The Book of Sirach furthers this notion, declaring that wisdom "is sweeter than honey, and the possession of [wisdom is] sweeter than the honeycomb" (Sir 24:20).

In the OT (A) Book of Sirach, the bee is used as an example of how appearances are deceiving. "The bee is small among flying creatures," states Sirach, "but her product is the best of sweet things" (Sir 11:3). In other

---

10. Griffin, "Cognition to Consciousness," 493.

words, out of the small bee comes a large amount of honey—and everything else in which it is used as a sweetener.

Bees and honey play one major role in the HB (OT) Book of Judges. Samson, the miracle child of Manoah and his unnamed wife, tears a young lion apart barehanded (cf. Judg 14:6) in order to demonstrate his strength. Walking by the lion's carcass at a later time, he sees "a swarm of bees in the body of the lion, and honey" (Judg 14:8), which he scrapes out into his hands and gives some to his parents. Later, Samson uses his experience in a riddle, telling the Philistines, "Out of the eater came something to eat. Out of the strong came something sweet" (Judg 14:14). The Philistines coax Samson's wife into getting the answer: honey in a lion's carcass (cf. Judg 14:18). Samson recognizes that he has been deceived.

One final biblical theme concerning bees is found in Moses' song near the end of the HB (OT) Book of Deuteronomy. The prophet sings about the LORD sustaining Jacob, that is, Israel, through the desert, nursing him with honey from the crags (cf. Deut 32:13) or, as some translations state, "with honey from the rock." Everyone knows that honey does not flow from a rock, but the phrase is meant to contrast the abundance of God's care for his people with the scarcity of the desert through which they wandered before arriving at the promised land. The phrase appears again in Psalm 81. The writer records God lamenting his people's inability to listen to him. If the Israelites would walk in the LORD's ways, God would feed his people with honey from the rock (cf. Ps 81:16).

"The Easter Proclamation," often referred to by its Latin name, *Exsultet*, sung only once a year during the night before Easter Sunday in Roman Catholic Churches, praises bees. The singer prays that that "holy Father" will "accept [the Paschal] candle, a solemn offering, the work of bees . . . [as a] gift from [God's] most holy Church."[11] Later, this hymn expresses how the large, lit candle's fire can be divided into many flames, that is, smaller candles can be lit from it and given to all the people present, yet the fire atop the Paschal Candle is never dimmed by the sharing of its light, "for it is fed by melting wax, drawn out by mother bees to build a torch so precious."[12]

Thus, the bee is portrayed as both harmful and helpful. With its stinger it can inject poison into its enemy, but it also dies as a result of this response. With its body it can produce honey and wax for humans. However, if all the honey and wax are stolen, the beehive dies. The bee serves the common good of the hive by gathering nectar from flowers near and far and producing honey that becomes the measure of sweetness. The bee also pollinates

---

11. "Easter," par. 19
12. Ibid.

the blossoms of many trees and plants so that they produce fruit. Those who are wise not only wander like the bee, but they imitate the bee, causing no harm to those with whom they share their wisdom.

Journal/Meditation: How are you like the bee? What can you learn from the bee?

Prayer: All-wise God, you created the bee to provide honey to your people as a sign of your abundant care. Teach me the lesson of service for the common good of the communities in which I live. In imitation of the bee, grant me the grace to praise your wisdom now and forever through Jesus Christ, your Son. Amen.

Camel

Text: "... Jesus looked around and said to his disciples, 'How hard it will be for those who have wealth to enter the kingdom of God! It is easier for a camel to go through the eye of a needle than for someone who is rich to enter the kingdom of God.'" (Mark 10:23, 25)

Reflection: A camel is a ruminant animal with either one hump or two humps on its back. It is adapted to arid climates and is used primarily as a beast of burden in deserts because it needs little water to survive. When it has only one hump, it is known as a dromedary (cf. Isa 66:20). Its light brown fur makes it very suitable for riders and for transporting goods in deserts.

Because of its large size, it is often contrasted to the smallness of a needle's eye, as in the above passage from Mark's Gospel. Jesus' saying about it being easier for a camel to pass through the eye of a needle than for a rich man to enter the kingdom of God is a hyperbole, an extravagant exaggeration, made to stress his point. Both the author of Matthew's Gospel (cf. Matt 19:24) and the author of Luke's Gospel (cf. Luke 18:25) copy the saying from Mark but slightly alter its context to emphasize the point to their respective readers: Keeping the commandments is not enough to insure life in God's kingdom. A person must become detached from everything and rely only upon God, if he or she wants to enter the kingdom of God. Those who have riches have to be about the task of managing their wealth; that is why it is easier for a camel to pass through a needle's eye than it is for a rich person to enter God's kingdom.

The Quran also mentions the camel passing through the eye of a needle, but in a slightly different context. God has given signs to people of their need to repent. "Verily for those who deny our signs and turn away in haughtiness from them," states God in *The Quran*, "the gates of heaven shall not be opened, nor will they enter paradise, not till the camel passes through the needle's eye" (*Quran* 7:40). While the saying is used here as an exaggeration—similar to the common phrase "until hell freezes over"—it emphasizes the need for people to obey Allah's words if they hope to enter heaven.

Hyperbole is also found in Matthew's unique woes or damnations of the Pharisees and scribes. The Matthean Jesus tells them, "You blind guides! You strain out a gnat but swallow a camel!" (Matt 23:24) Like the saying above, the smallness of the gnat, which is strained out of garden herbs, is contrasted to the largeness of the camel, which they swallow. The Pharisees and scribes are more concerned with tithes than they are with what Jesus teaches matters to God: justice, mercy, and faith.

In the ancient world, camels were used for transport of people. Jacob set his children and his wives on camels (cf. Gen 31:17). Likewise, Judith's enemy, Holofernes, takes a vast number of camels for transport as part of his war campaign (cf. Jdt 2:17). More importantly, however, camels are both a sign of wealth, especially when owned in large numbers, and they carry wealth from one desert community to another. Abraham's servant measures his master's wealth in, among other things, camels (cf. Gen 24:35). Jacob, when about to reconcile with his brother Esau over his stolen birthright, among other animals, presents thirty milch camels and their colts (cf. Gen 32:15). Likewise, Job, among his many possessions, counted "three thousand camels" (Job 1:3). Ezra leads some of the Babylonian captives, who were freed by King Cyrus of Persia, to Jerusalem along with 435 camels (cf. Ezra 2:67; Neh 7:69). Even the prophet Jeremiah mentions camels as booty, that is, wealth taken from one's enemy during war (cf. Jer 49:32). In book 8, hymn 46, of *The Rig Veda*, camels represent wealth; this hymn is addressed to "Indra, Lord of ample wealth" (*RV* 8:46:1) from whom the writer received "twenty hundred camels" (*RV* 8:46:22) of whom "a hundred camels" bleated for him (*RV* 8:46:31).

In biblical literature camels are known for carrying wealth. Abraham's servant loads ten of the camels he takes to Laban with all kinds of choice gifts (cf. Gen 24:10). After Joseph's brothers toss him into a pit, they see "a caravan of Ishmaelites coming from Gilead, with their camels carrying gum, balm, and resin, on their way to carry it down to Egypt" (Gen 37:25). The queen of Sheba comes to Jerusalem to see Solomon "with camels bearing spices and very much gold, and precious stones" (1 Kgs 10:2; 2 Chr 9:1).

The prophet Isaiah writes about the animals of the Negeb, that is, a desert, carrying their treasures on the humps of camels (cf. Isa 30:6). In Isaiah's vision of a restored Jerusalem, the prophet combines a large number of camels as a sign of wealth with camels burdened with goods: "A multitude of camels shall cover you, the young camels of Midian and Ephah; all those from Sheba shall come. They shall bring gold and frankincense, and shall proclaim the praise of the LORD" (Isa 60:6). For those who wonder about from where the camel in the Christmas Nativity crèche comes, they have their answer: Isaiah. Because the magi bring gold, frankincense, and myrrh as gifts to the infant Jesus in Matthew's Gospel (cf. Matt 2:1–12), the gold and frankincense of Isaiah 60:6 borne on camels results in at least one camel in the Christmas scene!

The Quran understands the camel as a beast of burden, created by God (cf. *Quran* 6:144). When narrating the story of Joseph, *The Quran* states that after his brothers come to get grain in Egypt from Joseph and return to their father Jacob, they discover that their money has been returned. So, they decide to go back to Egypt to get "a camel-load more of grain" (*Quran* 12:65), which they get and begin the journey back to their father. They are promised another "camel-load of grain" (*Quran* 12:72) if they find the master's goblet. However, *The Quran* also understands the camel, more specifically the she-camel, as a token or sign that people should "worship God, for [they] have no other god but he" (*Quran* 7:73; 11:64; 91:13).

While the Bible forbids the eating of camel meat (cf. Lev 11:4; Deut 14:7), *The Quran* seems to permit it. In 22:36 Allah says:

> We have made the camels signs of God for you. There is good for you in this. So pronounce the name of God over them as they stand with their forefeet in a line. When they have fallen (slaughtered) on their sides, eat of (their meat) and feed those who are content with little, and those who supplicate. That is why we have brought them under your subjugation so that you may be grateful. (*Quran* 22:36)

Following this command, there is an explanation: "It is not their meat or blood that reaches God: It is the fealty of your heart that reaches him. That is why he has subjugated them to you that you may glorify God for having shown you the way. So give glad tidings to those who are doers of good" (*Quran* 22:37).

In the CB (NT), John the Baptist is described as being "clothed with camel's hair" by the author of Mark's Gospel (Mark 1:6) to connect the prophet to the wilderness, desert, considered to be a place of renewal. His diet of locusts and wild honey (cf. Mark 1:6) further emphasize his desert origin. The author of Matthew's Gospel (cf. Matt 3:4) copies this verse from Mark as an ascetical contrast to the luxury of King Herod explained in the verses before it. Thus, while the HB (OT) does not mention using camel's hair for clothing, the CB (NT) uses it to portray John the Baptist as an ascetical prophet living in the desert.

The camel does not appear in *Grimm's Complete Fairy Tales*, but Aesop does have one story about a monkey and a camel. At a gathering of all the other animals, a monkey danced and entertained the assembly, receiving great applause. The camel became envious and decided to win the assembly's applause in the same way. "So he got up from his place and began dancing, but he cut such a ridiculous figure as he plunged about, and made such a grotesque exhibition of his ungainly person, that the beasts all fell upon him with ridicule and drove him away."[1] While Aesop attaches no moral to the tale, it seems to be that one should not attempt to dance before others with two left feet!

The camel, with one hump or two humps, represents what is huge, the impossible—like a camel passing through the eye of a needle—yet it accomplishes the impossible by bearing people and riches through the desert. In large herds, camels are a sign of wealth to other desert-dwelling people, even serving as a sign of God for some.

Journal/Meditation: With what qualities do you associate the camel? After reading this reflection on the camel, why do you think it is important to have one in a Christmas nativity scene? Or do you think the camel should be removed from the Christmas crèche? Why?

Prayer: God of the kingdom, you have given the camel as a sign of your love for people. Make me aware of how my wealth can occupy my time and cloud my vision. Fill me with the guidance of the wisdom of the Holy Spirit that it becomes possible for me one day to enter your kingdom, where you live, Father, with your Son and the Holy Spirit, one God, forever and ever. Amen.

---

1. Aesop, 131.

Dog

Text: "The young man [Tobias] went out and the [arch]angel [Raphael] with him; and the dog came out with him and went along with them. So they both journeyed along, and when the first night overtook them, they camped by the Tigris river." (Tob 6:1b–2)

Reflection: In the OT (A) Book of Tobit, a novel, a dog is mentioned two times as following Tobias and Raphael on their journey (cf. Tob 6:2a; 11:4b). While the dog serves no real narrative purpose, it is a faithful traveling companion on the important quest to retrieve money Tobias's father, Tobit, once loaned, to find a cure for Tobit's blindness, and to find a wife for Tobias. Because the dog is faithful to Tobias and Raphael, it has come to be known as man's best friend. Likewise, *Aesop's Fables* contains a short tale about a traveler and his dog that resembles the one in the Book of Tobit. A traveler is about to begin a journey when he tells his dog, "who was stretching himself by the door, 'Come. What are you yawning for? Hurry up and get ready: I mean [for] you to go with me.'"[1] But the dog wags his tail and says, "I'm ready, master: it's you I'm waiting for."[2]

    The dog is the domesticated form of the wolf, fox, coyote, etc. It is a carnivorous animal with a characteristic long muzzle, pointed ears, a fur coat, and a long fur-covered tail. The dog's call is a bark or a growl. The domestic animal named "dog," ranging in size from a few pounds to a hundred-plus pounds, has given rise to several phrases which will serve as the outline for this chapter: dog in the manger, a dog's life, dog eat dog, go to the dogs, let sleeping dogs lie, and put on the dog.

---

1. Aesop, 69.
2. Ibid.

Dog in the Manger

First, the phrase "dog in the manger" is taken from one of *Aesop's Fables* by the same name. Cattle discover a dog lying on the hay in their manger; the dog growls and snaps at them, keeping them from their food. "What a selfish beast," says one cow to another. "He can't eat himself and yet he won't let those eat who can."[3] "The Dog and the Shadow," another of *Aesop's Fables,* echoes this theme. As a dog is crossing a bridge over a stream with a piece of meat in his mouth, he sees his reflection in the water. Thinking it was another dog with a larger piece of meat, he drops the meat into the water and attacks the other dog, which is only his shadow. In the end, "he got neither: for one was only a shadow, and the other was carried away by the current."[4] Thus, the phrase "dog in the manger" refers to a person who cannot have or does not want to have something, but who tries to prevent another from having it.

A Dog's Life

Second, the phrase "a dog's life" refers to a wretched existence. *Grimm's Complete Fairy Tales* contains a story about "a sheep-dog whose master behaved ill to him and did not give him enough to eat."[5] A sparrow takes pity on the dog, leading him to the closest town. There, the sparrow gets the dog a piece of meat from two butchers' stalls and a piece of bread from a baker's stall. After being satiated, the dog and sparrow go out of the town and rest near a road. The sparrow rests in a tree, while the dog lays down in the road, where he falls asleep. A wagoner, driving three horses and a cart with casks of wine, runs over the dog, which "was crushed to death by the wheels."[6] Ultimately, the tricky sparrow destroys the wine, the wagon, and the wagoner.

The dog's wretched existence is synonymous with an insult in a lot of biblical books. Israelites and Jews referred derogatorily to Gentiles as dogs. In Israelite and Jewish culture, a dog is an unclean animal, that is, a person avoids contact with it. David, before killing the Philistine, is taunted by the giant, "Am I a dog, that you come to me with sticks?" (1 Sam 17:43) Likewise, Abner, commander of King Saul's army, asks Ishbaal, Saul's son, after Saul's death, "Am I a dog's head for Judah?" (2 Sam 3:8) Abner had

---

3. Ibid., 60.
4. Ibid., 75.
5. Grimm, 114.
6. Ibid., 115.

maintained loyalty to Saul's heir, but Ishbaal had accused him of sleeping with one of his father's concubines; Abner was innocent of the crime.

However, one of the best dog insults involves the prophet Elijah, King Ahab, and Queen Jezebel. The queen devises of plot to steal a vineyard from Naboth for Ahab, King of Israel. God sends Elijah to right this wrong. He delivers this message to Ahab: "Thus says the LORD: In the place where dogs licked up the blood of Naboth, dogs will also lick up your blood" (1 Kgs 21:19b). Later, Elijah adds, "Also concerning Jezebel the LORD said, 'The dogs shall eat Jezebel within the bounds of Jezreel'" (1 Kgs 21:23). A few years later, King Ahab is killed in battle in his chariot, from which the dogs lick his blood (cf. 1 Kgs 22:38). A few years after that, Jezebel is thrown out of a window. Her blood spatters on the wall, horses trample her body, and dogs eat her flesh (cf. 2 Kgs 9:30–37). In the Book of Mosiah in *Mormon*, the prophet Abinadi is sent by God to tell his people that "because of their iniquities," they will be slain "and the dogs . . . shall devour their flesh" (Mosiah 12:2). Likewise, those who refuse to repent "shall become meat for dogs" (Hel 7:19). There may be some remembrance in Helaman of the biblical account in Luke's unique story of a rich man, who never sees the poor man at his gate; "even the dogs would come and lick [the poor man's] sores" (Luke 16:21).

Even Jesus, a man of his own culture, refers to a Syrophoenician woman as a dog. When she asks him to heal her daughter, he tells her that it is not fair to take the children's food and throw it to the dogs (cf. Mark 7:27). "Children" refers to Jews; "dogs" refers to Gentiles. This unnamed woman counters Jesus with these words: "Sir, even the dogs under the table eat the children's crumbs" (Mark 7:28). Jesus rewards the woman's cleverness. The author of Matthew's Gospel copies this story from Mark, expanding it, and making the woman a Canaanite (cf. Matt 15:22) so the reader is clear about her non-Jewish status. Jesus states that he was sent only to the lost sheep of the house of Israel (cf. Matt 15:24). Then, Matthew copies Mark: "It is not fair to take the children's food and throw it to the dogs" (Matt 15:26). The woman replies, "Yes, Lord, yet even the dogs eat the crumbs that fall from their masters' table" (Matt 15:27). After praising the woman's faith, he heals her daughter reluctantly. Before this, the Matthean Jesus had told his disciples, "Do not give what is holy to dogs" (7:6a). In *Mormon*, Jesus is quoted as saying, "Give not that which is holy unto the dogs" (3 Ne 14:6). In other words, the disciples are not to give what is Jewish to Gentiles (that is, to non-Jews).

The HB (OT) Book of Proverbs contains a wisdom saying, comparing a fool to "a dog that returns to its vomit" (Prov 26:11). Quoting this saying, the author of the CB (NT) Second Letter of Peter refers to his opponent, one who after baptism returns to his former way of life, as a "dog turns back to its own vomit" (2 Pet 2:22). *Mormon* uses this saying to describe how "people had turned from their righteousness, like the dog to his vomit . . ." (3 Ne 7:8).

The Quran contains two references to a dog's life. Allah states that he gave signs to man so that man would turn back to him, but man ignored God's signs

> so that Satan came after him, and he went astray. We wished to exalt him, but he loved baseness and followed his lust. His likeness is that of a dog who hangs out his tongue if you drive him away, and still hangs it out if you leave him alone. Such is the case of the people who deny [God's] signs. (*Quran* 7:175–76)

The other reference is to the unclean quality of dogs. Again, the holy book refers to those believers who stray, like a dog. God says: "You may have thought that they were awake, yet they were asleep. We made them turn right and left, while their dog lay with his forelegs stretched across the threshold. If you had looked at them, you would have surely turned away and fled with horror at the sight" (*Quran* 18:18). According to Foltz, "dogs are classified as ritually unclean" in the Muslim world. This means that "a Muslim may not pray after being touched by a dog."[7] Even farmers who own guard or herder dogs do not touch them. Thus, upon seeing a dog stretched in front of a door, a devout Muslim should turn the other way so as not to touch the dog or let the dog touch him.

Over twenty of *Aesop's Fables* feature the wretched life of a dog. "The Mischievous Dog" is one such tale about a dog "who used to snap at people and bite them without any provocation, and who was a great nuisance to everyone who came to his master's house."[8] The dog's master "fastened a bell round his neck to warn people of his presence."[9] Thinking that the bell was a badge of honor, the dog didn't realize that it was a warning to people approaching his master's house. "Notoriety is often mistaken for fame," says Aesop.[10] Another tale about "The Blacksmith and His Dog" explains how the ironworker's small dog slept while his master worked, "but was very

---

7. Foltz, "She-camel," 157.
8. Aesop, 3.
9. Ibid.
10. Ibid.

wide awake indeed when it was time for meals."[11] According to Aesop, the moral is this: "Those who will not work deserve to starve."[12]

Dog Eat Dog

Third, the phrase "dog eat dog" refers to ruthless competition between people. Just as a dog will eat whatever meat it can find, even another dog, so do people compete for positions of power and things. Again, three of *Aesop's Fables* illustrate this point. In one story, "The Wolves and the Dogs," the wolves convince the dogs that they have been ill treated by their master. So, the dogs hand over the flocks to the wolves, who promise the dogs a feast. However, when the dogs enter the wolf den, the wolves tear them to pieces, literally one dog eating another one.[13] In "The Dog and the Wolf," the dog escapes being eaten by the wolf by promising him a feast at a later time. When the wolf comes looking for the feast, all he finds is the dog on the stable's roof. The wolf has been tricked.[14] And in "The Dog Chasing a Wolf," the dog thinks that the wolf is scared of him, and that is why he is running away from him. However, the wolf tells him, "Don't you imagine I'm running away from you, my friend: it's your master I'm afraid of."[15] The implication is that the wolf will be chasing, capturing, and eating the dog soon.

Go to the Dogs

The final stage of the gradual decline of a business, friendship, or argument is often captured by the phrase "go to the dogs." Qoheleth, meaning "Teacher" or "Preacher" and the author of the HB (OT) Book of Ecclesiastes, attempts to illustrate this phrase after reflecting on the same fate of both the righteous and the wicked, namely, death. He concludes that the only difference between the good dead and the evil dead is that "whoever is joined with all the living has hope, for a living dog is better than a dead lion" (Eccl 9:4). The Teacher explains that the living know that they will die, but the dead know nothing; the dead have no more reward, and even the memory of them is lost to others (cf. Eccl 9:5). Aesop, too, illustrates

---

11. Ibid., 73
12. Ibid.
13. Cf. Ibid., 147.
14. Cf. Ibid., 177.
15. Ibid., 219.

this concept in "The Gardener and His Dog." The gardener's dog falls into a well, from which he attempts to extract him with the rope and bucket hanging over the well. After lowering himself into the well to get the dog, the dog bites the gardener; the gardener climbs out of the well, and lets it go to the dog.[16] A farm comes close to going to the dogs in "The Farmer and His Dogs." After a huge snowstorm, which prevented him from getting out to procure provisions for himself and his family, a farmer, successively, kills and eats his sheep, goats, and oxen. After observing this, the dogs decided to leave the farm, because they think that it has come to them, and they will be the next food for the farmer and his family.[17] Thus, this is the meaning of the fourth phrase "go to the dogs."

Let Sleeping Dogs Lie

The fifth phrase employing the word "dogs" is "let sleeping dogs lie." This phrase means that one should take no action in a seemingly peaceful, but potentially troublesome, situation. Nelson explains that in Hindu literature the dog is considered a "despised species."[18] Nelson narrates a tale about "a dog who was faithful to [Yudhisthira]," a king known for his piety as Dharmaraja (meaning "righteous king"), who made a pilgrimage to the Himalayas. Indra, the king of heaven in Hinduism, meets him on a mountain and tells him that he has come to take him to heaven; however, he will have to abandon the dog. After pleading with Indra, Yudhisthira declares that he will never abandon the dog. According to Nelson, "At that point the dog, who had been listening to the conversation, changed appearance, manifesting his true form as the god Dharma," Yudhisthira's god-father.[19] After mounting Indra's chariot, he entered into heaven. True righteousness is like a companion dog, which follows one to the end. Even Indra learns to let sleeping dogs lie.

Put on the Dog

Sixth, to "put on the dog" refers to making a display of wealth or knowledge ostentatiously or pretentiously. In "The Dogs and the Fox," one of *Aesop's Fables*, a few dogs put on the dog. A fox happens upon a group of dogs

---

16. Cf. Ibid., 171–72.
17. Cf. Ibid., 199.
18. Nelson, "Cows," 188.
19. Ibid.

chewing on a lion's skin. The fox tells them, "You think yourselves very brave, no doubt; but if that were a live lion, you'd find his claws a good deal sharper than your teeth."[20] Confucius discusses this concept in *The Analects*. In a commentary on how good birth is not enough to make a man a gentleman, Confucius states, "Culture is just as important as inborn qualities; and inborn qualities, no less important than culture. Remove the hairs from the skin of a tiger or panther, and what is left looks just like the hairless hide of a dog . . ." (*Analects* 12:8). In other words, even a man of good birth needs to add culture to his hide.

Care of Parents

Besides the six phrases about dogs explained above, religious literature uses the dog as an example for the care of parents in their old age. In *The Analects*, Confucius explains that "filial sons . . . are people who see to it that their parents get enough to eat." Then he adds: "But even dogs . . . are cared for to that extent. If there is no feeling of respect, wherein lies the difference?" (*Analects* 2:7) Likewise, "The Man, the Horse, the Ox, and the Dog" in *Aesop's Fables* narrates a story about a horse, an ox, and a dog that beg a man for shelter during a snow storm. The man lets them into his home, lights a fire to warm them, and feeds them. According to the fable, they showed their gratitude to the man.

> They divided the life of man among them, and each endowed one part of it with the qualities which were peculiarly his own. . . . [T]he dog took old age, which is the reason why old men are so often peevish and ill-tempered, and, like dogs, attached chiefly to those who look to their comfort, while they are disposed to snap at those who are unfamiliar or distasteful to them.[21]

Spiritual Medium

According to Sterckx, in pre-Buddhist China, the dog, more than any other animal, acted as a spiritual medium. "Dogs embodied familiarity and proximity between the human and animal world. They lived on the threshold of the realms of the living and the dead, and their mediating role between the domestic world and the world outside is well attested."[22] Sterckx also narrates

20. Aesop, 187.
21. Ibid., 189.
22. Sterckx, "Tawny Bull," 263.

a story about a "white dog operating as the agent of an underworld official."[23] The dog is sent to dig up a burial pit from which a deceased man has been released to rejoin the world of the living. Again, "the role of the dog [is that of] guardian or mediator for the passage into different territory. . . ."[24] The Egyptian jackal (dog) god Anubis protected the dead, warding off tomb scavengers, and was also credited with the invention of embalming. A statute of Anubis, either in the likeness of a dog or of a man with a dog's head, was often placed in front of tombs. In *The Rig Veda*, the god of the dead is Yama, who shows souls to the home of the departed. The dead are told: "Run and out speed the two dogs, Sarama's offspring, brindled, four-eyed upon your happy pathway" (*RV* 10:14:10). Sarama is the female dog of the chief Hindu deity, Indra. Sarama gave two dogs to Yama to be "watchers, four-eyed, who look on men and guard the pathway" (*RV* 10:14:11) to the abode of the departed. Thus, while the Hindu god is not in the form of a dog, the Lord of the Dead has two dogs assisting him.

While dogs are considered spiritual mediums in China and protectors of the dead in Egypt and India, in the CB (NT) they are used as metaphors for those who pervert the gospel. For example, in his Letter to the Philippians, Paul tells his readers to beware of the dogs (cf. Phil 3:2). Remember, in Jewish circles the term "dog" was applied to Gentiles and other outsiders. Likewise in the Book of Revelation, the author states that outside the new Jerusalem are the dogs (cf. Rev 22:15). The holy is inside the city; the non-holy is outside, the realm of the dogs. Hinduism's *The Rig Veda* sees dogs similarly. "Drive . . . away the dog, my friends, drive the long-tongued dog away," begins one hymn (*RV* 9:101:1). The purpose is to keep the dog from drinking the soma juice, the celestial nectar and drink of the gods. Another hymn begs Indra, the supreme Hindu deity, to hurl his "bolt of stone" (*RV* 7:101:19) from heaven at the "demon dogs" (*RV* 7:101:20) and to "destroy the fiend . . . in the form of [a] dog . . ." (*RV* 7:101:22).

Man's best friend or companion appears as the subject of many fables and is used as a metaphor for describing people who keep others from having what they want or need. "Dog" is used to describe a wretched existence, ruthless competition, decline, leaving good enough alone, and ostentation. The way a person cares for a dog informs the way he or she should care for parents. The dog can serve as a spiritual medium and a metaphor for perversion.

23. Ibid.
24. Ibid., 264.

Journal/Meditation: What images and metaphors does the word "dog" evoke in you? What has been your experience with a dog? In what ways has a dog served as a spiritual guide for you?

Prayer: Creator God, you gave the dog as a companion to people, to protect and to guide them. Grant that I may learn authentic faithfulness from this creature and care more deeply for all you have created. Hear this prayer in the name of your Son, Jesus Christ, who lives and reigns with you and the Holy Spirit, one God, forever and ever. Amen.

Dove (Turtledove)

Text: ". . . [W]hen Jesus had been baptized, just as he came up from the water, suddenly the heavens were opened to him and he saw the Spirit of God descending like a dove and alighting on him." (Matt 3:16)

Reflection: Except for biblical literature and a few verses in *The Rig Veda*, the dove is not known in other sacred writings. The verse above from Matthew's Gospel uses the dove as a metaphor for the Holy Spirit. The author of Matthew's Gospel copied the metaphor from Mark (cf. Mark 1:10) as did the author of Luke's Gospel. However, Luke's Gospel states that the Holy Spirit descended upon Jesus in bodily form like a dove (cf. Luke 3:22). John's Gospel portrays John the Baptist stating that he saw the Holy Spirit descend from heaven like a dove (cf. John 1:32). Thus, in much Christian iconography, murals, and paintings a dove can be seen depicting the Holy Spirit. In many old churches, a dove may be painted on the ceiling of the sanctuary indicating the descent of the Holy Spirit.

A dove is a bird of the pigeon family with a heavy body, a small head, and a cooing call. A turtledove is a bird with black and chestnut upper parts, a pink breast, and a black and white neck, noted for its purring call. These characteristics give rise to the various metaphors employing the dove. For example, the dove is a sign of innocence. In his missionary instructions to his disciples, the Matthean Jesus uniquely tells them to be innocent as doves (cf. Matt 10:16).

The dove is also a sign of peace. In the HB (OT) book of Genesis, Noah sends a dove from the ark three times to see if the flood waters have subsided. The first time the dove returns to Noah because there is no place for the bird to land. The second time the dove returns with an olive leaf. And the third time the dove does not return, indicating to Noah that it is now safe to leave the ark because the dove has found a place to land (cf. Gen 8:8–12). The flight of the dove to a tree inspired the author of Psalm 55 to compare the dove's roosting place to a person's resting place. "O that I had wings like a dove!" declares the psalmist. "I would fly away and be at rest" (Ps 55:6). In a similar vein, the prophet Jeremiah exhorts the inhabitants of Moab to "be like the dove that nests on the sides of the mouth of a gorge" (Jer 48:28).

The cooing sound made by the dove gives rise to two more metaphors: moaning and mourning. The prophet Isaiah records a psalm-like prayer of King Hezekiah, who, after he had been sick and had recovered from his illness, declares, "I moan like a dove" (Isa 38:14). In one of the prophet Ezekiel's prophecies about the end of Israel, he writes, "If any survivors escape, they shall be found on the mountains like doves of the valleys, all of them moaning over their iniquity" (Ezek 7:16). Likewise, the prophet Nahum says that the inhabitants of Nineveh will moan like doves (cf. Nah 2:7). Isaiah combines the moaning and mourning dove metaphors, stating "like doves we moan mournfully" (Isa 59:11b), describing the Jews without God's protection of Jerusalem and the temple.

The dove also becomes a term of endearment, that is, an affectionate name for a loved one. The HB (OT) book known as the Song of Solomon or the Song of Songs records the male lover telling his beloved that "the voice of the turtledove is heard in [the] land" (Song 2:12). He addresses her as "O my dove, in the clefts of the rock, in the covert of the cliff, let me see your face, let me hear your voice; for your voice is sweet, and your face is lovely" (Song 2:14). Later in the book he refers to her again as his dove (cf. Song 5:2; 6:9). Also both lovers repeatedly declare that the other's eyes are doves (cf. Song 1:15; 4:1, 5:12).

The most extensive biblical use for dove or turtledove is that of a sacrificial animal. God seals the covenant with Abram using a turtledove (cf. Gen 15:9). The HB (OT) book of Leviticus specifies that the Israelites who cannot afford to offer God cattle or sheep may offer the LORD "a burnt offering of birds," choosing "from turtledoves or pigeons" (Lev 1:14). Usually "two turtledoves or two pigeons" (Lev 5:7, 14:22; 15:14, 29; Num 6:10) will suffice.

The HB (OT) Book of Exodus states that the LORD told Moses to "consecrate to [him] all the firstborn; whatever is the first to open the womb among the Israelites, of human beings and animals, is [his]" (Exod 13:2). The author of Luke's Gospel in the CB (NT) seems to have combined that idea with that of the instruction in Leviticus about the purification of a woman who conceives and bears a male child (cf. Lev 12:1–8). Luke alludes to Jesus being presented in the temple instead of Mary's ceremonial

Dove (Turtledove) 31

uncleanness being removed after childbirth (cf. Luke 2:22–23). Because Joseph and Mary are poor, according to Luke, they "offered a sacrifice" of "a pair of turtledoves or two young pigeons" (Luke 2:24) as specified for Mary's purification in Leviticus 12:8.

Doves were being used for sacrifice during Jesus' adult ministry. All four gospels in the CB (NT) record the event of Jesus entering the temple and driving out those who were selling and those who were buying in the temple (cf. Mark 11:15). However, he overturns "the seats of those who sold doves" only in Mark's Gospel (Mark 11:15) and in Matthew's Gospel (cf. Matt 21:2). The author of Luke's Gospel records the event but does not mention doves. In John's Gospel this event happens at the beginning of his ministerial career—in contrast to it occurring near the end of it in Mark, Matthew, and Luke. Jesus sees people selling doves (cf. John 2:14). John uniquely records, "He told those who were selling the doves, 'Take these things out of here! Stop making my Father's house a marketplace!'" (John 2:16)

In *The Rig Veda*, the dove appears in only one hymn, number 165 in book 10. All five verses of the hymn mention the dove. However, the dove is considered an ill-omened bird; the "harmless bird" (*RV* 10:165:2) is "the envoy of destruction" (*RV* 10:165:1) which has flown into a house and "beside the fireplace, on the hearth it settles" (*RV* 10:165:3). Those who see this messenger of death are told, "Drive forth the dove, chase it with holy verses . . ." (*RV* 10:165:5). The hymn concludes: "Let the swift bird fly forth and leave us vigor" (*RV* 10:165:5).

The dove can serve as a sign of God's Holy Spirit as well as innocence and peace. Its cooing sound gives rise to using it as a metaphor for moaning and mourning. Used as a term of endearment, it serves as an affectionate name for a loved one. Two doves or turtledoves were often specified as a sacrifice for the poor, who could not afford to offer cattle or sheep to God. In Hinduism's scriptures, the dove is an omen of death that flies into a room and settles on the hearth of the fireplace. Such is the variegated spirituality represented by the dove.

Journal/Meditation: Which of the following uses of the dove do you like the best: Holy Spirit, innocence, peace, moaning and mourning, term of endearment, sacrifice, omen of death? What does the use tell you about yourself? about your spirituality?

Prayer: LORD God, your Spirit's image of a dove brings me innocence and peace. Accept this prayer as one from a poor man (woman), and grant that at the end of my life I may hear you summon me as your dove, your beloved, to the kingdom of heaven, where you live with my Lord Jesus Christ and the Holy Spirit forever and ever. Amen.

Eagle

Text: "... Moses went up to God; the LORD called to him from the mountain, saying, 'Thus you shall say to the house of Jacob, and tell the Israelites: You have seen what I did to the Egyptians, and how I bore you on eagles' wings and brought you to myself.'" (Exod 19:3–4)

Reflection: The eagle is a large and powerful bird of prey with a hooked bill and a broad wingspan. The eagle, noted for its keen eyesight and majestic soaring flight, hunts by day. In various cultures the eagle represents power and, as such, appears as an image on standards, seals, and money. In particular, as noted in the passage from the HB (OT) Book of Exodus above, the eagle's wings represent God's power to rescue. The LORD tells Moses that he delivered the Israelites from Egyptian slavery by carrying them on eagles' wings through all the events of the exodus and bringing them to himself at Mount Sinai (Horeb). In the HB (OT) Book of Deuteronomy, Moses recites the words of a song praising God for choosing Jacob (the Israelites). In one verse he declares, "As an eagle stirs up its nest, and hovers over its young; as it spreads its wings, takes them up, and bears them aloft on its pinions, the LORD alone guided [Jacob]" (Deut 32:11–12a).

The very same idea is found in the *Book of Doctrine and Covenants* of the Reorganized Church of Jesus Christ of Latter Day Saints. In a revelation given to Joseph Smith on January 19, 1841, God declares that it is his will that his servant, Lyman Wight, "should continue in preaching for Zion, in the spirit of meekness, confessing [him] before the world, and [he] will bear him up as on eagle's wings, . . . that when he shall finish his work, that [God] may receive him unto [him]self . . ." (*D&C* 107:7).

The rescuing aspect of the eagle is enshrined in Aesop's fable about the serpent and the eagle. After swooping down upon a snake and capturing it, the eagle discovers that the serpent has coiled around the bird; "and then there ensued a life-and-death struggle between the two."[1] A man, however, came to the eagle's rescue, freeing the eagle from the snake, which spat poison into the man's drinking water. Just as the man was about to take a drink "the eagle knocked [the water container] out of his hand and spilled its contents upon the ground."[2] According to the moral, "one good turn deserves another."[3] Also, it is important to note that in this story the eagle rescues the man, just as God rescues people.

Kemmerer records a Christian legend about an eagle sheltering St. Medard from a rainstorm with her great wings;[4] St. Menard is a sixth-century French preacher and missioner. Opoku records that the emblem for the Asakyiri clan of the Akan of Ghana is an eagle, representing powerful vigilance.[5] And Lawrence narrates a story about a wren that hid itself in an eagle's feathers in a contest to determine which bird could fly the highest. Using the eagle's power, the wren emerges just as the eagle is about to declare itself the winner of the race. The wren "flew a few inches upward and declared itself winner of the race and king of all the birds."[6] According to Lawrence, ". . . [T]he tale expresses the idea that through cunning and strategy the smallest and most unpromising contestant defeated the largest and most powerful creature."[7]

The reason the eagle is used as an image of power is because of its ability to mount the wind currents, to fly to great heights, and to soar. In the same revelation from the *Book of Doctrine and Covenants* noted above, God describes his servant William Law as one he shall lead "in paths where the poisonous serpent cannot lay hold upon his heel, and he shall mount up in the imagination of his thoughts as upon eagle's wings" (*D&C* 107:30). The Bible contains several references to the eagle's ability to mount up to its nest on high (cf. Job 39:27). The prophet Isaiah, offering hope to his readers, puts it this way: ". . . [T]hose who wait for the LORD shall renew their strength, they shall mount up with wings like eagles, they shall run and not be weary, they shall walk and not faint" (Isa 40:31).

Closely allied with the eagle's ability to mount is its ability to fly. This is due to its huge wingspan. This attribute is employed in the HB (OT) Book of

1. Aesop, 216–17.
2. Ibid., 217.
3. Ibid.
4. Cf. Kemmerer, *Animals*, 230.
5. Cf. Opoku, "African Mythology," 357.
6. Lawrence, "Hunting the Wren," 407.
7. Ibid.

Proverbs. Chapter 23 presents dining etiquette that focuses on moderation. When eating with a ruler, a diner should not be focused on the delicacies or riches. According to Proverbs, when a diner's eyes light upon delicacies or riches, they are gone; for suddenly they take wings to themselves, "flying like an eagle toward heaven" (Prov 23:5c). In a comment later, the author of the book adds that there are four things he cannot understand; one of those is "the way of an eagle in the sky" (Prov 30:19a), that is, the effortless way it seems to fly.

The prophet Habakkuk describes the Babylonian war machine getting ready to descend upon Judah, declaring that their horsemen fly like an eagle swift to devour its prey (cf. Hab 1:8b). John of Patmos employs this idea when he describes the woman who gives birth to the male child destined to rule the nations. God gives her "two wings of the great eagle" (Rev 12:14) so that she can fly away from the great red dragon into the wilderness.

The eagle's ability to fly is also employed by *The Rig Veda*. Indra, the supreme deity in Hinduism, declares in one hymn that he will delay the Maruts, his attendants, "on their journey [by] sweeping—with what high spirit!—through the air like eagles" (*RV* 1:165:2b). In another hymn, the stones used to press the leaves of an unidentified plant to make soma juice, a ritual drink, are compared to eagles. "The eagles have sent forth their cry aloft in heaven; in the sky's value the dark impetuous ones have danced," states the hymn. "Then downward to the nether stone's fix[ed] place they sink, and, splendid as the sun, effuse their copious stream" (*RV* 10:94:5). The rising sun is described as having "eagle pinions" in another hymn (*RV* 1:163:1); a pinion is the terminal section of a bird's wing, otherwise known as its flight feathers.

The CB (NT) Book of Revelation records John of Patmos narrating his vision of an eagle. Besides the bird's ability to fly, John records it speaking. He writes that he heard an eagle crying with a loud voice as it flew in mid-heaven (cf. Rev 8:13). Here, John is comparing the screeching sound of the eagle to the woeful forces about to be unleashed on the earth.

The eagle's ability to soar is employed by the prophet Obadiah in his single speech against the nation of Edom. The prophet tells the Edomites, "Though you soar aloft like the eagle, though your nest is set among the stars, from there I will bring you down, says the LORD" (Obad :4). In other words, the soaring nation of Edom will fall because it took advantage of the nation of Judah's weaknesses after it was destroyed by the Babylonians.

Aesop narrates a fable about "The Tortoise and the Eagle." The tortoise begs the eagle to teach him to fly. The eagle attempts to dissuade the tortoise, until he presses him "with entreaties and promises of treasure, insisting that it could only be a question of learning the craft of the air."[8] Finally, the eagle consents, picking up the tortoise in his talons. "Soaring with him to a great height in the sky he then let him go, and the wretched tortoise fell headlong and was dashed to pieces on a rock."[9]

Closely allied to the eagle's soaring is the eagle's swiftness. In the HB (OT) Book of Second Samuel, King Saul and his son Jonathan are hymned by David after their deaths. He describes them as being swifter than eagles (cf. 2 Sam 1:23b). Jeremiah declares that his mythic foe-from-the-north's "horses are swifter than eagles" (Jer 4:13c). The Book of Lamentations echoes the prophet's words, describing the Babylonians as the "pursuers" who "were swifter than the eagles in the heavens" (Lam 4:19a).

In a rather strange fable, Aesop lauds the swiftness of eagle feathers. In "The Eagle and the Arrow," an eagle, perched on a high rock, keeps looking for prey but fails to see a huntsman, who shoots an arrow and hits the eagle in the breast. To the arrow the eagle says, "Ah! Cruel fate that I should perish thus: but oh! fate more cruel still, that the arrow which kills me should be winged with an eagle's feathers!"[10]

Jeremiah combines the mounting aspect of the eagle with its ability to swoop when describing the destruction of the Edomites in his poems against Judah's neighboring nations which often were her enemies. God declares that he will mount up and swoop down like an eagle, spreading his wings against Edom (cf. Jer 49:22). This image uses the eagle's sweeping movement as it makes a sudden attack on prey to describe how fast God will destroy Judah's enemies. Job, too, alludes to this motion of the eagle in one of his speeches. In describing how fast his life passes, Job compares his days to an eagle swooping on prey (cf. Job 9:26). Likewise, in the sections on the curses God will place upon the Israelites for their disobedience, Moses states, "The LORD will bring a nation from far away, from the end of the earth, to swoop down on your like an eagle . . ." (Deut 28:49). Thus, the swooping motion of the eagle becomes a metaphor for destruction in the Bible.

Likewise, Aesop narrates a fable about "The Eagle and the Cocks." Two roosters in the same farmyard fight to decide who is the master. The beaten one hides in a corner while the winner flies to the roof of the stable and crows loudly. A high-flying eagle spies him and swoops down and carries him off.[11]

8. Aesop, 67.
9. Ibid.
10. Ibid., 88.
11. Cf. Ibid., 114.

Eagle

The prophet Ezekiel has a vision of four living creatures, each of which has four faces. One of the four faces is that of an eagle (cf. Ezek 1:10; 10:14). The eagle's face represents divine mobility, meaning that God can move from one place to another, just as an eagle can fly from one place to another. This same image is used by the author of the CB (NT) Book of Revelation to describe the four living creatures surrounding God's throne. The fourth living creature is like a flying eagle (cf. Rev 4:7). As in Ezekiel, so here the eagle represents God's mobility. The fact that there are four of these creatures indicates that God is able to be everywhere in heaven and on earth. While it is not biblical, popular iconography represents John's Gospel with an eagle. As is often seen on the cover of a *Book of Gospels*, four creatures with wings (a lion, a man, an ox, and an eagle) appear. Each creature is paired with a gospel (lion, Mark; man, Matthew; ox, Luke; and eagle, John); thus, each creature serves as an icon or image for a specific gospel. The same four living creatures can also be found "on the tympani of medieval cathedrals or on the pages of medieval manuscript illuminations."[12]

The prophet Ezekiel also uses the eagle in an allegory. The allegory begins: "A great eagle with great wings and long pinions, rich in plumage of many colors, came to the Lebanon. He took the top of the cedar, broke off its topmost shoot; he carried it to a land of trade; set it in a city of merchants" (Ezek 17:3-4). The eagle is King Nebuchadnezzar of Babylon. The cedar is a reference to the Davidic palace in Jerusalem. The topmost shoot is King Jehoichin, whom Nebuchadnezzar exiled to Babylon, the land of trade. The analogy continues: "There was another great eagle, with great wings and much plumage" (Ezek 17:7a). This great eagle is the Egyptian Pharaoh Psammetichus II, to whom Zedekia, Jehoichin's uncle, who was set up as king in Jehoichin's place, turned for support in his revolt against Nebuchadnezzar. Thus, the great eagle serves as an analogy for rulers. Likewise, the prophet Daniel has a vision of a lion with eagles' wings (cf. Dan 7:4), representing the Babylonian Empire.

Thus, God's bearing his people on eagles' wings demonstrates his potency, as does the eagle's ability to mount, fly, and soar. Just as God saves, he also destroys, as seen in the eagle's swooping upon prey in all its swiftness. God's mobility is demonstrated by the living creature with the face of an eagle. And if the eagle can be used to portray a ruler, how much more can an eagle be used to portray the healing, illumination, and power of God.

---

12. Apostolos-Cappadona,"*Dynamis* of Animals," 448.

Journal/Meditation: Which characteristic of the eagle do you think about first when seeing an eagle in the wild or on television? How does that characteristic inform your spirituality?

Prayer: Heavenly God, on eagles' wings you brought your chosen people to yourself. Deepen my awareness of your presence everywhere, and grant that as I patiently wait for you, my strength may be renewed. May I one day swiftly fly with wings like an eagle's to the kingdom, where you live and reign as Father, Son, and Holy Spirit, forever and ever. Amen.

Elephant

Text: "[The house of Emer] had horses, and asses, and there were elephants . . . ; all of which were useful unto man [and woman], and more especially the elephants . . . ." (Ether 9:19)

Reflection: The elephant is the largest living land animal. It is usually gray in color or grayish brown mammal with a long flexible trunk, large prominent ears, thick legs, and pointed tusks. In the sacred literature of the religions of the world, the elephant is considered a war animal, whose training is often associated with human mindfulness teaching. *Mormon's* Book of Ether mentions the elephant only one time, as can be seen above. In this supposed history of early Americans, called Jaredites, who left the tower of Babel (cf. Gen 11:1–9) and traveled by barge to north America, the elephant is understood to be a work animal, a beast of burden, and a pack animal, like a horse or donkey.

Hinduism's *The Rig Veda* often uses the elephant as a metaphor. For example, the storm deities, called the Maruts, are "like the wild elephants" that "eat the forests up when [they] assume [their] strength among the bright red flames" (*RV* 1:64:7). In other words, the lightning that sets the forests on fire, which devours them, is like the wild elephants, which eat the trees and devour them. Similarly, Agni, the god of fire, is compared to a bull elephant that "consumes the trees" (*RV* 1:140:2).

Indra, the lord of heaven and Hindu supreme deity, is the god of rain and thunderstorms. Riding on a white elephant, Indra wields a lightning thunderbolt. Thus, is it is not surprising to find Indra compared to a wild and stately elephant. Hymn 16 of book 4 of *The Rig Veda* declares that Indra is "a wild elephant with might invested" (*RV* 4:16:14). "As a wild elephant rushes on, this way and that way, mad with heat, none may compel [Indra]," states hymn 33 of book 8, because the god "moves mighty in [his] power" (*RV* 8:33:8). Whoever seeks Indra's enmity, according to hymn 45 of book 8, "will battle like a stately elephant on a hill" (*RV* 8:45:5). But the stately elephant, Indra's antagonist, will not be powerful enough to beat the god who rides the white elephant.

As Vargas makes clear, "The image of the elephant is often the insignia of India, symbolizing royalty and supremacy."[1] Vargas continues: "Cosmologically, eight or sixteen elephants support the physical universe . . . . It was also the exclusive privilege of a king to be carried by an elephant, and so images of the Buddha with elephants remind the reader of his own royal pedigree."[2]

Likewise, worshipers of the Asvins, vedic gods symbolizing the shining of sunrise and sunset and averting misfortune and sickness in Hinduism, are like "hunters [who] follow two wild elephants" (*RV* 10:40:4). Another hymn in the same book states that the Asvins "are like two mad elephants bending their forequarters and smiting the foe" (*RV* 10:106:6).

The power of the sacred drink named soma or Soma Pavamana in *The Rig Veda* leaves those who sip it feeling "like a docile king of elephants" (*RV* 9:57:3). In other words, those who imbibe the sacred intoxicant feel like a pious king among his retinue, or like an elephant king, or like a stately and noble elephant. This helps to understand Harris's statement about "the close connection between elephant ownership and kingship."[3] Furthermore, "being able to ride an elephant . . . is said to be the sign of high merit, and in an interesting metaphor the training of an elephant is compared to the meditative techniques associated with the . . . foundations of mindfulness."[4] More about the elephant as a metaphor of mindfulness can be found below.

In the OT (A) books of First and Second Maccabees, the elephant is considered a war machine. The elephant then was equivalent to a tank now. The Syrian King Antiochus IV Epiphanies ruled Palestine at the time of the Maccabees (175 BCE). He "invaded Egypt with a strong force, with chariots and elephants and cavalry and with a large fleet" (1 Macc 1:17). Before leaving for Persia, he left Lysias, a man of royal lineage, in charge of the king's affairs (cf. 1 Macc 3:32), giving him "half of his forces and the elephants" (1 Macc 3:34); the Second Book of Maccabees tells the reader that he had

---

1. Vargas, "Snake-Kings," 220.
2. Ibid.
3. Harris, "Recycling Plant," 208.
4. Ibid.

eighty elephants (cf. 2 Macc 11:4), and later he attacks Judea with twenty-two elephants (cf. 2 Macc 13:2).

In 163 BCE, according to the First Book of Maccabees, after Antiochus IV Epiphanies's death, his son, Antiochus IV Eupator, defeated Judas Maccabeus with, among other forces, "thirty-two elephants accustomed to war" (1 Macc 6:30). After Judas and his troops flee Jerusalem, Antiochus pursues them. According to the biblical account, the king gets ready for battle by offering "the elephants the juice of grapes and mulberries to arouse them for battle" (1 Macc 6:34). Then, "with each elephant [Antiochus's troops] stationed a thousand men armed with coats of mail, and with brass helmets on their heads; and five hundred picked horsemen were assigned to each beast" (1 Macc 6:35). Furthermore, "on the elephants were wooden towers, strong and covered; they were fastened on each animal by special harness, and one each were four armed men who fought from there, and also its Indian driver" (1 Macc 6:37). Thus, the elephant tank approached Eleazar, one of Judas's troops, who "got under the elephant, stabbed it from beneath, and killed it; but it fell to the ground upon him and he died" (1 Macc 6:46). According to the Second Book of Maccabees, it was Judas who stabbed the leading elephant and its rider (cf. 2 Macc 13:15b).

Elephants were so important in warfare that a soldier was in command of the elephants (cf. 2 Macc 14:12), which in battle were strategically stationed (cf. 2 Macc 15:20). In one battle, the narrator of the Second Book of Maccabees states that Judas Maccabeus sees "the savagery of the elephants" (2 Macc 15:21) and begins to pray that God will assist him and his troops in battle.

The importance of elephants as weapons of war can be seen in the other references to them in the books of Maccabees. Rome is admired for its ability to conquer people, even those armies "who went to fight . . . with one hundred twenty elephants" (1 Macc 8:6). Capturing the enemy's elephants gives control of a city to the conqueror (cf. 1 Macc 11:56).

Buddhism's *The Dhammapada* also views the elephant as an animal of war, dedicating a whole chapter (23) of fourteen strophes of four verses each to it. The elephant serves as an example of mindfulness. For example, the writer declares that he "shall endure the unwarranted word" of those who "are of poor virtue, . . . like an elephant in battle" (*Dhp* 23:320). In other words, just as a well-disciplined elephant endures attacks in battle, so will the disciplined person practicing Buddhism deflect the harsh "unwarranted word" (*Dhp* 23:321) of others. "Excellent are tamed . . . tuskers, great elephants. But better than them is one who has subdued oneself" (*Dhp* 23:322) by the four noble paths. Even a tamed elephant cannot take a person to that place where only "a well-subdued, disciplined self" can go (*Dhp* 23:323).

The mind is like a "tusker . . . deep in rut, . . . hard to control. Bound, the tusker does not eat a morsel, but remembers the elephant forest" (*Dhp* 23:324). According to *The Dhammapada*, the mind wanders wherever it wishes and according to its pleasure, but it must be disciplined "like one seizing a goad" to restrain "an elephant in rut" (*Dhp* 23:326). Mindfulness is the desire of the Buddhist, who delights in awareness, keeping watch over the mind, "like a tusker, sunk in mire" (*Dhp* 23:327), lifts itself from the mud pit to stand on firm ground.

A "mature companion" (*Dhp* 23:328) is recommended, that is, one who is wise and disciplined. Not having such a person means that the Buddhist wanders alone, "like the elephant in the . . . forest" (*Dhp* 23:329). In other words, just as the great elephant goes about comfortably wherever it will in the forest, unattached, "with little exertion," so can a person "wander alone and do no wrongs" while living "a life of solitude" (*Dhp* 23:330).

Chapter 23 of *The Dhammapada* ends with a series of blessings that result from practicing awareness or being mindful:

> A blessing is contentment with whatever [there be],
> A blessing is the wholesome deed at the end of life,
> A blessing it is to relinquish all sorrow.
>
> A blessing in the world is reverence for mother,
> A blessing, too, is reverence for father,
> A blessing in the world is reverence for the recluse,
> A blessing, too, the reverence for the *brahmana*.
>
> A blessing is virtue into old age,
> A blessing is faith established,
> A blessing is the attainment of insight-wisdom,
> A blessing it is to refrain from doing wrongs." (*Dhp* 23:331–33)

This series of blessings illustrates the results of mindfulness. One is content, whole, without sorrow. A person reverences his or her parents and takes care of them in their older years; he or she also has great respect for the person who lives alone and for the one who speaks sacred words. The blessings of virtue in old age, faith, insight both ordinary and transcendent, and refraining from wrong-doing are the result of years and years of practicing mindfulness, just like one trains an elephant.

Thus, the elephant in world religions manifests a spirituality of work and serves as a metaphor for the wild power of Hindu deities. The elephant also represents royalty, supremacy, and nobility. As a war machine in biblical literature, it becomes an example of a well-disciplined mind in Buddhist literature. This largest of land animals teaches about the power of subduing oneself, and that is a spiritual practice.

Journal/Meditation: What is it about the power of the elephant that gets your attention? How would you characterize that spiritual trait?

Prayer: Almighty God, you have created the tuskers, great elephants, to manifest your strength, supremacy, nobility, and power. Grant that my meditation may be as disciplined as an elephant and that my self-control may enable me to delight in your royal presence. I ask this in the name of my Lord, Jesus Christ, who lives and reigns with you and the Holy Spirit, one God, forever and ever. Amen.

Fox

Text: "A farmer was greatly annoyed by a fox, which came prowling about his yard at night and carried off his fowls. So he set a trap for him and caught him; and in order to be revenged upon him, he tied a bunch of tow to his tail and set fire to it and let him go. As ill-luck would have it, however, the fox made straight for the fields where the corn was standing ripe and ready for cutting. It quickly caught fire and was all burnt up, and the farmer lost all his harvest. Revenge is a two-edged sword."[1]

Reflection: The fox is a wild carnivorous mammal of the dog family which has a pointed muzzle, large ears, a long bushy tail, and usually reddish-brown or gray fur. Being a night hunter, the fox relies on cunning and an acute sense of hearing and smell. Such is the way the fox is described in Aesop's fable above. He prowls around the yard at night, catches chickens, and carries them away. However, even though the farmer catches the fox, the fox, nevertheless, manages to live up to its fame as a trickster. Instead of getting revenge on the fox, the farmer ends up destroying his own crop of corn with the fire he sets to the tow on the fox's tail.

This particular fable is echoed in the biblical story of Samson in the HB (OT) Book of Judges. In taking revenge upon his Philistine father-in-law for having given his wife to Samson's companions, the famous judge

> went and caught three hundred foxes, and took some torches; and he turned the foxes tail to tail, and put a torch between each

---

1. Aesop, 117.

pair of tails. When he had set fire to the torches, he let the foxes go into the standing grain of the Philistines, and burned up the shocks and the standing grain, as well as the vineyards and olive groves. (Judg 15:4–5)

Thus, the foxes were a way of spreading the fire very widely and very quickly.

Aesop features almost thirty fables featuring a fox. As indicated above, most of the stories narrate a fox's ability to trick; however, there are also a number of accounts of another animal tricking the fox. As a trickster, the fox cunningly praises a crow with cheese in "The Fox and the Crow." The crow is so flattered that she drops the cheese when she begins to caw, and the fox snatches it and eats it.[2] In "The Fox and the Goat," a fox falls into a well and tricks a goat to jump in to taste the water. Once the goat is in the well, the fox climbs out by jumping on the goat's back, leaving the stupid goat in the well.[3] A fox, which had been trapped but escaped without his tail, attempts to trick the other foxes to cut off their tails in "The Fox without a Tail."[4] In "The Lion, the Wolf, and the Fox," the wolf tells the infirm-with-age lion that all the other animals of the forest, except the fox, are concerned about his health. When the fox finally shows up, he tells the lion that he can be cured if he is wrapped in a wolf's skin. The lion kills the wolf while the fox laughs to himself.[5] A fox tricks a big stag to enter a lion's den in "The Lion, the Fox, and the Stag"; the stag is killed and eaten by the lion. However, the fox tricks the lion by filching the stag's brains.[6]

The trickster quality of the fox is also found in *Grimm's Complete Fairy Tales*. In "The Wolf and the Fox," the fox is identified as the weaker of the two who once lived together, but also as the one who does all the work. The first time the wolf tells the fox, "Red fox, get me something to eat, or I shall eat you,"[7] the fox gets him one of two lambs. However, the wolf desires the other lamb as well, gets it, and is beaten by an old sheep. The next day the wolf says the same thing to the fox, which brings him six pancakes. However, the wolf wants more. When he attempts to get them, he surprises the farmer's wife, who raises an alarm which brings people with sticks and clubs to beat the wolf. A third time the wolf tells the fox to get him something to eat. So, the fox leads the wolf to freshly butchered meat in a cellar. The wolf gorges himself on the fresh meat. When the farmer shows up, the fox dashes

2. Cf. Ibid., 6.
3. Cf. Ibid., 42.
4. Cf. Ibid., 68.
5. Cf. Ibid., 203–04.
6. Cf. Ibid., 212–14.
7. Grimm, 136.

through the hole they had used to enter the cellar, but when the wolf tries to get through the hole, he is too bloated to get through and, consequently, gets stuck in the hole. The farmer promptly kills him. The fox makes it back to the woods in safety and rejoices to be freed from his living companion.[8] In "Gossip Wolf and the Fox," the fox tricks a wolf to attempt to steal sheep and then tricks him again to carry him to her house.[9]

In "How Mrs. Fox Married Again," "an old fox with nine tails, who wished to put his wife's affection to proof" pretends to be dead.[10] Once word is out that Mrs. Fox is a widow suitors begin to appear. The first is a one-tailed young fox, which is rejected by Mrs. Fox. The second suitor is two-tailed fox, which is rejected by Mrs. Fox. The line of suitors continues with the third fox having three tails, the fourth having four, etc. until the ninth fox appears with nine tails, like the old fox which had pretended death. Upon the nine-tailed fox being let into the house, the old fox jumps up and drives away all the suitors he had tricked into thinking he was dead. After the old fox dies, another line of suitors appear at Mrs. Fox's door: a wolf, a dog, a stag, a hare, a bear, a lion, and several other wild animals; she rejects all of them. At last there comes a young fox, which she marries.[11]

A fox tricks a lion using a horse in "The Fox and the Horse." After meeting an old horse which could not work anymore, the farmer challenges the horse to bring him a lion and he will maintain him in his old age. After the horse leaves his stable, he meets a fox which tricks him into playing dead while the fox goes off to get a lion. Because the horse is so big, the fox offers to fasten the supposed-dead horse to the lion so the lion can drag the horse to its den. However, the fox tied together the lion's legs with the horse's tail. After this, the horse jumped up and began to drag the lion back to the stable. When the horse's master saw the lion, he remembered his promise to the horse and gave him plenty to eat until he died.[12]

The fox's trickster ability is also found in the CB (NT). Insultingly, Jesus refers to Herod Antipas as a fox (cf. Luke 13:32). By identifying Herod as a fox, Jesus both insults him and refers to his ability to deceive.

Kienzle states that in the polemical literature of the twelfth and early thirteenth centuries, foxes were used to represent heretics. The fox was a type "of the heretic *par excellence*."[13] According to Kienzle, the wolf and

---

8. Ibid., 136–38.
9. Cf. Ibid., 139–40.
10. Ibid., 143.
11. Cf. Ibid., 143–46.
12. Cf. Ibid., 147–48.
13. Kienzle, "Bestiary," 106.

the fox "probably represent evil tendencies and behavior more than any other animals."[14] She adds that the fox "has a reputation for deceit and destruction."[15]

Also in the CB (NT), Jesus refers to the dens in which foxes live when speaking about not having a home himself. Both the author of Matthew's Gospel and the author of Luke's Gospel, employing material found in Q (from *Quelle*, meaning a source used by Matthew and Luke but not known to Mark or John), portray Jesus telling a person who wanted to follow him, "Foxes have holes, and birds of the air have nests; but the Son of Man has nowhere to lay his head" (Matt 8:20; Luke 9:58).

Besides living in a den in the ground and often being portrayed as a trickster, the fox is also often seen as gullible, the one tricked. In *Aesop's Fables*, there is the story "The Fox and the Stork." At first the fox tricks the stork, which he has invited to dinner, by serving soup in a large flat dish from which the fox easily laps it up, but the stork with its long bill has none of the broth. Later, however, the stork invites the fox to dinner; the fox serves it in a pitcher with a long narrow neck into which the stork could insert its bill and eat, but into which the fox's head would not fit.[16] "The Fox and the Monkey" features a monkey who tricks a fox.[17] In "The Dog, the Cock, and the Fox," the dog and the rooster travel together as friends; the dog sleeps at the foot of the tree and the cock in its branches. A fox attempts to get the rooster to fly down so that the fox can eat him, but the cock tells the fox he has to awaken the porter at the foot of the tree. The fox awakens the dog, which tears him to pieces. And thus, the fox is tricked by the cock.[18]

Even a grasshopper can trick a fox. In "The Fox and the Grasshopper," the fox attempts to get the grasshopper in the branches of a tree to come down by praising her song. However, the grasshopper has seen fellow grasshoppers' wings strewn about the entrance to the fox's den, and she will not be tricked by empty praise into coming down.[19] In "The Swollen Fox," the fox is tricked by food. After finding bread and meat in a hollow tree, the fox slips through the narrow opening and proceeds to eat all of it. However, when he attempts to leave through the same narrow opening, he cannot get out because he has increased in size.[20]

14. Ibid., 107.
15. Ibid.
16. Cf. Aesop, 23.
17. Cf. Ibid., 26–27.
18. Cf. Ibid., 29.
19. Cf. Ibid., 163.
20. Cf. Ibid., 56.

The fox is tricked by geese in "The Fox and the Geese." After spotting a flock of geese, a fox makes his way to them to devour them one after another. The geese request that the fox grant them their last wish, namely, to pray. The first prayed for a long time. The second prayed for a long time. The third prayed for a long time. "When they have done praying, the story shall be continued further, but at present they are still praying, and they show no sign of stopping."[21] A cat tricks a fox in "The Fox and the Cat." An arrogant fox teases a cat, which tells him that he can climb a tree and escape the hounds. The fox states, "I am master of a hundred arts, and have into the bargain a sack full of cunning."[22] A hunter with four dogs approaches, and the cat climbs a tree. "Open your sack, Mr. Fox, open your sack," said the cat. However, the dogs had already seized the fox.[23]

Harris narrates the tale of "How Mr. Rabbit was too Sharp for Mr. Fox," another story about a fox being tricked. A little boy asks Uncle Remus, "Did the fox kill and eat the rabbit when he caught him with the Tar-Baby?"[24] This gives Uncle Remus the opportunity to tell the story: Briar Rabbit keeps telling the fox that he doesn't care what the fox does with him as long as he doesn't fling him into the briar patch. At first the fox decides to barbecue the rabbit, then he decides, consecutively, to hang him, drown him, and skin him. After the fox tells the rabbit what he intends to do, the rabbit tells him he can do anything he wants, but he asks that he not toss him into the briar patch. Of course, that is exactly what the fox does, and the rabbit escapes, declaring that he was bred and born in a briar patch and was able to escape from the fox with ease.[25]

In *The Analects of Confucius*, the great teacher explains how a gentleman is to dress properly. When wearing "a yellow robe," the gentleman wears "fox fur" (*Analects* 10:6). Confucius explains that "the thicker kinds of fox [fur] . . . are for home wear" (*Analects* 10:6). Thus, *The Analects* disclose that the Chinese not only hunted the fox, but used its fur for clothing.

Kemmerer preserves a tale about the sixth-century Irish St. Ciaran of Clonmacnoise, who founded a monastery and became its first abbot. Ciaran often took wild animals as disciples, such as the fox, which "was sorely challenged by discipleship, and slunk away to the wild lands to chew on the Bible, only to be pursued by hounds, which forced him back to St. Ciaran."[26]

21. Grimm, 146.
22. Ibid., 148.
23. Ibid.
24. Harris, "Mr. Rabbit," 175.
25. Cf. Ibid., 175–78.
26. Kemmerer, *Animals*, 231.

After a while, the fox again abandons his monastic vows, slinking away to chew the saint's shoe. The abbot sends the badger to bring back the fox "to his discipleship, noting that such thievery becomes not monks."[27] Through thick and thin, St. Ciaran, the fox, and his other animal disciples "lived together in community until the end of their days."[28]

The fox is featured in a riddle in book 10 of *The Rig Veda*. The chief Hindu god, Indra, sings, "Resolve for me, O singer, this my riddle: . . . The fox steals up to the approaching lion . . ." (*RV* 10:28:4). As we have seen in other stories about the fox, the busy-tailed, cunning creature usually knows where to stop, especially when a powerful lion is present.

The fox reminds the reader of the ability to be cunning. But the trickster is also tricked, revealing his gullibility. Cleverness is not always a benefit. However, repentance and training in discipleship can change the most cunning fox into one of the best animals, exemplifying spiritual discretion.

Journal/Meditation: What emotions do you associate with the fox? What quality of the fox can foster your own spirituality?

Prayer: Of all your creatures, O God, the fox may be the cleverest. Share with me the same wisdom that you have instilled in this bushy-tailed, wild animal that I may learn from my failings. All praise be to you, Father, Son, and Holy Spirit, one God, forever and ever. Amen.

---

27. Ibid.
28. Ibid.

Goat

Text: "A thousand heads has Purusa, a thousand eyes, a thousand feet. On every side pervading earth he fills a space ten fingers wide. This Purusa is all that yet has been and all that is to be; the lord of immortality which waxes greater still by food. So mighty is his greatness; yes, greater than this is Purusa. All creatures are one-fourth of him, three-fourths eternal life in heaven. From that great general sacrifice [with Purusa as the gods' offering] the dripping fat was gathered up. He formed the creatures of the air; and animals both wild and tame. From it were horses born, from it all cattle with two rows of teeth; from it were generated kine, from it the goats and sheep were born." (*RV* 10:90:1–3, 8, 10)

Reflection: Hymn 90 of book 10 of *The Rig Veda* is dedicated to Purusa, a Hindu concept meaning embodied spirit, man's personified consciousness, soul, original source of the universe, and the life-giving principle in all animated beings. The hymn states that Purusa has one thousand eyes and feet, indicating that his presence cannot be counted because he represents all created life. For human kind his presence is as wide as the heart of a person, wherein the soul was located by ancient people. Furthermore, Purusa is lord of immortality, which grows greater through the sacrifices made by people. All creatures have been made by him from his own sacrificed self. From the curds and butter of dripping fat he created all the animals, both wild and tame. Also, from it the goats were born. Thus, Purusa is an abstract essence of self, spirit, and the universal principle that is eternal, indestructible, unchanging, without form, and all pervasive. Purusa connects everything and everyone. He is the being who becomes a sacrificial victim of gods and whose sacrifice creates all life forms, including human beings.

In Greek mythology, Pan, the god of nature, pastures, flocks, and forests is depicted with a human torso and head with hind legs, ears, and horns of a goat. Pan's Roman equivalent is Faunus, the god of nature, farming, and fertility. Thus, it is not difficult to see the resemblance between Purusa, Pan, and Faunus.

In book 6 of *The Rig Veda*, the god Pusan is identified as the "lord of the path" (*RV* 6:53:1), that is, custodian of roads and the guide of travelers. He also helps those find their lost property (cf. *RV* 6:54:1–2). He is "the lord of riches, who listens to . . . prayers." He is "the strong whose wealth is never lost" (*RV* 6:54:8). Pusan, a "bright god whose steeds are goats" (*RV* 6:55:3, 4), is "a stream of wealth, a treasure-heap, the friend of every pious man" (*RV* 6:55:3). The singer asks that "the sure-footed goats come nigh, conveying Pusan on his car[t], the god who visits mankind" (*RV* 6:55:6).

Several other hymns speak about how the "goats are the team that draws" Pusan's chariot (*RV* 6:57:3). In hymn 67 of book 9, the writer asks that "Pusan, drawn by goats, be [the] protector . . . on all his paths" (*RV* 9:67:10; cf. 1:138:4). And in book 10, hymn 26, the writer prays, "O Pusan, may those goats of yours turn hitherward your chariot . . . . Friend of all suppliants are you, born in old time, and firm and sure" (*RV* 10:26:8).

The other major use of goat in *The Rig Veda* is that as a sacrifice. Hymn 162 of book 1 refers to "the dappled goat [that] goes straightforward, bleating," as a sacrifice for a horse (*RV* 1:162:2). The hymn declares that the goat is dear to all the gods (cf. *RV* 1:162:3) before it is led before the horse and announced as a sacrifice to the gods (cf. *RV* 1:162:4). The next hymn even explains the order of the sacrificial procession: the goat is led before the horse and "the sages and the singers follow after" (*RV* 1:163:12). Doniger explains this ritual, stating that "the goat carries away the evil from the horse."[1]

In the HB (OT), the goat is the sacrifice *extraordinaire* to the LORD, Israel's God. A female goat three years old (cf. Gen 15:9) is one of the three animals Abram cuts in two and between which God walks to make a covenant with Abram. As a sacrifice, the goat must be at least eight days old (cf. Lev 22:27) and it cannot be the first-born because the first-born is holy, that is, it belongs to God (cf. Num 18:17). A goat may be brought to God as an offering of well-being. After laying his hand on the goat's head, the donor

---

1. Doniger, "Symbol," 340.

slaughters it, and the priests sprinkle its blood on the sides of the altar. Most of its entrails are burned as a food offering by fire for a pleasing odor to God (cf. Lev 3:16a). The donor consumes the rest of the goat meat as a covenant of well-being, that is, peace between him and God. If the goat is offered as a burnt offering, then the whole goat is cut into pieces and burned on the altar (cf. Lev 1:10–13).

The goat is most often used as a sin offering. The person making the offering lays his hand on the goat's head, signifying that he is transferring his guilt to the goat. Then, the goat is slaughtered and burned on the altar by the priest. Sometimes only part of the goat is burned and the rest eaten by the donor, and at other times all of the goat is burned on the altar. No matter what the case, the priest makes atonement for the donor for his sin, and he is forgiven (cf. Lev 4:22–31; 5:1–6; 9:1–17; etc.). The HB (OT) Book of Numbers often refers to a male goat serving as a sin offering (cf. Num 7:16, 22, 28, etc.), as well as a female goat serving as such for a person who sins unintentionally (cf. Num 15:27).

"The Goat and the Vine" in *Aesop's Fables* narrates a tale about a goat to be sacrificed. As a goat is eating the tender shoots of a vine with grapes in a vineyard, the vine asks the goat why he is harming it. No reply is recorded by the goat, but the vine continues by telling him that even if he eats all the vine's leaves, the vine will "produce wine enough to pour over [the goat] when [he] is led to the altar to be sacrificed."[2]

Chapter 16 of the Book of Leviticus in the HB (OT) describes the procedure that is known as the scapegoat. After choosing two goats, Aaron, the first priest, sets them "before the LORD at the entrance of the tent of meeting; and Aaron . . . casts lots on the two goats, one lot for the LORD and the other lot of Azazel" (Lev 16:7–8). In other words, Aaron decides by rolling dice or picking the longest or shortest straw which goat will serve as a burnt offering for the LORD. The other goat, designated for Azazel, a demon who was thought to inhabit the desert, is presented alive to God. Then, Aaron lays "both his hands on the head of the live goat, and confesses over it all the iniquities of the people of Israel, and all their transgression, all their sins, putting them on the head of the goat, and sending it away into the wilderness by means of someone designated for the task" (Lev 16:21). The goat, bearing all the iniquities of the people, is led to the desert and set free; when it dies there, the sins of the people die with it.

While most people know that the animal used to celebrate Passover was a sheep, it could also be a goat. According to the instruction in the HB (OT) Book of Exodus, it could be taken either from the sheep or the goats.

2. Aesop, 99.

It had to be a year-old male and without blemish (cf. Exod 12:5). This agile ruminant mammal is both wild and domesticated; it has backward curving horns, straight hair, and a short tail. As a sign of wealth, the goat was raised for wool, meat, and milk.

In the ancient world, a flock of goats represents wealth. After tricking his father-in-law, Laban, into giving him all the spotted and speckled among the goats (cf. Gen 30:32), Jacob engages in some primitive genetic engineering of goats. As a result he "grew exceedingly rich, and had large flocks" (Gen 30:43). As Jacob goes to meet his brother, Esau, in order to be reconciled with him for having stolen his birthright (cf. Gen 27:1–46), he brings with him "two hundred female goats and twenty male goats" (Gen 32:14) among other gifts. In the narrative about Moses instructing the Israelite army to defeat the Midianites, the LORD explains to Moses how he wants the booty distributed. The half-share, the portion of those who had gone out to war, was 337,500 sheep and goats, and the LORD's tribute of sheep and goats was 675. As for the Israelites' half, which Moses separated from that of the troops, the congregation's half was 337,500 sheep and goats (cf. Num 32:36–37, 42). Likewise, the First Book of Samuel describes a very rich man who had one thousand goats (cf. 1 Sam 25:2). The Second Book of Chronicles narrates the story of Arabs bringing King Jehoshaphat 7,700 male goats (cf. 2 Chr 17:11). According to the Book of Proverbs, goats can provide their owner with the price of a field (cf. Prov 27:26).

Mormon also understands a flock of goats to represent wealth. In the Book of Enos, the prophet records that "the people of Nephi did . . . raise . . . flocks of . . . goats and wild goats" (Enos 1:21). Likewise, the First Book of Nephi mentions that in the promised land Nephi found "the goat and the wild goat . . . which were for the use of men" (1 Ne 18:25).

The goat was food for ancient people. Israel's God, the LORD, permitted the people to eat both the domestic goat and the wild goat (cf. Deut 14:4–5). The OT (A) Book of Tobit records that Tobit's wife, Anna, who wove cloth, was partially paid with a young goat for a meal (cf. Tob 2:12). In the CB (NT), Luke's unique story about a prodigal son (cf. Luke 15:11–32) also demonstrates that a young goat was used for feasting. The elder son complains to his father that his father has "never given [him] even a young goat so that [he] might celebrate with [his] friends" (Luke 15:29). The Book of Ether in *Mormon* likewise demonstrates that under the reign of King Emer the people "became exceeding[ly] rich" (Ether 9:16), having "goats and . . . many other kinds of animals which were useful for the food of man" (Ether 9:18). In a similar way, Moses reminds the Israelites how the LORD, their God, fed his people in a variety of ways, even giving them goats (cf. Deut 32:14). The wisdom found in the HB (OT) Book of Proverbs exhorts the reader to "know well the condition of [his] flocks" so that "there will be enough goats' milk for [his] food, for the food of [his] household, and nourishment for [his] servant-girls" (Prov 27:23a, 27). Gentiles also used goats for food. In the OT (A) Book of Judith, the narrator explains that Holofernes, general of the Babylonian King Nebuchadnezzar, sets out on a campaign with innumerable goats for food for his troops (cf. Jdt 2:17). Even *The Rig Veda* mentions milking a goat for food (cf. RV 8:59:15).

Both goat's hair, today known as a type of wool, and goat's skin were used by biblical people. The HB (OT) Book of Exodus records the LORD telling Moses to ask the Israelites to make an offering of goats' hair out of which curtains would be made for a tent over the tabernacle (cf. Exod 25:4; 26:7). Later, in the same book, goats' hair is requested again (cf. Exod 35:6), and the Israelites respond by donating more (cf. Exod 35:23); out of the goats' hair the women used their skill and spun the goats' hair to make eleven curtains of goats' hair for a tent over the tabernacle (cf. Exod 35:26; 36:14).

The narrator of the First Book of Samuel in the HB (OT) tells a story about Michal, David's wife, who saved her husband from her father, King Saul, by putting an idol in his bed and putting "a net of goats' hair on its head" (1 Sam 19:13). When Saul's messengers discovered the idol in place of David, whom Saul wanted to kill, Saul realized that he had been deceived by his own daughter. Likewise, the Letter to the Hebrews in the CB (NT) attests to the fact that people "went about in skins of sheep and goats" (Heb 11:37).

The First Book of Samuel also mentions a place named "Rocks of the Wild Goats" (1 Sam 24:2), which implies that wild goats lived among the rocky ground there. This is confirmed in God's first speech to Job when the LORD asks him, "Do you know when the mountain goats give birth?" (Job 39:1) Likewise, Psalm 104, which praises God for all his creative work, states, the high mountains are for the wild goats (cf. Ps 104:18a), because, as *The Rig Veda* notes, the mountain goat is sure footed (cf. RV 10:134:6).

In the Song of Solomon (Song of Songs) in the HB (OT), the goat serves as a metaphor for beauty. The man tells his female lover that her hair "is like a flock of goats, moving down the slopes" (Song 4:2, 6:5b). In the OT (A) Book of Sirach, King David is described as one who "played with lions as though they were young goats" (Sir 47:3a), thus emphasizing his youthful strength. The Book of Proverbs in the HB (OT) identifies things that are stately in their stride and stately in their gait; among these is "the he-goat" (Prov 30:31). The Book of Alma in *Mormon* describes how people fled the presence of Alma and Amulek "even as a goat flees with her young from two lions" (Alma 14:29), once God set them free from prison.

The prophet Ezekiel uses the goat metaphor to describe God's judgment of his people: "As for you, my flock, thus says the Lord GOD: I shall judge between sheep and sheep, between rams and goats" (Ezek 34:17). Uniquely, the author of Matthew's Gospel portrays the Son of Man coming in glory and separating "people one from another as a shepherd separates the sheep from the goats, [putting] the sheep at his right hand and the goats at [his] left" (Matt 25:32–33). The placing of the goats on the left indicates that is the side for those who are going off to eternal punishment (cf. Matt 25:46). There may be a reference here to goat-demons (cf. Lev 17:7; 2 Chr 11:15; Isa 13:21; 34:14), which is another way to write about Azazel, a spirit thought to live in the desert; some Israelites may have treated the demons as idols or other gods.

In "The Lord's Animals and the Devil's" in *Grimm's Complete Fairy Tales*, the devil "created goats with fine long tails,"[3] while God created the other animals. The goats' tails got caught in the hedges; this meant that the devil had to disentangle them. However, God became perturbed as he observed the destructive quality of the goats and sent the wolves to eat some of them. After this the devil approached God, wanting compensation for his goats, but God tricked the devil by sending him on a trip. When he returned, he took the eyes of the remaining goats and exchanged them for his own. This story is a myth, because it ends with the following sentence: "This is why all goats have devil's eyes, why their tails are bitten off, and why he likes to assume their shape."[4] Thus, goats are associated with evil.

In the HB (OT) Book of Daniel, a male goat represents power because he is identified as the king of Greece (cf. Dan 8:21). In the prophet's vision, "a male goat appeared from the west, coming across the face of the whole earth.... The goat had a horn between its eyes" (Dan 8:5–6); the horn, too, represents power. This "male goat [who] grew exceedingly great" (Dan 8:8) is Alexander the Great, who swept through Persia in the third century BCE and Hellenized the then-known world.

A wise goat appears in Grimm's "One-Eye, Two-Eyes, and Three-Eyes" Cinderella-like story. There is a mother with three daughters; one has one eye, one has two eyes, and one has three-eyes. The two odd-eyed ones mistreat their two-eyed sister, who every day takes the goat to the field. A woman appears to the two-eyed sister, giving her a magic formula to use to get food and then make it disappear. She is told to say, "Bleat, my little goat, bleat, cover the table with something to eat." Then, after eating from the well-spread table, she is to say, "Bleat, bleat, my little goat, I pray, and take

---

3. Grimm, 392.
4. Ibid., 393.

the table quite away."⁵ Thus, with the proper chant the magical goat makes food appear and disappear until two-eyes' sisters discover that she is eating better than they are.

Their mother in a fit of jealously kills the goat. But as fate would have it, two-eyes is instructed to bury the goat's entrails, from which a tree sprouts with silver leaves and gold apples. The tree will let only two-eyes pick its golden fruit. A knight comes along and asks the mother and the two sisters for a branch from the tree, but they are not able to break off one. However, two-eyes is able to break off a branch with silver leaves and gold apples. In payment for the branch, the knight takes her with him to his castle, where he marries her. Meanwhile, her two sisters grudge her good fortune, while the tree with the silver leaves and gold fruit follows her to the castle.

After a few years pass, two poor women appear at the castle's gate. Two-eyes recognizes them as her sisters, who had fallen into such poverty that they had to wander about and beg for bread from door to door. However, two-eyes did not return evil for evil; she welcomed them, was kind to them, and took care of them. They repented of the evil they had done to her because of her good fortune with a goat.

While Aesop's "The Wolf and the Goat" is not about a magical goat that makes food appear and disappear, it is about a wise goat which a wolf is trying to trick down from the top of a steep rock where the goat is grazing. The wolf explains to the goat how she is risking her life on the ledge; he invites her to come down where he is because there is plenty of food there. However, the goat is smarter than the wolf. She replies, "It's little you care whether I get good grass or bad; what you want is to eat me."⁶

Aesop also narrates two fables about goatherds. In "The Goatherd and the Goat," one goat strays from the flock, and the goatherd tries several ways to get her back. When nothing works, he throws a stone at her, breaking one of her horns. The goatherd begs her not to tell his master. However, using a pun, the goat tells the goatherd, ". . . [M]y horn would cry aloud even if I held my tongue."⁷ In "The Goatherd and the Wild Goats," wild goats mingle with the goatherd's domestic ones. At the end of the day he puts all of them into the same pen and feeds them, giving little to the domestic goats and much to the wild ones in the hope that they would stay and not want to leave. The next day he takes all of them to pasture, where the wild goats separate themselves from the domestic ones and scamper away. The goatherd accused the wild goats of ingratitude. But one of the wild goats turns

5. Ibid., 177.
6. Aesop, 140.
7. Ibid., 166.

around and explains that it was the goatherd's generosity that put them on their guard. "If you treat newcomers like ourselves so much better than your own flock," explained one of the wild goats, "it's more than likely that, if another lot of strange goats joined yours, we should then be neglected in favor of the last comers."[8]

Thus, a Hindu god gives birth to goats, while another god is pulled in his chariot by them. Not only is the goat a sacrifice in Hinduism, but in the HB (OT) one is used in the covenant-making ceremony with Abram and as an offering of well-being, a sin offering, and a scapegoat. The goat represents wealth, even while it is used for food, shelter, and clothing. As a metaphor, the goat can reference beauty, strength, stride, flight, judgment, and power. In fables, it is known for its tenacity, diligence, and wisdom. It even has the ability with the right chant to make food appear and disappear. For the spiritual traveler, the goat provides sustenance in a variety of ways.

Journal/Meditation: Which of the following characteristics of the goat do you find worthy of journaling or meditation: sacrifice, scapegoat, food, shelter, metaphor, wisdom?

Prayer: You provided a ready means for your people to seek reconciliation with you, O God, by giving them goats from the flock. In the fullness of time, you sent your Son, Jesus Christ, as the scapegoat for the human race. Taking upon himself my sins, he carried them to the cross. Grant that I may live fully the peace he has brought with his self-sacrifice. He lives and reigns with you and the Holy Spirit, one God, forever and ever. Amen.

---

8. Ibid., 223.

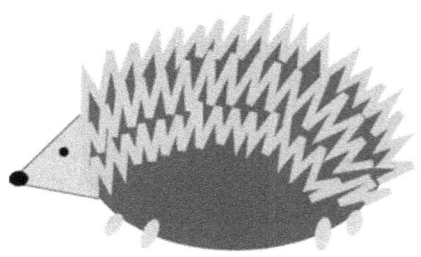

Hedgehog

Text: "I will rise up . . ., says the LORD of hosts, and will cut off from Babylon name and remnant, offspring and posterity, says the LORD. And I will make it a possession of the hedgehog, and pools of water, and I will sweep it with the broom of destruction, says the LORD of hosts." (Isa 14:22–23)

Reflection: While the hedgehog is usually associated with self-preservation, happiness, and industriousness, the two times the small creature appears in biblical literature it is associated with wilderness, abandonment, and despair. It is amazing that the small spiny mammal with a pointed head and round body with spines on the back—which protect it when it rolls itself into a ball under attack—should be associated with such diverse meanings. As can be seen in the passage above from the HB (OT) prophet Isaiah, the hedgehog is given Babylon for its possession once God has destroyed that great nation. Later in Isaiah, God explains the divine punishment that will be visited upon Edom, a nation that played a treacherous role after the destruction of Jerusalem by Babylonian forces in 587 BCE. God promises to devastate the land so that "the hedgehog shall posses it" (Isa 34:11a).

Only one of *Aesop's Fables* features a hedgehog, which is presented in a more positive light than in Isaiah. In "The Fox and the Hedgehog," a fox, swimming across a river, is swept away by the current, carried down the stream, and, after getting bruised and exhausted, scrambles onto dry ground. A swarm of horseflies settle on him and suck his blood, but he is too weak to shoe them away. A hedgehog sees the fox and offers to brush away the flies, but the fox declines his offer, stating, "[I]f you drive them off, another swarm of hungry ones will come and suck all the blood I have left and leave me without a drop in my veins."[1]

Grimm's Complete Fairy Tales contains two long stories about a hedgehog. The first, "The Hare and the Hedgehog," which portrays the hedgehog as a trickster, narrates how a male hedgehog emerges from his den on a Sunday morning ready to go and inspect his turnip patch, when he meets a rabbit which is off to inspect his cabbage patch. After being insulted by the rabbit because of his small size, the hedgehog challenges the rabbit to a race; the winner would take away a golden Louis-d'Or and a bottle of brandy. Thinking that this is a no-brainer, the rabbit accepts the challenge, and both animals agree to meet in the field's furrows in thirty minutes.

The hedgehog hurries home. He instructs his wife, who looks exactly like him, to position herself at the end of the field in a furrow. When she sees the rabbit, she is to say to him, "I am here already!"[2] Once the race is begun, the male hedgehog slows down and dunks into a furrow; when the rabbit arrives at the end of the furrow, the female hedgehog shows herself and declares that she has won the race. The rabbit is truly puzzled. So, he decides to run the race again back the way he came. When he gets back to the starting point, the male hedgehog appears and declares to have won the race. The rabbit insists on running the race again, again, and again, until he has run back and forth in the field seventy-four times and drops dead. According to the tale,

> The moral of this story . . . is, firstly, that no one, however great he may be, should permit himself to jest at any one beneath him, even if he be only a hedgehog. And, secondly, it teaches, that when a man marries, he should take a wife in his own position, who looks just as he himself looks. So whosoever is a hedgehog let him see to it that his wife is a hedgehog also, and so forth.[3]

"Hans the Hedgehog" is a transformation-trickster tale that may be better classified as a rags-to-riches story on several levels. After being taunted by the peasants of a town for not having children, a rich countryman goes home and states, "I will have a child, even if it be a hedgehog."[4] His wife gives birth to a child "that was a hedgehog in the upper part of his body, and a boy in the lower;"[5] they name him Hans the Hedgehog, and, after his

---

1. Aesop, 206
2. Grimm, 113.
3. Ibid., 113–14.
4. Ibid., 484.
5. Ibid.

christening, a bed is prepared for him with straw behind the stove because he could not get into any ordinary bed with his spikes or quills.

When he was eight years old, his father bought him bagpipes. Then, Hans asked his father to "get the cock shod"[6] so he could ride away and never come back. He left for the forest, taking with him some of his father's pigs and donkeys. The cock took him to a high tree in the forest. From that spot for years he played his bagpipes as he watched over his herds which increased to many pigs and donkeys.

One day a king lost in the forest heard him playing the bagpipes. The king, following the music, found him and asked the hedgehog if he knew the way to the king's kingdom. Hans told him he did, and "if the king would write a bond and promise him whatever he first met in the royal courtyard as soon as he arrived at home,"[7] the hedgehog would help him. The king tricks the hedgehog by not writing what he promised. When the hedgehog gets the king home, he spies his daughter, the princess, who should have been Hans's bride, but she tells her father that even if he had not tricked Hans, she would not have gone with him. Because he was tricked, all Hans could do was return to the forest to his herds and sit in the tree playing his bagpipes.

A while later, another king appeared in the forest; he, too, was lost. But he heard the bagpipes, found the hedgehog, and asked him for help. The hedgehog agreed to help the king and his retinue get home "if he would give him for his own whatsoever first met him in front of his royal palace."[8] The king agreed and wrote and signed a document attesting to the same. When Hans, the hedgehog-boy who had become a hedgehog-man, got the king to his palace, the king's only daughter was the first person he saw; this meant that she belonged to him. However, Hans left the king and went back to the forest to care for his herds and play his bagpipes.

By this time, Hans's herds filled the forest. So, he resolved to take his wealth to his father. So, he mounted the cock and drove the herds before him to the village, and he gave the herds to the peasants who lived there. He asked his father to re-shod the cock, and he would leave and never return again. His father granted his wish, and Hans took off to visit the first king he had helped in the forest in order to collect what the king had promised him. After persuading his daughter to go with Hans, the king gives her a carriage with six horses and attendants together with gold and possessions, and they leave together. When they are a few miles away from the palace, Hans stops

---

6. Ibid., 485.
7. Ibid.
8. Ibid., 486.

the carriage, removes the princess' rich clothing, and pierces her with his quills until she bleeds over all. "That is the reward of your falseness," states Hans. "Go your way. I will not have you!"[9]

After this, he went to visit the second king he had helped find his way through the forest to his palace. Here, Hans was welcomed, given the princess who also greeted him, and married her. However, in the evening when it was time to go to bed, she was afraid of his quills. He, however, had informed the king that "when he entered the room and was about to get into bed, he would creep out of his hedgehog's skin and leave it lying . . . by the bedside, and that the men [the king was to appoint] were to run nimbly to it, throw it in the fire, and stay by it until it was consumed."[10] All took place as planned. Hans "was delivered, and lay there in bed in human form, . . . a handsome young man."[11] As a result, Hans inherited his father-in-law's kingdom. A few years later, he returned to his father, explained all that had happened to him, and brought his father to live with him in his kingdom.

"Hans the Hedgehog" is a transformation-trickster tale. The countryman is transformed from being childless to possessing a son, who albeit is half-hedgehog and half-boy. Hans is transformed from being a creature sleeping behind the stove to the owner of a forest full of herds of pigs and donkeys. Hans is further transformed into a handsome man by slipping out of his hedgehog skin and having the king's men destroy it. And, finally, Hans is transformed from son-in-law to king. The trickster note appears when the first king attempts to trick him by not writing what he was promising and drawing his only daughter into his plot to cheat Hans.

The rags-to-riches dimension of the fable is found in Hans's progress from owning nothing to having huge herds of pigs and donkeys. It is further echoed in his transformation from a hedgehog man to a handsome young man. And it reaches its culmination when Hans, who was one-half hedgehog and one-half boy, becomes king in his father-in-law's place. Thus, the hedgehog illustrates the qualities of self-preservation, happiness, and industriousness even if it displays quills on its back and represents desolation in biblical literature. This small creature is fittingly associated with being helpful and trickery.

Journal/Meditation: Which story above about the hedgehog got your attention? Why? What hedgehog qualities connect with your own spirituality?

---

9. Ibid., 487.
10. Ibid., 488.
11. Ibid.

Prayer: Even your smallest creature gives you praise, O LORD. Give me the voice to praise you for your watchful care, and grant that I may serve you happily, like the hedgehog. I ask this through my Lord Jesus Christ, your Son, who lives and reigns with you and the Holy Spirit, one God, forever and ever. Amen.

Ibex

Text: "These are the animals you may eat: the ox, the sheep, the goat, the deer, the gazelle, the roebuck, the wild goat, the ibex, and the antelope, and the mountain sheep" (Deut 14:4–5).

Reflection: In the entire Bible, the ibex, a wild mountain goat with long knobby backward-curving horns, is mentioned but one time, and that reference is to include the animal among those the Israelites may kill and eat, as seen above. The ibex lives in mountains. It is very agile and hardy, able to climb on rock and survive on sparse vegetation. It is a ruminant with a four-chambered stomach, which enables it to capture almost every nutrient of what it consumes. The male sports a beard, and most taxonomists identify nine species living in Europe, Asia, and northern Africa.

Ancient peoples domesticated the ibex for natural weed control and to provide hair for weaving and meat and milk for food. Skins could be used for water and wine, as well as parchment for writing. Francke records that in Buddhism rock carvings, the horns of ibex were once used as a charm to encourage childbearing or to give thanks for a child. He narrates how the people of a Buddhist village made ibexes from flour and butter and gave them to the parents upon the birth of a child. This custom of a thank offering helped him to understand the rock carvings of ibexes at places associated with Buddhism; Buddhists went to the rock-carved places to pray to be blessed with a child.[1]

---

1. Cf. Francke, *Antiquities*, 95–96.

Thus, even though there are no biblical references to ibexes, other than the one found in the HB (OT) Book of Deuteronomy, this wild mountain goat with backward-curving horns represents agility and survival. The image of the ibex carved on rock, and marking a place of prayer where Buddhists could seek the conception of a child, ties into the survival aspect of the ibex. Indeed, if this mountain goat could thrive in the mountains, those who lived below would see it as an image of the survival of their own kind and give thanks to it when a child was born.

Journal/Meditation: What quality of the ibex enhances your spirituality? Explain.

Prayer: Heavenly God, in the mountains your agile ibexes thrive. Grant what I need to survive here below that I may move with ease in your service until I enter into the kingdom, where you live and reign with your Son, my Lord Jesus Christ, and the Holy Spirit, one God, forever and ever. Amen.

Jackal

Text: "Resolve for me, O singer, this my riddle: the jackal drives the wild boar from the brushwood" (*RV* 10:28:4).

Reflection: The resolution of the riddle is found in Indra's power to alter the course of nature. Indra, Hinduism's supreme god, is the deity of rain and thunderstorms, wielding a lightning thunderbolt and riding on a white elephant. Because he is the chief god, he is able to reverse the normal course of natural events, like the wild boar driving away the jackal. As *The Rig Veda* makes clear, the jackal drives the wild boar from the woods. In another hymn from book 10 of *The Rig Veda*, the god Agni, an important Hindu deity and the god of fire, is portrayed as the one who devours all things—sacrifices made to Agni are burned and he, as messenger from and to the gods, brings the sacrifice to the appropriate god—and brings healing to anyone wounded by a jackal (cf. *RV* 10:16:6). Agni is able to heal because he is forever young, that is, the fire is started every day.

The jackal is a wild, carnivorous mammal resembling a dog with long legs, large ears, and a bushy tail. As an opportunistic omnivore, however, the jackal will hunt and eat small and medium-sized animals, such as mammals, birds, and reptiles; it is a very proficient scavenger. The jackal is also a good long-distant runner and can usually be spotted at dawn and dusk alone or in a pack devouring a carcass.

Because the jackal prefers uninhabited places, in the Bible it is often described as living in ruins. The phrase "haunt of jackals" is used often to describe deserted or ruined places (cf. Ps 44:19; Isa 34:13; 35:7). The prophet Jeremiah describes destroyed Jerusalem as "a lair of jackals" (Jer 9:11; 10:22; 49:33) and Babylon as "a den of jackals" (Jer 51:37). Isaiah states that "jackals [will cry] in the pleasant palaces" of Babylon once it is destroyed (Isa 13:22). The Book of Lamentations states that "jackals prowl over" Mount Zion, upon which Jerusalem was built and destroyed (Lam 5:18).

The HB (OT) Book of Job portrays Job complaining to God because he is not heard. He states, "I am a brother of jackals" (Job 30:29a); in other words, Job thinks of himself as a jackal in the wilderness, howling, but not being heard. Likewise, are the LORD's words of the prophet Malachi about Edom, Esau's heritage: "I have made his hill country a desolation and his heritage a desert for jackals" (Mal 1:3). Ezekiel pushes the metaphor even further, portraying God as stating, "Your prophets have been like jackals among the ruins, O Israel" (Ezek 13:4). Nevertheless, the creator of all things declares that the jackals will honor him (cf. Isaiah 43:20); that is to say that God's glory will be manifest even in places where no one lives.

In the Bible, the jackal is depicted as a scavenger. Psalm 63 portrays the singer declaring that those who sought to destroy his life "shall be prey for jackals" (Ps 63:10). In Lamentations, the singer laments that there is not enough food in Jerusalem to feed the children whereas "[e]ven the jackals offer the breast and nurse their young" (Lam 4:3a). The prophet Micah references the howl of the jackal when he records God telling Israel that he "will lament and wail; . . . [he] will make lamentation like the jackals" (Mic 1:8), that is, he will mourn, when the Assyrians destroy the northern kingdom. The prophet Jeremiah describes a drought during which "[t]he wild asses stand on the bare heights [and] pant for air like jackals" (Jer 14:6).

Schimmel narrates one of Rumi's poems about a jackal which took himself "to a dyer's vat and stayed in the vat an hour or so."[1] When he got out of the vat, "his hide was all colors."[2] "'I am a peacock of Paradise!' he cried," because "[h]e saw himself red and yellow and green and blue and put himself the jackal on show."[3] Then, he called upon his companion to look at his brightness and his luster and call him "pride of the world" and "pillar of faith."[4] "In me blazes the light of God's favor, shining out," he said. "I was of God's brilliance the paraphrase . . . ."[5] However, his companion was smart enough to see through him. It is not a rainbow-colored jackal that the God-seeker should admire, but God himself and those who live together in their nearness to God.

1. Schimmel, *Rumi*, 76.
2. Ibid., 77.
3. Ibid.
4. Ibid.
5. Ibid.

In other myths and legends the jackal is often depicted as a clever sorcerer. However, in Egypt there is the jackal-headed god, Anubis, associated both with mummification and the afterlife. Anubis appears as either a male Egyptian holding a staff in one hand and an ankh, a sign of eternal life, in the other with the head of a jackal or as a recumbent jackal on a tall platform before a tomb's entrance to indicate that he is a protector of the grave. He is depicted in black, which is not the color of the coat of real jackals. Black represents the discoloration of the corpse that occurs after treatment with embalming fluid and the smearing of the wrapping with a resinous substance during the mummification process. Black is also the color of the silt of the Nile River which symbolizes fertility and rebirth in the afterlife.

The association of a jackal with embalming and protecting tombs probably comes from the association of jackals as scavengers in cemeteries, especially where the dead were placed in shallow graves; the jackals often uncovered the bodies and ate them. In an effort to protect the dead through mummification and in the tomb, a jackal god, Anubis, was created.

During various periods of Egyptian history, Anubis was associated with several other roles. For example, he measured the heart of the dead, determining whether the person was worthy of entering the realm of the dead. He also weighed the soul to be sure that it was lighter than an ostrich feather in order to ascend to heavenly bliss. Anubis guided the dead across the threshold from this world to the afterlife. Thus, in funerary contexts, he is depicted as attending to the deceased person's mummy or sitting on top of the tomb to protect it.

Thus, the jackal represents strength, survival, and solitude. Its strength comes from its ability to run. Its survival comes from its ability to scavenge. And its solitude comes from its living in uninhabited places. In Egyptian mythology these qualities give rise to Anubis, the god associated with mummification of the dead, leading the dead from this world to the next, and guardian of the dead.

Journal/Meditation: What quality of the jackal do you find most appealing? What quality of the jackal do you find most repulsive?

Prayer: Eternal Father, you bestowed strength, survival, and solitude upon the jackal which led some of your people to associate him with death. Give me a greater appreciation for the ways of all your creatures. Hear me through my Lord Jesus Christ, your Son, who lives and reigns with you and the Holy Spirit, one God, forever and ever. Amen.

Kudu (Antelope)

Text: "Come like a thirsty antelope to the drinking place: drink soma to your heart's desire." (*RV* 8:4:10a)

Reflection: The kudu is a large antelope native to Africa. The male sports long spiraling horns. Kudus live in herds in the savannas, relying on thickets for protection, especially for the young. Their brown and striped pelts help to camouflage them. Males are usually found in groups—although many live solitarily—only leaving the group during mating season. The females leave the herd to give birth, keeping the calf hidden for several weeks and then gradually integrating into the herd. Kudu are great runners, great kickers, and great jumpers. They browse on leaves and shoots and various wild fruits.

In the verse from *The Rig Veda* above, the kudu or antelope is employed as a metaphor for speed. The hymn invites Indra, the chief Hindu god, to run like a thirsty antelope to drink soma juice, a ritual drink squeezed from an unknown plant and having energizing qualities. The writer of the hymn knew that the antelope could run fast. In another hymn, the writer uses the antelope's beauty, stating that the Maruts, Hindu storm deities and attendants of Indra, are as "beauteous as antelopes" (*RV* 1:64:8a).

The Bible mentions the antelope two times. In the HB (OT) Book of Deuteronomy, the antelope is listed among the animals that the Israelites may eat (cf. Deut 14:5). While affirming this fact, Opoku says that there is a metaphysical reality to the antelope. ". . . [T]he relationship between . . .

people and the antelopes is not characterized by opposition, but by agreeable continuity, incessant interaction, and harmonious integration," writes Opoku.[1] "[T]he antelope represents . . . the presence of the sacred."[2]

The prophet Isaiah employs the image of catching an antelope using a net to describe the people remaining in destroyed Jerusalem. Referring to its citizens, Jerusalem's "children have fainted; they lie at the head of every street like an antelope in a net," states the prophet (Isa 51:20). The Israelites have been captured by their enemies, the Babylonians.

The kudu are hunted for their meat, similar in taste to venison; for their hides, used to make coverings; and for their horns, used to make a musical instrument for playing.

Thus, the qualities of speed, beauty and grace, rapid advancement, and representing the presence of the sacred are delivered by the kudu or antelope. Certainly, speed is a spiritual quality, especially if it is done with beauty and grace. Speed enables the runner to advance rapidly on whatever he or she desires to accomplish. Taken together, these identify the kudu (antelope) as an animal that displays the sacred, especially when its horns are used to call people to worship.

Journal/Meditation: What particular project or goal requires speed, beauty, and grace from you? How can you learn these spiritual disciplines from the kudu (antelope)?

Prayer: With great speed, your Holy Spirit comes upon me, almighty God, filling me with grace and enabling me to achieve your will. Keep me rapidly advancing on the way to your kingdom, where you live with your Son, my Lord Jesus Christ, and the Holy Spirit, one God, forever and ever. Amen.

---

1. Opoku, "African Mythology," 356.
2. Ibid.

Leviathan (Behemoth, Rahab, Dragon)

Text: "... God created the great sea monsters and every living creature that moves, of every kind, with which the waters swarm...." (Gen 1:21a)

Reflection: From verse 21 of the first chapter of the Book of Genesis, it becomes very clear that God made sea monsters, which are subject to his control. The psalmist further emphasizes this point when he sings, "Praise the LORD from the earth, you sea monsters and all deeps" (Ps 148:7). The biblical, mythological monsters, the monsters of chaos, are called Leviathan and Behemoth. Leviathan is most likely the crocodile, and Behemoth is probably the hippopotamus.[1] These monsters, "despite their massive strength and attendant fearlessness," according to McGinnis, "are but pets in the hand of God, reinforcing the sense that God checks the potentially destructive forces in the world and holds them within bounds."[2]

Leviathan

Leviathan represents the forces of watery chaos which God conquers, as Psalm 74 makes clear: "[God] crushed the heads of Leviathan" (Ps 74:14a). Likewise, in Psalm 104, the writer sings about the sea which God made "and Leviathan that [he] formed to sport in it" (Ps 104:26). According to the prophet Isaiah, one day in the future "the LORD with his cruel and great

---

1. Cf. McGinnis, "Job's Dialogue," 90.
2. Ibid., 90–91.

and strong sword will punish Leviathan the fleeing serpent, Leviathan the twisting serpent . . ." (Isa 27:1).

Other biblical texts mention a sea monster or a sea serpent without naming it Leviathan. For example, the prophet Jeremiah writes that King Nebuchadrezzar of Babylon swallows kingdoms like a monster (cf. Jer 51:34). The narrator of the story of Jonah states that "the LORD provided a large fish to swallow up Jonah; and Jonah was in the belly of the fish three days and three nights" (Jonah 1:17). In Matthew's Gospel in the CB (NT), Jesus refers to Jonah, stating he was "three days and three nights in the belly of the sea monster" (Matt 12:40). The prophet Amos portrays God's judgment as all encompassing on the earth and in the sea; should people attempt to hide at the bottom of the sea, God says that he will command the sea serpent, and it shall bite them (cf. Amos 9:3). In *The Rig Veda*, the "flood-obstructing serpent" is known as Vrtra (*RV* 6:72:3), the personification of drought. Indra, Hinduism's chief god, and Agni, the god of fire, are petitioned to "slay him who stays the waters, [to] slay the serpent" (*RV* 7:94:12). More will be provided on the Hindu monsters below.

The fullest biblical treatment of Leviathan occurs in the Book of Job in the HB (OT). After cursing the day of his birth, Job states, "Let those curse [the day of his birth] who curse the sea, those who are skilled to rouse up Leviathan" (Job 3:8). Near the end of the book the LORD speaks to Job out of a whirlwind, asking a series of questions about Leviathan:

> Can you draw out Leviathan with a fishhook, or press down its tongue with a cord? Can you put a rope in its nose, or pierce its jaw with a hook? Will it make many supplications to you? Will it speak soft words to you? Will it make a covenant with you to be taken as your servant forever? Will you play with it as with a bird, or will you put it on leash for your girls? Will traders bargain over it? Will they divide it up among the merchants? Can you fill its skin with harpoons, or its head with fishing spears? (Job 41:1–7)

Then, God tells Job, "Lay hands on it; think of the battle; you will not do it again! Any hope of capturing it will be disappointed; were not even the gods overwhelmed at the sight of it? No one is so fierce as to dare to stir it up. Who can stand before it? Who can confront it and be safe?—under the whole heaven, who?" (Job 41:8–11)

The LORD continues to describe Leviathan to Job, saying:

> I will not keep silence concerning its limbs, or its mighty strength, or its splendid frame. Who can strip off its outer garment? Who can penetrate its double coat of mail? Who can

open the doors of its face? There is terror all around its teeth. Its back is made of shields in rows, shut up closely as with a seal. One is so near to another that no air can come between them. They are joined one to another; they clasp each other and cannot be separated. Its sneezes flash forth light, and its eyes are like the eyelids of the dawn. From its mouth go flaming torches; sparks of fire leap out. Out of its nostrils comes smoke, as from a boiling pot and burning rushes. Its breath kindles coals, and a flame comes out of its mouth. In its neck abides strength, and terror dances before it. The folds of its flesh cling together; it is firmly cast and immovable. Its heart is as hard as stone, as hard as the lower millstone. (Job 41:12–24)

Now that God has described the monster he created, he continues to tell Job about how others respond to it, when they try to kill it, saying:

When it raises itself up, the gods are afraid; at the crashing they are beside themselves. Though the sword reaches it, it does not avail, nor does the spear, the dart, or the javelin. It counts iron as straw, and bronze as rotten wood. The arrow cannot make it flee; sling stones, for it, are turned to chaff. Clubs are counted as chaff; it laughs at the rattle of javelins. (Job 41: 25–29)

The description of Leviathan resumes: "Its underparts are like sharp potsherds; it spreads itself like a threshing sledge on the mire. It makes the deep boil like a pot; it makes the sea like a pot of ointment. It leaves a shining wake behind it; one would think the deep to be white-haired" (Job 41:30–32). Then, God summarizes his description of the monster, stating: "On earth it has no equal, a creature without fear. It surveys everything that is lofty; it is king over all that are proud" (Job 41:33–34).

Behemoth

Earlier in the Book of Job, The LORD described Behemoth to Job, telling him: "Look at Behemoth, which I made just as I made you; it eats grass like an ox. Its strength is in its loins, and its power in the muscles of its belly. It makes its tail stiff like a cedar; the sinews of its thighs are knit together. Its bones are tubes of bronze; its limbs like bars of iron" (Job 40:15–18). Only the Book of Job mentions the monster named Behemoth, which, "is the first of the great acts of God" (Job 40:19a). This means that "only its maker can approach it with the sword" (Job 40:19b).

Next, God describes that "the mountains yield food for it where all the wild animals play" (Job 40:20). He continues: "The lotus trees cover it for shade; the willows of the wadi surround it. Even if the river is turbulent, it is not frightened; it is confident though Jordan rushes against its mouth" (Job 40:20–23). Finally, about Behemoth, the LORD asks Job, "Can one take it with hooks or pierce its nose with a snare?" (Job 40:24/25)

Rahab

Another name for Leviathan and Behemoth is Rahab, not to be confused with the prostitute who appears in the HB (OT) Book of Joshua and elsewhere in the HB (OT) and in the CB (NT). According to McKenzie, this Rahab is "a mythological being . . . associated or identified with the monster of chaos which is slain by the creative deity in ancient Semitic myths of creation."[3] When Rahab is mentioned in biblical literature, it is, of course, God who conquers it, as Job states: "By his power he stilled the sea; by his understanding he struck down Rahab" (Job 26:12). Psalm 89 states it this way: "You [, O LORD God,] crushed Rahab like a carcass" (Ps 89:10a). Echoing both Job and Psalm 89, the prophet Isaiah puts it in the form of a question: "Was it not you [, LORD,] who cut Rahab in pieces, who pierced the dragon?" (Isa 51:9c) Isaiah also uses Rahab in a derogatory form, naming Egypt as "Rahab who sits still" (Isa 30:7). McKenzie explains that the prophet is referring to the country as "a monster of threatening appearance which is really inactive."[4] In other words, when help was needed, Egypt did not respond.

Monsters

Leviathan, Behemoth, and Rahab are no different from other cultural monsters. Babylon had its Tiamat; North America has its Bigfoot; Canada has its Nuk-luk; Nepal has its Yeti or Abominable Snowman; and Scotland has its Nessie, the Loch Ness Monster, just to name a few of the more than twenty-five world monsters usually found on lists of such creatures.

Mormon mentions monsters. The Second Book of Nephi refers to the "awful monster . . . [of] death and hell" (2 Ne 9:10); later it declares that God delivers "his saints from that awful monster the devil, and death, and hell, and that lake of fire and brimstone" (2 Ne 9:19; 9:26). The Book of Alma states that some people thought that a character named Ammon, sent from the Nephites, was a monster (cf. Alma 19:26). The angel Maroni states

---

3. McKenzie, *Dictionary*, 719.
4. Ibid.

that the Jaredites "were driven forth; and no monster of the sea could break them" (Ether 6:10).

The Rig Veda also mentions monsters. In one hymn the dawn "drives away the darksome monster" (*RV* 1:92:5); in another the sun makes "each monster fall and cease from troubling" (*RV* 6:71:5), that is, the terrors of the night. Even dark storm clouds are called the monster begotten by the Maruts, the Hindu storm gods (cf. *RV* 1:168:9). Repeatedly the chief god, Indra, is said to have defeated monsters. Vrtra, "the flood-obstructing serpent" (*RV* 6:72:3), that is, a water monster, is defeated by him (cf. *RV* 2:11:10), as well as the fiend of drought, which Indra "did strike the monster Susna dead" (*RV* 10:22:7). Likewise, Indra "cleft asunder the head of Arbuda the watery monster" (*RV* 10:67:12), demolishing "the works of the great watery monster" (*RV* 10:111:4). Other monsters in *The Rig Veda* include the demon Ahi (cf. *RV* 8:82:14). And in hymn 87 of book 10, Agni, the god of fire, is petitioned to destroy "the insatiable monsters" (*RV* 10:87:14).

Dragon

The material describing monsters gives rise to another mythological beast known as the dragon, usually a scaly green dinosaur-like or lizard-like creature with a long tail and wings that breathes fire. Psalm 74 attributes to God not only the division of the sea by his might, but the fact that he "broke the heads of the dragons in the waters" (Ps 74:13), thus demonstrating his control over all chaos. Likewise, Job asks God, "Am I the Sea, or the Dragon, that you set a guard over me?" (Job 7:12) Job is referring to the storm god of other cultures who had to defeat a monster to become chief god; however, Job's God is already supreme. The Greek version of the Book of Esther narrates a dream of Mordecai, a Jew living in the city of Susa during the time of Artaxerxes, as consisting of "two great dragons" coming forward, "both ready to fight, and they roared terribly" (Esth 11:6). At the end of the book, the two dragons are identified as Haman, a high official in Artaxerxes's court who desires to destroy all Jews in Susa, and Mordecai (cf. Esth 10:7).

Four other biblical books mention dragons: Isaiah, Ezekiel, Daniel, and Revelation. In the prophet Isaiah, like in Psalm 74 and Job 7, it is the LORD who "will kill the dragon that is in the sea" (Isa 27:1), who in days of old "pierced the dragon" (Isa 51:9; cf. 2 Ne 8:9). The prophet Ezekiel prefers to name the Pharaoh, the king of Egypt. who failed to rescue Jerusalem from the Babylonians as "the great dragon sprawling in the midst of [the Nile's] channels" (Ezek 29:3). Then, extending the metaphor to all of Egypt, Ezekiel portrays God condemning the land. The Lord GOD states:

> I will put hooks in your jaws, and make the fish of your channels stick to your scales. I will draw you up from your channels, with all the fish of your channels sticking to your scales. I will fling you into the wilderness, you and all the fish of your channels; you shall fall in the open field, and not be gathered and buried. To the animals of the earth and to the birds of the air I have given you as food. (Ezek 29:4–5)

Later in the book, Ezekiel again declares Pharaoh to be like a dragon in the seas (cf. Ezek 32:2). He continues, "[Y]ou thrash about in your streams, trouble the water with your feet, and foul your streams" (Ezek 32:2). Now, God says what he is going to do:

> I will throw my net over you; and I will haul you up in my dragnet. I will throw you on the ground, on the open field I will fling you, and will cause all the birds of the air to settle on you, and I will let the wild animals of the whole earth gorge themselves with you. I will strew your flesh on the mountains, and fill the valleys with your carcass. I will drench the land with your flowing blood up to the mountains, and the watercourses will be filled with you. (Ezek 32:3–6)

In the Greek version of the Book of Daniel, there is a humorous story about the prophet and a dragon that lives near the temple of the Babylonian god Bel, otherwise known as Marduk (cf. Dan 14:23). Daniel tells the Babylonian king that he "will kill the dragon without sword or club" (Dan 14:26). The narrator of the story states: "Daniel took pitch, fat, and hair, and boiled them together and made cakes, which he fed to the dragon. The dragon ate them, and burst open" (Dan 14:27). Bel, who had won his place in the Babylonian pantheon by killing the chaos dragon of the deep, Tiamat, is not only represented by a dragon, but is also killed by a Jewish prophet feeding food to an idol which cannot eat!

However, of all the biblical books mentioning dragons the CB (NT) Book of Revelation is by far the most comprehensive. In this book, the dragon is the enemy of God and, as it is in other biblical literature, it needs to be defeated. The "great red dragon with seven heads and ten horns, and seven diadems on his heads" (Rev 12:3) that appears in the heaven is a composite of every Greek and Roman emperor the Jews and Christians consider to be their enemies. Because the dragon's appearance is a portent, that is, an astrological sign, with his tail he sweeps away a third of the stars of heaven and throws them to the earth. Thus, clearly this is a cosmic battle between evil (the dragon) and good, the male child (the Messiah) that the woman is about to bear (cf. Rev 12:4–5). However, as war breaks out in heaven,

Michael, a name which means "who is like God," appears and fights the dragon, throwing "that ancient serpent, who is called the Devil and Satan, the deceiver of the whole world" (Rev 12:9), down to the earth, where he pursues the woman, but she is able to fly away (cf. Rev 12:13–14).

Then—as is typical of a sea monster—"from his mouth the serpent poured water like a river after the woman to sweep her away with the flood. But the earth came to the help of the woman; it opened its mouth and swallowed the river that the dragon had poured from his mouth" (Rev 12:15–16). This makes the dragon angry, so he goes off to make war on the woman's other children (cf. Rev 12:17). Then—again in typical monster fashion—"the dragon took his stand on the sand of the seashore" (Rev 12:18).

In the next scene, the author of the book, John of Patmos, narrates that he saw a beast rising out of the sea. The beast has ten horns and seven heads; on its horns are ten diadems, and on its heads are blasphemous names (cf. Rev 13:1). The beast is, of course, the ancient sea monster, Leviathan, who was already used as a model for the dragon in chapter 12. Now, using Daniel's details about beasts and dragons, the author states that the dragon gave the beast his power, throne, and authority. People worship "the dragon, for he had given his authority to the beast . . ." (Rev 13:4). Another beast rises out of the earth; "it had two horns like a lamb and it spoke like a dragon" (Rev 13:11).

The next time that the dragon is mentioned is part of the sixth plague on the great river Euphrates. John narrates that he "saw three foul spirits like frogs coming from the mouth of the dragon, from the mouth of the beast, and from the mouth of the false prophet" (Rev 16:13). Again, here, the dragon is associated with water. Cavendish records a similar figure in Scotland mythology. "There are stories about chiefs who practiced witchcraft," he writes, "with a familiar spirit in the form of a monstrous frog hopping from wave to wave in the wake of the chief's ship, and a gigantic figure whistling him out of his deathbed, so that only the strongest man in the clan could prevent the dying man running out to join his master the Devil."[5]

The final appearance of the dragon in the Book of Revelation occurs when an angel comes down from heaven, holding in his hand the key to the bottomless pit and a great chain (cf. Rev 20:1). He seized "the dragon, that ancient serpent, who is the Devil and Satan, and bound him for a thousand years, and threw him into the pit, and locked and sealed it over him, so that he would deceive the nations no more, until the thousand years were ended" (Rev 20:3). The final word about the dragon is this: "After that he must be let out for a little while" (Rev 20:3).

---

5. Cavendish, *Legends*, 205.

Two books in *Mormon* use the dragon as an image of power. The people of Limhi are described as fighting like dragons (cf. Mosiah 20:11), as well as did the Lamanites, their enemies (cf. Alma 43:44).

The Rig Veda contains over fifty references to dragons. However, most of them are about the god Indra slaying Vrtra (also called Ahi), the serpent. With his thunderbolt Indra strikes a cloud and sets free the rain. This is best illustrated in hymn 32 of book 1 of *The Rig Veda*. In verse 1 of the hymn, the singer chants: "I will declare the manly deeds of Indra, the first that he achieved, the thunder-wielder. He slew the dragon, then disclosed the waters, and cleft the channels of the mountain torrents" (*RV* 1:32:1). Verse 2 repeats the idea of verse 1, stating, "He slew the dragon lying on the mountain; his heavenly bolt of thunder Tvastar fashioned. . . . [I]n rapid flow descending the waters glided downward to the ocean" (*RV* 1:32:2). The artist of the gods, Tvastar, fashioned the lightning bolt and gave it to Indra, who "grasped the thunder for his weapon, and smote to death this first-born of the dragons" (*RV* 1:32:3b). All the mentions of dragon in this hymn are to Vrtra, as can be seen in verse 5: "Indra with his own great and deadly thunder smote into pieces Vrtra, worst of Vrtras" (*RV* 1:32:5a); thus, "low on the earth so lies the prostrate dragon" (*RV* 1:32:5b). "There as he lies, like a bank-bursting river, the waters taking courage flow above him. The dragon lies beneath the feet of torrents which Vrtra with his greatness had encompassed" (*RV* 1:32:8). "Nothing availed him lightning, nothing thunder, hailstorm of mist which had spread around him; when Indra and the dragon strove in battle, Maghavan gained the victory for ever" (*RV* 1:32:13). The one who rides the clouds, Maghavan, that is, Indra, was not seen by anyone when he avenged "the dragon," nor did fear possess his heart "when he had slain him" (*RV* 1:32:14).

Other more poetic references to Indra slaying the dragon, Vrtra (Ahi), include a verse from hymn 51 of book 1. The verse, addressed to Indra, states: "You have unclosed the prisons of the waters; you have in the mountain seized the treasure rich in gifts. When you had slain with might the dragon Vrtra, you, Indra, did raise the sun in heaven for all to see" (*RV* 1:51:4). A verse from hymn 52 of book 1 puts it this way: "Then heaven himself, the mighty, at that dragon's roar reeled back in terror when, Indra, his thunderbolt . . . had struck off with might the head of Vrtra, tyrant of the earth and heaven" (*RV* 1:52:10). In hymn 80 of book 1, Indra is addressed as the "mightiest, thunder-armed, [who] has driven by force the dragon from the earth, lauding [his] own imperial sway" (*RV* 1:80:1). And a few verses later, the singer says, "When with the thunder you did make your dart and Vrtra meet in war, your might, O Indra, fain to slay the dragon, was set firm in heaven, lauding your own imperial sway" (*RV* 1:80:13).

In book 4, there are two poetic statements about Indra slaying the dragon Vrtra (Ahi). Hymn 19 states: "You slew Ahi who besieged the waters, and dug out their all-supporting channels. The dragon stretched against the seven prone rivers, where no joint was, you rent with your thunder" (*RV* 4:19:2b, 3b). Hymn 22 states it this way: "These are your great deeds, Indra, your . . . mighty deeds to be told aloud at all libations. That you, O hero, bold and boldly daring, did with your bolt, by strength, destroy the dragon" (*RV* 4:22:5). The last of the more poetic presentations of Indra's slaying of the dragon is found in book 5, hymn 29: "[Indra] grasped his thunderbolt to slay the dragon, and loosed, that they might flow, the youthful waters" (*RV* 5:29:2b).

"Now, verily, will I declare the exploits, mighty and true, of [Indra] the true and mighty," begins hymn 15 of book 2. "In the [first three days of a festival] he drank the soma; then in its rapture Indra slew the dragon" (*RV* 2:15:1). Hymn 19 of book 2 states, "Indra, this mighty one, the dragon's slayer, sent forth the flood of waters to the ocean" (*RV* 2:19:3). Here is how hymn 17 of book 4 narrates the deed:

> Great are you, Indra; yes, the earth with gladness, and heaven confess to you your high dominion. You in your vigor, having slaughtered Vrtra, did free the floods arrested by the dragon. Moreover, when you first were born, O Indra, you struck terror into all the people. You, Maghavan, rent with your bolt the dragon who lay against the water-floods of heaven. (*Rig Veda* 4:17:1, 7)

In two successive verses, hymn 17 of book 6 states:

> Yes, even that heaven itself of old bent backward before your bolt, in terror of its anger, when Indra, life of every living creature, smote down within his lair the assailing dragon. Yes, strong one, Tvastar turned for you, the mighty, the bolt with [a] thousand spikes and [a] hundred edges, eager and prompt at will, wherewith you crushed the boasting dragon, O impetuous hero. (*RV* 6:17:9–10)

"Indra, you set free the many waters that were encompassed . . . by the dragon," begins verse 3 of hymn 21 in book 7. "Down rolled, as if on chariots borne, the rivers; through fear of you all things created tremble" (*RV* 7:21:3). And hymn 82 of book 8 describes Indra's deed this way: "When in their terror all the gods shrank from the dragon's furious might, fear of the monster fell on them. Then [Indra] was my defender, then, invincible, whose foe is not, the Vrtra-slayer showed his might" (*RV* 8:82:14–15).

Leviathan (Behemoth, Rahab, Dragon)

The Rig Veda contains other references to Indra "slaying the dragon" (*RV* 1:61:8; 1:165:6; 2:12:3; 5:29, 3, 8), "slaying Vrtra the dragon who enclosed the waters" (*RV* 6:20:2), "blowing the great dragon from the air" (*RV* 8:3:20), "destroying the dragon" (*RV* 10:133:2), and rescuing "from the dragon's grasp" (*RV* 10:48:2). Other references include: "Floods great and many, compassed by the dragon, you bade swell and set free, O hero," Indra (*RV* 2:11:2); "Who slew the dragon putting fort his vigor, the demon lying there, he, men, is Indra" (*RV* 2:12:11); "Indra with wondrous powers subdued the dragon, the guileful lurker who beset the waters" (*RV* 5:30:6); "The fountain-depths obstructed in their seasons, you, thunderer made flow, the mountain's udder. Strong Indra, you by slaying even the dragon that lay extended there have shown your vigor" (*RV* 5:32:2); "What time, O Indra, in your arms you took your wildly rushing bolt to slay the dragon" (*RV* 8:85:5); Indra, "[y]ou did free rivers swallowed by the dragon; and rapidly they set themselves in motion, those that were loosed and those that longed for freedom. Excited now to speed they run unresting" (*RV* 10:111:9); and "When, bearing warlike weapons, fain to win your praise, you met Vrtra, yes, the dragon, for the fight" (*RV* 10:113:3).

Other interesting phrases about dragons include chastising dragons (cf. *RV* 10:138:1), "the female dragon's path" (*RV* 10:144:4), and pursuing dragons (cf. *RV* 10:139:6). Even the god of fire, Agni, gets into the picture of dragons, as hymn 113 in book 10 states, ". . . [A]ll the gods extolled, with eloquence, [Indra's] deeds of manly might. As Agni eats the dry food with his teeth, he ate Vrtra, the dragon, maimed by Indra's deadly dart" (*RV* 10:113:8).

Besides Indra, the other major dragon in *The Rig Veda* is Ahibudhnya, referred to as "the great dragon of the deep" (*RV* 1:186:5; 2:31:6; 5:41:16; 7:35:13; 10:66:11; 10:92:12; 10:93:5). Ahibudhnya is a divine being that dwells in and presides over the firmament in Hindu mythology. In other words, he dwells in the depth of air; he is the regent of the depths of the firmament. "With lauds I sing the dragon born of floods," states the singer of hymn 34 of book 7, "he sits beneath the streams in middle air" (*RV* 7:34:16). Some translators refer to Ahibudhnya as the Leviathan of the sea of heaven, the distant invisible and deified being who presides over the firmament much like the biblical Leviathan presides over the ocean.

Thus, there are monsters named Leviathan, Behemoth, Rahab, Vrtra, and Ahibudhnya. All of them represent chaos, usually in terms of water—sea, ocean, rivers. Sometimes these monsters are called sea serpents, sea monsters, or dragons. Biblically, the LORD God controls monsters; in *The Rig Veda*, Indra slays the monsters or dragons. Mythological monsters and dragons represent the chaos that forever enters people's lives; the fact that there is some god that eliminates the chaos gives hope to those who experience it.

Journal/Meditation: What name do you give to the monsters or dragons that entered your life in the past few days? After identifying a few of them, specifically identify how your conquered each one of them. What spiritual virtue did you employ?

Prayer: Almighty God, you created the great sea monsters and every living creature that moves on the earth. You defeated the dragon that threatened your people, demonstrating that out of chaos you bring control. Fill me with the gift of your Holy Spirit that I may calm the chaos that surrounds me with the good news of the death and resurrection of your Son, Jesus Christ, who lives and reigns with you, Father, and the Holy Spirit, one God, forever and ever. Amen.

Lion

Text: "A slave ran away from his master, by whom he had been most cruelly treated, and, in order to avoid capture, betook himself into the desert. As he wandered about in search of food and shelter, he came to a cave, which he entered and found to be unoccupied. Really, however, it was a lion's den, and almost immediately, to the horror of the wretched fugitive, the lion himself appeared. The man gave himself up for lost: but to his utter astonishment, the lion, instead of springing upon him and devouring him, came and fawned upon him, at the same time whining and lifting up his paw. Observing it to be much swollen and inflamed, he examined it and found a large thorn embedded in the ball of the foot. He accordingly removed it and dressed the wound as well as he could; in the course of time it healed up completely. The lion's gratitude was unbounded; he looked upon the man as his friend, and they shared the cave for some time together."

"A day came, however, when the slave began to long for the society of his fellow men, and he bade farewell to the lion and returned to the town. Here he was presently recognized and carried off in chains to his former master, who resolved to make an example of him, and ordered that he should be thrown to the beasts at the next public spectacle in the theater. On the fatal day the beasts were loosed into the arena, and among the rest a lion of huge bulk and ferocious aspect; and then the wretched slave was cast in among them. What was the amazement of the spectators, when the lion after one glance bounded up to him and lay down at his feet with every expression of affection and delight! It was his old friend of the cave! The audience clamored that the slave's life should be spared; the governor of the town, marveling at such gratitude and fidelity in a beast, decreed that both should receive their liberty."[1]

Reflection: Aesop's famous story above about the slave and lion is but one of over twenty-five fables that feature a lion in *Aesop's Fables*. It is reminiscent of the HB (OT) prophet Isaiah's idyllic picture of harmony where he writes about "the calf and the lion and the fatling together" (Isa 11:6; cf. 2 Ne 15:29) and the lion eating straw like the ox (cf. Isa 11:7; 65:25; 2 Ne 30:13; 21:7). Natural enemies would exist in peace—such was the prophet's messianic hope that the large wild member of the cat family with its tawny yellow coat and shaggy mane for the male would live in harmony with the tame animals it usually killed and devoured.

Very similar to Aesop's fable above is the story about St. Jerome pulling a thorn from a lion's paw. Because of Jerome's good deed, the lion agreed to protect Jerome's donkey. When the donkey went missing, Jerome presumed that the lion had eaten him. Meanwhile, the lion searched for the donkey and found him captured by thieves, who "fled when they saw a lion approaching, abandoning their string of camels, which the lion delivered to the monastery along with the donkey."[2] Chapple narrates a similar story about two Jaina monks who instructed a lion "in the value of kindness and admonished him to refrain from killing."[3] The lion was so affected by the monks' lecture "that he renounced hunting and killing for food and eventually starved to death. [However,] [h]e was reborn in heaven, and later became Mahavira," widely regarded as the founder of Jainism, but more properly regarded as a reformer of Jainism.[4]

In the HB (OT) Book of Daniel is found the story of the prophet Daniel willingly being thrown into a den of lions rather than worship King Darius. After having sealed Daniel in the lions' den all night, the king arrives the next morning to discover Daniel still alive. Daniel tells the king that his "God sent his angel and shut the lions' mouths so that they would not hurt [him], because [he] was found blameless before [God], and also before . . . [the] . . . king" (Dan 6:22). After Daniel is released from the lions' den, those who had accused him, along with their wives and children, are thrown into the den, and the lions devour them.

---

1. Aesop, 31–32.
2. Kemmerer, *Animals*, 229.
3. Chapple, "Inherent Value," 242.
4. Ibid.

Strength

In other biblical literature, the lion is known for its strength, but not as much as Samson, one of the judges. After hearing a young lion roar at him, "[the] spirit of the LORD rushed on him, and he tore the lion apart barehanded as one might tear apart a kid" (Judg 14:6a). Later, Samson sees "the carcass of the lion, and there was a swarm of bees in the body of the lion, and honey. He scraped it out into his hands, and went on, eating as he went" (Judg 14:9a). Not only does the death of the lion serve to reveal Samson's strength, but it becomes the basis for a riddle: "Out of the eater came something to eat. Out of the strong came something sweet" (Judg 14:14).

Aesop narrates a fable about a man and a lion who were companions on a journey. As they made their way, they began to boast about their strength to each other; "each claimed to be superior to the other in strength and courage."[5] Coming upon a crossroad, the man spied a statue of a man strangling a lion. Pointing toward the statue, the man declared that the statue proved his point that he was stronger. "Not so fast, my friend," said the lion; "that is only your view of the case. If . . . lions could make statues, you may be sure that in most of them you would see the man underneath."[6]

In "The Wolf and the Lion," Aesop narrates another tale about a lion's strength. After stealing a lamb, a wolf meets a lion, "who took his prey away from him and walked off with it."[7] Likewise, in "The Archer and the Lion," all animals except the lion flee from the archer. The lion challenges the archer to a fight. However, after getting stung by one arrow, the lion runs away.[8] Even *The Quran* notes the strength of a lion from which other animals flee (cf. *Quran* 74:51).

The lion's strength is also narrated in the HB (OT) First Book of Kings. An unnamed "man of God" disobeys the LORD's words about not eating or drinking. As he is going away, a lion meets him on the road and kills him. Then the lion stands beside the body (cf. 1 Kgs 13:25). When word is brought to an old prophet, he declares, "It is the man of God who disobeyed the word of the LORD; therefore the LORD has given him to the lion, which has torn him and killed him according to the word that the LORD spoke to him" (1 Kgs 13:26). The old prophet finds the body thrown in the road with the lion standing beside the body, which the lion had not eaten (cf. 1 Kgs 13:28). The prophet gathers the body and buries it in his own grave.

---

5. Aesop, 66.
6. Ibid.
7. Ibid., 96.
8. Cf. Ibid., 135.

The lion's strength is also attested in the HB (OT) Book of Proverbs. The author states that the lion "is mightiest among wild animals and does not turn back before any" (Prov 30:30). Such strength is used to describe the tribe of Judah in the HB (OT) Book of Genesis. Among Jacob's last words to his sons are these addressed to Judah: "Judah is a lion's whelp; from the prey, my son, you have gone up. He crouches down, he stretches out like a lion, like a lioness—who dares rouse him up?" (Gen 49:9) Balaam compares the Israelites to a lioness in the HB (OT) Book of Numbers, stating that the people rise up like a lioness; they rouse themselves like a lion (cf. Num 23:24a). In another oracle he declares, "[Israel] crouched, he lay down like a lion, and like a lioness; who will rouse him up?" (Num 24:9a) Balaam's comparison of Israel to a lion is echoed in Moses' blessing of the Israelites in the HB (OT) Book of Deuteronomy. Moses declares, "Gad lives like a lion; he tears at arm and scalp" (Deut 33:20), and "Dan is a lion's whelp that leaps forth . . ." (Deut 33:22). The psalmist asks God to deliver him from his pursuers, who, like a lion, will tear him apart and drag him away, with no one to rescue him (cf. Ps 7:2).

The lion's strength instills fear in others, because the lion usually kills whatever it attacks. Aesop narrates at least ten fables about lion's killing someone or something. For example, "The Ass, the Fox, and the Lion" narrates how a fox tricks a donkey into falling into a pit and how the lion finished off the fox "and then at his leisure proceeded to feast upon the ass."[9] In "The Ass, the Cock, and the Lion," the lion eats the donkey.[10] In "The Pack-Ass, the Wild Ass, and the Lion," the lion eats the wild donkey.[11] "The Old Lion" is about an elderly lion feigning to be sick and tricking other animals into his cave, where he promptly kills them and eats them—until a fox notices that no footprints lead away from the cave.[12] "The Lion and the Three Bulls" is a story about a lion fomenting jealousy and distrust among three bulls, which separated from and avoided each other. This gave the lion the opportunity to kill them one by one and eat them.[13] "The Wily Lion" is a story about a bull being tricked by a lion, which ends up eating the bull.[14] A stag is featured in two fables. In "The stag and the Lion," the stag runs into a cave only to find a hungry lion there.[15] And in the lengthy "The Lion,

---

9. Ibid., 15–16.
10. Cf. Ibid., 127–28.
11. Cf. Ibid., 158–59.
12. Cf. Ibid., 54.
13. Cf. Ibid., 98.
14. Cf. Ibid., 93.
15. Cf. Ibid., 194.

the Fox and the Stag" fable, the fox tricks the stag into entering the lion's den, where the lion "overpowered him, and feasted right royally upon his carcass."[16]

God Is Like a Lion

The lion's strength becomes a metaphor for God's strength and the strength of certain biblical people. The shepherd boy David declares that the LORD has saved him "from the paw of the lion" (1 Sam 17:37) when he was tending sheep. In the Book of Job, Eliphaz tells Job that God can destroy "the roar of the lion, the voice of the fierce lion, and the teeth of the young lions are broken" (Job 4:10). He adds, "The strong lion perishes for lack of prey, and the whelps of the lioness are scattered" (Job 4:11). Later in the book Job tells God that the Holy One is as bold as a lion hunting him (cf. Job 10:16a). God answers Job, asking him, "Can you hunt the prey for the lion, or satisfy the appetite of the young lions, when they crouch in their dens, or lie in wait in their covert?" (Job 38:39–40) Of course, Job cannot. The prophet Hosea says that God "will be like a lion to Ephraim, and like a young lion to the house of Judah" (Hos 5:14a). He will tear and go away; he will carry off, and no one will rescue (cf. Hos 5:14b). Later in the book the prophet states that "the LORD . . . roars like a lion" (Hos 11:10) and that he "will devour . . . like a lion" (Hos 13:8c). King Hezekiah of Judah, after being ill and recovering, wrote a psalm naming God to be "like a lion [who] breaks all [his] bones" (Isa 38:13). And in the CB (NT) the author of the Second Letter to Timothy states that he "was rescued from the lion's mouth" by God (2 Tim 4:17), a reference to Psalm 22:21 in which the pray-er asks God to save him from the lion's mouth (cf. Ps 22:21).

Jeremiah the prophet also compares God's anger to a lion. "Like a lion he has left his covert" writes the prophet (Jer 25:38). Later, Jeremiah portrays God saying, "Like a lion coming up from the thickets of the Jordan against a perennial pasture, I will suddenly chase Edom away from it" (Jer 49:19; 50:44). In one lament for destroyed Jerusalem, God's wrath is compared by the singer to "a lion in hiding [which] led [him] off [his] way and tore [him] to pieces" (Lam 3:10b–11a).

The Bible offers some of the characteristics of the lion and applies them to people. The valiant warrior is described as one having a heart "like the heart of a lion" (2 Sam 17:10). Likewise, *Mormon* describes warriors in a battle fighting "like lions for their prey" (Mosiah 20:10). In fact, killing a lion demonstrates how strong one really is (cf. 2 Sam 23:20; 1 Chr 11:22).

---

16. Ibid., 212–14.

Mattathias is described as being "like a lion in his deeds, like a lion's cub roaring for prey" (1 Macc 3:4). The psalmist describes his enemy to be "like a ravening and roaring lion" (Ps 22:13). The writer of the Book of Proverbs compares a wicked ruler over poor people to "a roaring lion" (Prov 28:15), but he also states that a king's anger is like "the growling of a lion" (Prov 19:12; 20:2). The prophet Isaiah describes the nation which God will bring to punish Israel as roaring like a young lion (cf. Isa 5:29a). Later in the same book the phrase "lioness and roaring lion" is used again (Isa 30:b), and the prophet declares that God will come to fight upon Mount Zion "as a lion or a young lion growls over its prey" (Isa 31:4). God is not terrified by the shouting of shepherds, nor is he daunted by their noise (cf. Isa 31:4). *Mormon* portrays those whom God uses to manifest his anger as "roaring like a lion" (2 Ne 15:28). "They shall roar like young lions; . . . they shall roar, and lay hold on the prey, and shall carry away safe, and none shall deliver" (2 Ne 15:29).

Mormon describes Jesus stating that his people "are a remnant of Jacob . . . among the Gentiles, . . . in the midst of them as a lion among the beasts of the forest, as a young lion among the flocks of sheep . . ." (3 Ne 21:12; cf. 3 Ne 20:16). The same idea is found in the fifth chapter of the Book of Mormon in which the people are exhorted to repent "lest a remnant of the seed of Jacob shall go forth among [them] as a lion, and tear [them] to pieces . . ." (Morm 5:24).

The prophet Ezekiel declares that the princes of Judah "are like a roaring lion tearing the prey" because "they have devoured human lives" (Ezek 22:25). Likewise, the prophet Amos in announcing the punishment that God is about to bring upon his people, asks, "Does a lion roar in the forest, when it has no prey? Does a young lion cry out from its den, if it has caught nothing?" (Amos 3:4) The reader has to answer both questions with "No." Then Amos declares, "The lion has roared; who will not fear? The LORD God has spoken . . ." (Amos 3:4). Later, Amos will announce that the day of LORD will be "as if someone fled from a lion, and was met by a bear" (Amos 5:19). In the CB (NT), the author of the First Letter of Peter says that it is the devil which prowls around like a roaring lion looking for someone to devour (cf. 1 Pet 5:8). Commenting on this passage, Kienzle states that the word "'lion' designates the animal, and the animal signifies the devil."[17] "The lion as ravenous beast represent the devil," she writes.[18] She adds, "While the lion generally assumed a high-ranking position in beast literature, exegetes reading 1 Peter 5:8 counted it with numerous other animals

---

17. Kienzle, "Bestiary," 105.
18. Ibid., 106.

that could represent evil."[19] And in the Book of Revelation, John of Patmos describes an angel descending from heaven and giving "a great shout, like a lion roaring" (Rev 10:3). Later in the same book, the author describes the beast rising out of the sea as having a mouth "like a lion's mouth" (Rev 13:2).

Prowling

Another characteristic of the lion is prowling or lurking; both of these are applied to people. For example, the psalmist says that the wicked "lurk in secret like a lion in its covert" (Ps 10:9). Likewise, in Psalm 17 the wicked are declared to be "like a lion eager to tear, like a young lion lurking in ambush" (Ps 17:12). The prophet Jeremiah compares Judah's foe to a "lion . . . gone up from its thicket" (Jer 4:7) or as "a lion from the forest [which] shall kill them" (Jer 5:6a). God laments that his people have become like a lion in the forest (cf. Jer 12:8a).

Lying in wait is another characteristic of a lion used in biblical literature. In the OT (A) Book of Sirach, sin's teeth are like lion's teeth (cf. Sir 21:2). Later in the same work, the author states, "A lion lies in wait for prey; so does sin for evildoers" (Sir 27:10). Even vengeance lies in wait for the proud like a lion (cf. Sir 27:28). In the prophet Jeremiah, God accuses Jerusalem of using her own sword "like a ravening lion" to kill the prophets he sent (Jer 2:30b).

Royalty

The prophet Ezekiel presents an allegory using the image of a lion. He writes:

> What a lioness was your mother among lions! She lay down among your lions, rearing her cubs. She raised up one of her cubs; he became a young lion, and he learned to catch prey; he devoured humans. The nations sounded an alarm against him; he was caught in their pit; and they brought him with hooks to the land of Egypt. When she saw that she was thwarted, that her hope was lost, she took another of her cubs and made him a young lion. He prowled among the lions; he became a young lion, and he learned to catch prey; he devoured people. And he ravaged their strongholds, and laid waste their towns; the land was appalled, and all in it, at the sound of his roaring. The nations set upon him from the provinces all around; they spread

---

19. Ibid., 105.

their net over him; he was caught in their pit. With hooks they put him in a cage, and brought him to the king of Babylon; they brought him into custody, so that his voice should be heard no more on the mountains in Israel. (Ezek 19:2–9)

In the analogy, the lion represents the tribe of Judah and the royal line of King David. The lioness is Judah. The first cub is King Jehoahaz, who was exiled to Egypt. The second cub is King Jehoiakim, who succeeded Jehoahaz. Jehoiakim's failed revolt led to his exile. His successor, King Jehoiachin, was taken into captivity and brought to Babylon. The prophet Micah, like Ezekiel, saw "the remnant of Jacob . . . among the nations . . . like a lion among the animals of the forest, like a young lion among the flocks of sheep, which, when it goes through, treads down and tears in pieces, with no one to deliver" (Mic 5:7a, 8). And, of course, the CB (NT) Book of Revelation refers to Jesus as "the Lion of the tribe of Judah, the Root of David" (Rev 5:5); he is the one who has conquered and is worthy to break the seven seals on the scroll. Kienzle notes the "the lion of Judah signifies the King of Kings,"[20] while Foltz makes clear that in the Iranian tradition lion figures are associated with monarchy and appear on many public buildings, even on religious ones.[21]

Aesop's Fables contains three tales identifying the lion with royalty. In "The Lion and the Wild Ass," after the two creatures hunt together, the lion divides the spoils into three portions. The lion declares that he is entitled to more because he is the "king of beasts."[22] "When the lion reigned over the beasts of the earth," begins "The Kingdom of the Lion," "he was never cruel or tyrannical, but as gentle and just as a king ought to be."[23] And in "The Gnat and the Lion," after the gnat triumphs "over the king of the beasts," he gets caught in a spider web and is eaten by the spider.[24]

Besides the lion representing the royal line of David, it was also used by other rulers to signify their power. Ezekiel identifies a Pharaoh of Egypt who considered himself a lion among the nations (cf. Ezek 32:2). The prophet Daniel narrates a vision of four great beasts, one of which "was like a lion and had eagles' wings" (Dan 7:4); the lion represents Babylon. This is made clear in the OT (A) Book of Esther; in her prayer to God for strength to face her husband the king, she says, "Put eloquent speech in my mouth before the lion . . ." (Esth 14:13). The prophet Nahum refers to the king of Nineveh

20. Ibid., 106.
21. Cf. Foltz, "She-camel," 155.
22. Aesop, 85.
23. Ibid., 145.
24. Ibid., 198–99.

as a lion filling caves with his plunder. "What became of the lions' den, the cave of the young lions, where the lion goes, and the lion's cubs, with no one to disturb them?" asks Nahum (Nah 2:11). Then, he answers, "The lion has torn enough for his whelps and strangled prey for his lionesses; he has filled his caves with prey and his dens with torn flesh" (Nah 2:12).

In *The Rig Veda* the lion is associated with the god Agni. Both heaven and earth "reverence the lion" (*RV* 1:95:5) or the one "born as a lion" (*RV* 3:2:11), "couched like a lion in his lair" (*RV* 3:9:4), around whom the ancestors "stand as round an angry lion" (*RV* 5:15:3). Indra, too, is depicted as a lion, that is, "a dread lion" (*RV* 4:16:4).

Lion Imagery

Maybe the best use of the lion imagery is that found in the prophet Ezekiel which is borrowed by the author of the Book of Revelation. Among Ezekiel's many visions is one of four living creatures or wheels, each of which has four faces; one of the four faces is that of a lion (cf. Ezek 10:14; 1:10). In another vision, the prophet sees cherubim and each has two faces, one being that of a young lion (cf. Ezek 41:19). In a vision, the author of the Book of Revelation refers to Ezekiel's four living creatures (cf. Rev 4:6b) and names the first one as being "like a lion" (Rev 4:7). In later Christian iconography, a winged lion came to represent Mark's Gospel. Thus, the cover on a *Book of Gospels* often displays four creatures with wings, and one of those is a lion, which represents Mark's Gospel. Apostolos-Cappadona states, "The Western Christian classification of animals as emblems is attested to by the lion" which signifies one of the four evangelists "found on the tympani of medieval cathedrals or on the pages of medieval manuscript illuminations, such as those in the *Book of Kells*."[25]

Alongside the strong lion is the weak lion. In "The Lion and the Bull," the supposedly-strong lion prepares to entice a fat bull to his den under the pretense of sacrificing a sheep. However, upon arrival the bull notices no sheep and leaves the lion with his empty saucepans and spits, which had been meant for the bull.[26] And many people know the fable about "The Lion and the Mouse." Just when the lion was about the kill the mouse, the mouse asks for mercy, which the lion grants. Later, the mouse finds the lion entangled in a net, which he gnaws until the ropes break and the lion is free.[27] In "The Lion, the Mouse, and the Fox," a mouse runs over the back

---

25. Apostolos-Cappadona, "*Dynamis* of Animals," 448.
26. Cf. Aesop, 113.
27. Cf. Ibid., 16.

of a lion asleep in his den. The fox watches and harasses the lion about not doing anything about it. The lion states that he is only concerned about the mouse's manners.[28] And in "The Lion and the Boar," the two creatures stop quarrelling about who should be first to drink from a stream and become friends.[29]

Thus, the lion represents strength and weakness. Lions both kill and spare potential victims. People are often attributed with anger like that of a lion, as well as God. A soldier is often portrayed as being a lion-hearted warrior. The lion's roar, indicating its fierceness, is attributed to people, as well as the lion's prowling, lurking, and lying in wait characteristics. Monarchies often display the lion on coats-of-arms and describe rulers as lions.

Journal/Meditation: Which lion characteristic best describes you? How specifically?

Prayer: Mighty God, you made your Son the Lion of the tribe of Judah and the Root of David through his suffering, death, and resurrection. Give me the strength of the lion that I may never cease to praise you and always confess that Jesus Christ, who lives and reigns with you and the Holy Spirit, is King of kings and Lord of lords, forever and ever. Amen.

---

28. Cf. Ibid., 105.
29. Cf. Ibid., 65.

Mule Deer

Text: "As a deer longs for flowing streams, so my soul longs for you, O God." (Ps 42:1–2a)

Reflection: The mule deer displays a grayish-brown coat, some white under parts, a black tail, and long ears. As one of more than forty species of deer, it is a mammal distinguished by the branched antlers on males. Males are often referred to as stags, that is, adult male red deer; females are often referred to as hinds. In the HB (OT) Book of Psalms, the longing of the deer to drink from a flowing stream of water is compared to the longing or thirst that the singer of the song has for the living God. The psalmist can compare his thirst for God to that of the way a deer thirsts for water because the deer was considered a clean animal, that is, one which the Israelites could eat (cf. Deut 14:5; 12:15, 22; 15:22). Included in the clean animal category was the roebuck, a male roe deer (cf. Deut 14:5). Both deer and roebuck are mentioned as part of King Solomon's daily provisions (cf. 1 Kgs 4:23).

Aesop's Fables, which usually refer to the male deer as a stag, demonstrate that people enjoyed venison. In "The Stag and the Ox-Stall," a stag, being chased by dogs, takes refuge in a stable where several oxen are in stalls. The deer hides under a haystack, but the tip of his antlers can still be seen. When the owner comes to feed the oxen, he removes hay from the stack and sees the stag, which he has seized and killed for his table.[1] In "The Stag with One Eye," Aesop demonstrates how misfortune often assails one from an unexpected quarter. A stag with only one eye grazes near the sea

---

1. Cf. Aesop, 24–25.

shore with his good eye focused on land in order to spot any dog that may approach. While watching the land, the deer does not notice the sailors on the shore who spy the deer, shoot it with an arrow, and kill it for food.[2] A huntsman shoots a stag with an arrow and kills it in "The Stag and the Vine." After concealing himself under cover of a thick vine, the deer begins to eat the leaves, only to expose himself to the hunter.[3] A sick stag dies because his friends eat all the grass around him, and he is "too feeble to get up and go in search of fodder; and thus he perished miserably of hunger owing to the thoughtlessness of his friends."[4]

Kemmerer narrates a Buddhist tale of a stag which intercedes with a king who loves to hunt every day, "descending on the quiet forest . . . with flying arrows, chasing the deer through thick forests with intent to kill, and wounding many in the process."[5] The story continues:

> The deer decide that it is better to volunteer death than to be hunted, so they draw straws each day to determine who must go to the palace to be killed and consumed. From then on, a deer goes willingly to the king to be killed each day for his feast. One day a doe with a tiny fawn draws the short stick. She pleads with the leader not to send her off to the chopping block, knowing that her fawn cannot survive without her. He sends her back to nurse her little one, granting reprieve, then turns toward the palace to offer his own life in exchange. The king, impressed by the generous gift of the stag—one the king would not likely offer his subjects—spares the stag's life.[6]

Instead of leaving immediately, the stag speaks with the king, asking him to spare the lives of the other deer. The king grants the stag's request. Then, the stag asks for mercy for the other animals in the forest. Amazed at the stag's compassion, he agrees not to pursue or kill any other creatures in the forest. The stag continues to ask the king to spare the birds, then the fish, and the king does. Kemmerer continues: "The stag's willingness to die for others, and to speak up on behalf of all sentient beings, moves the king to compassion. He ultimately agrees to stop killing all creatures . . . ."[7] Once love entered the heart of the king, he stopped killing all animals. As Kemmerer notes, "The stag is, of course, the Buddha in one of his innumerable

   2. Cf. Ibid., 119.
   3. Cf. Ibid., 138.
   4. Ibid., 140.
   5. Kemmerer, *Animals*, 112.
   6. Ibid.
   7. Ibid., 113.

future lives, teaching against the deadly horrors of hunting."[8] Vargas says that animals are active agents of enlightenment. "... [A]nimals were active witnesses to an event that marks the Buddhist tradition and were hearers of the teachings."[9]

Kemmerer narrates another story about animals voicing opposition to hunting.

> [A] crow, a pigeon, a mouse, a tortoise, and a deer, all of whom are friends, work together to escape a cruel and greedy hunter. When deer becomes caught in a hunter's trap, crow quickly carries mouse over to chew through the bindings. Tortoise comes along, slowly, to see if his friend is safe, but as deer is released, the hunter arrives, taking the slow-moving tortoise away in fresh binds. The remaining friends hatch a scheme to save tortoise: Deer lies by a nearby lake, as if freshly dead, with crow pretending to peck his eyes. The greedy hunter drops tortoise and rushes over to claim the "dead" deer. Meanwhile, mouse chews through the leather bindings to free tortoise, who slips into the lake. Deer then leaps up and dashes off, as does mouse, while crow lifts onto the wind.[10]

In *Aesop's Fables*, the deer is usually fleeing from hounds or dogs. For example, in "The Fawn and His Mother," the hind tells her son that he has "a powerful body and a stout pair of horns" and that she cannot imagine that he would "run away from the hounds."[11] However, as soon as she hears a pack of dogs, the hind runs away as fast as she can. In "The Stag and the Lion," a stag takes refuge in a cave from the hounds chasing him only to discover that a hungry lion lives in the cave.[12]

Aesop narrates the fable of "The Stag at the Pool," which echoes the opening passage from Psalm 42. However, seeing "his own reflection in the water," the stag is "struck with admiration for his fine spreading antlers, but at the same time [feels] nothing but disgust for the weakness and slenderness of his legs."[13] While caught in self-absorption, a lion sees him, attacks him, and the stag gives chase. "... [C]oming presently to a wood, he was caught by his antlers in the branches, and fell a victim to the teeth and claws

---

8. Ibid.
9. Vargas, "Snake-Kings," 219.
10. Kemmerer, *Animals*, 68–69.
11. Aesop, 71.
12. Cf. Ibid., 194.
13. Ibid., 74.

of his enemy."[14] His last words are these: "Woe is me! (sic). I despised my legs, which might have saved my life, but I gloried in my horns, and they have proved my ruin."[15] This fable echoes the story about King David's son, Absalom, who, while riding his mule, "went under the thick branches of a great oak" and "his head caught fast in the oak, and he was left hanging between heaven and earth, while the mule that was under him went on" (2 Sam 18:9–10). Joab, David's army commander, seizes the opportunity to kill the young man, who had attempted to usurp his father's throne.

Kemmerer records two stories about deer protected by Catholic saints. One concerns St. Maedoc, who "was in prayer when a stag came dashing into his hermitage for protection."[16] The saint covered the deer with the corner of his cloak, and the dogs ran past. Like St. Maedoc, St. Godric "harbored a hunted stag in his forest hermitage."[17] In gratitude, the stag returned regularly to the hermitage to visit the saint.[18] According to Anderson and Raphals, there is a magical or a spiritual quality to deer.[19]

In *The Rig Veda*, the "spotted deer" draw the chariots of the Maruts, the storm gods who number from twenty-seven to thirty-six. The gods ride in golden chariots pulled by "spotted deer" (*RV* 1:37:2; 1:39:6; 1:64:8; 1:85:4; 1:165:5; 2:34:3; 3:26:4; 5:52:8; 5:53:1; 5:54:5; 5:55:6; 5:57:3; 5:60:2; 8:7:29). Some mythologists think that Santa Claus's sleigh pulled by reindeer may have some foundation in the Maruts's chariots being pulled by "spotted deer."

Run Like a Deer

The use of the mule deer in the literature of world religions give rise to metaphors and similes applied to human beings. For example, King David praises God for having made his feet like those of deer (cf. 1 Sam 22:34; Ps 18:33). Likewise, the prophet Habakkuk records this prayer: "GOD, the Lord, is my strength; he makes my feet like the feet of a deer, and makes me tread upon the heights" (Hab 3:19). In *The Rig Veda*, soma, a Vedic ritual drink, is said to run "like a darting deer" (*RV* 9:32:4). Those who do not approach the god Indra with the sacred soma are said to "chase him as hunters chase a deer" (*RV* 8:2:6). Likewise, the sacrificial horse is described as

14. Ibid.
15. Ibid.
16. Kemmerer, *Animals*, 226.
17. Ibid.
18. Ibid.
19. Cf. Anderson, "Daoism and Animals," 278.

having "limbs of the deer" (*RV* 1:163:1). In the Book of the Prophet Isaiah, the day of deliverance is characterized by the lame leaping like a deer (cf. Isa 35:6a). And the HB (OT) Book of Proverbs tells a young man to "rejoice in the wife of [his] youth, a lovely deer, a graceful doe" (Prov 5:18–19). In other words, the man's wife is as beautiful in her movements as a deer is elegant in its bounding.

In some Native American tribes, members dance the deer dance "to appease the spirit guiding the animals and ask its permission to track and kill some of the creatures."[20] "Only with the help of the spirit, they believe, could there be a successful hunt."[21] The source of the dance is traced to a herdsman who becomes a hunter. The legend among the Yaqui Indians narrates how he watched three deer—two large and one small—along the bank of a river. The two large deer faced each other, interlocking their antlers, scraping against each other and creating music that caused the small deer to jump into the air. The hunter "believed that the big deer were singing and that they were using the antlers as musical instruments to accompany their song. And the small deer, he felt certain, was dancing to the music."[22] After the deer disappeared into the woods, the hunter headed home and found an abandoned fawn, which he picked up and took with him. "When he reached his village, he talked with his friends and explained to them that he wanted to sing the deer song. Using two sticks, he showed his friends how to mimic the music of deer antlers. Then he taught a young boy how to dance in the same manner as the small deer he had watched."[23] Thus, the Yaqui people explain the origin of the deer dance which ensured the success of the hunt and provided food and hides for clothing and tents. But even more, the people believed that the deer possessed far-reaching powers to cure illness and infertility, and, similar to the Maruts in *The Rig Veda*, to summon rain, thunder, and lightning.[24]

Another tribe of Indians, the Hupa, conduct the White Deerksin Dance. Dressing in pelts of killed albino deer, they participate in the annual world renewal ceremony which demonstrates thanks for the blessings of the past and petitions the power for good fortune in the future.[25] The Mandans enact a deer calling ceremony. Men, dressed in deer hides and antlers, crawl on all fours to a place where they can be good targets for the hunters, and,

20. *Spirit*, 51.
21. Ibid.
22. Ibid., 49.
23. Ibid.
24. Cf. Ibid., 51.
25. Cf. Ibid., 54.

one by one, they are killed symbolically, as the hunters hope the deer seen during the hunt will be killed.[26]

A creation story of the Wichitas Indians explains that the world began when a voice sang to the great hunter, named "Star That Is Always Moving," instructing him to shoot the third deer that leaped out of the primordial waters.

> The first deer was a white as the moon, the second as black as the night sky, and the third a combination of black and white. Star That Is Always Moving shot the black-and-white deer, wounding it with his arrow. And so began the alternation of day and night. The hunter then chased the wounded deer and its two companions into the sky, where they became stars.[27]

In an attempt to retrieve his arrow, the hunter pursued the wounded deer and continues to pursue it. When he finally catches his prey, the world will end.

The mule deer represents food and future existence in terms of sustenance. While some cultures tell stories designed to stop hunting the deer, others tell tales about how saints have protected the hunted animal or how the hunt began with a dance. The deer represents swiftness, speed, sensitivity, and gentleness. The way it seeks streams of water, its swiftness, and its docility deserve spiritual imitation by those who want to find God.

Journal/Meditation: If you are a hunter, how is killing a deer a sacred rite for you? If you are not a hunter, what do you learn from the deer about your quest for God?

Prayer: O God, as the mule deer longs for flowing streams of water, so I long for you. Deepen within me the gentleness of the hind, but give me the courage of the stag. Hear my prayer in the name of your Son, Jesus Christ, who lives and reigns with you and the Holy Spirit, one God, forever and ever. Amen.

---

26. Cf. Ibid., 70–71.
27. Ibid., 35.

Nighthawk

Text: "The mighty flowing soma-draft, brought by the hawk, has gladdened you; that is your strength, O Thunderer; you have struck down Vrtra from the floods, lauding your own imperial sway." (*RV* 1:80:2)

Reflection: The nighthawk, a bird with long pointed wings and black, white, and buff plumage, feeds on insects usually after dark. Its plumage, looking like bark or leaves, is designed to conceal it during the day when it perches in a tree or when it nests on the ground. While the nighthawk is a smaller bird than what most people think of in terms of a hawk, it is one of many types of nocturnal birds which hunt for prey in flight at night or while there is still some light in the sky. There are at least ten species of nighthawk. This entry will be focused on the "hawk" of nighthawk.

In *The Rig Veda*, the hawk is responsible for bringing the purified ritual drink, known as soma, to Indra, the chief Hindu god. With the energizing juice of an unknown plant, Indra, the Thunderer, is able to defeat Vrtra, a serpent or dragon which personifies drought. Thus, the chaos of drought is destroyed, and Indra is praised for having conquered evil. In hymn 32 of book 1, Indra's deed is posed as a question: "Who saw you avenge the dragon, Indra, that fear possessed your heart when you had slain him; that, like a hawk affrighted through the regions, you crossed nine-and-ninety flowing rivers?" (*RV* 1:32:14) Again, in hymn 44 of book 5, "the hawk is [the] full course, girth-stretching, rapturous drink [for the gods]. They ever seek a fresh draft so that they may come, know when [their] time to halt and drink [their] fill is near" (*RV* 5:44:11). The hymns mention "the hawk [that] rent . . . the stalk that gladdens" (*RV* 6:20:6), "that which the hawk brought in his claw, inviolate, through the air to . . . drink" (*RV* 8:71:9), and "soma, your juice has been effused and poured into the pitcher; like a rapid hawk it rushes on" (*RV* 9:67:15).

The purified soma, known as Pavamana, is "power in streams . . . as a hawk on trees" (*RV* 9:86:35). The purified soma is "sped by the hawk" (*RV* 9:89:2) to Indra. After drinking the mystical juice, Indra is compared to the hawk which "comes in body to the soma; armed with his iron claws he slays the [enemy]" (*RV* 10:99:8). Earlier in *The Rig Veda*, the "mighty Dadhikras," a personification of the morning sun, "the giver of many gifts, who visits all people," is called an "impetuous hawk, swift and of varied color, like a brave king whom each true man must honor" (*RV* 4:38:2).

In *Aesop's Fables*, the hawk is portrayed as a bird of prey in three tales. In "The Mouse, the Frog, and the Hawk," a mouse, which lives on land, and a frog, which lives on land or in water, become friends. After the frog tied himself to the mouse, he jumped into the water and drowned the mouse, which floated to the surface and "was spied by a hawk, who pounded down on him and seized him in his talons. The frog was unable to lose the knot which bound him to the mouse, and thus was carried off along with him and eaten by the hawk."[1] In "The Nightingale and the Hawk," a hungry hawk spies a nightingale sitting on a bough of an oak and darts to the spot, seizing her in his talons. She begs the hawk to spare her life, telling him to seek prey among bigger birds. "You must think me very simple," said the hawk, "if you suppose I am going to give up a certain prize on the chance of a better of which I see at present no signs."[2] Thus, the hawk is known for its "dogged patience, stern vigilance, and amazing celerity . . . that, high in the skies, focuses its sharp eyes on its prey and, with incredible speed, swoops down and captures it with its unsparingly sharp talons."[3] Finally, stupid pigeons, preyed upon by a kite, invite "a hawk into the dovecote to defend them against their enemy" in "The Hawk, the Kite, and the Pigeons." Of course, "the hawk killed more of them in a day than the kite had done in a year."[4]

In the HB (OT), the hawk is considered an unclean animal (cf. Lev 11:16; Deut 14:15); this means that it is not be eaten by the Israelites. It is mentioned by the prophet Isaiah in that context when he declares that the land of Edom will be given over to the hawk as part of divine punishment

---

1. Aesop, 57.
2. Ibid., 187–88.
3. Opoku, "African Mythology," 357.
4. Aesop, 220.

(cf. Isa 34:11). The only other mention of this bird is found in the HB (OT) Book of Job. God asks Job, "Is it by your wisdom that the hawk soars, and spreads its wings toward the south?" (Job 39:26) Of course, God's question is meant to put Job in his place and demonstrate God's absolute wisdom. Thus, the hawk is often associated with awareness and truth, the results of wisdom.

So, the nighthawk, one of many species of hawks that preys upon insects, is also one of many kinds of hawks that prey on other creatures. In Hinduism the hawk is revered because it brings from heaven the precious energizing drink that enables Indra to defeat the dragon, while in Judaism the hawk is considered an unclean bird. When *The Rig Veda* compares the rising sun to a hawk, it is marking the animal as an emblem of vigilance and patience.

Journal/Meditation: Of what is the nighthawk an emblem for you?

Prayer: Father, Lord of all creation, every morning your sun greets me like the wings of a nighthawk darting through the sky. Make me more aware and more grateful for the gift of grace from the Holy Spirit given to me through your Son, Jesus Christ, who lives and reigns with you in Holy Trinity, forever and ever. Amen.

Owl

Text: "An owl, who lived in a hollow tree, was in the habit of feeding by night and sleeping by day; but her slumbers were greatly disturbed by the chirping of a grasshopper, who had taken up his abode in the branches. She begged him repeatedly to have some consideration for her comfort, but the grasshopper, if anything, only chirped the louder. At last the owl could stand it no longer, but determined to rid herself of the pest by means of a trick. Addressing herself to the grasshopper, she said in her pleasantest manner, 'As I cannot sleep for your song, which, believe me, is as sweet as the notes of Apollo's lyre, I have a mind to taste some nectar, which Minerva gave me the other day. Won't you come in and join me?' The grasshopper was flattered by the praise of his song, and his mouth, too, watered at the mention of the delicious drink, so he said he would be delighted. No sooner had he got inside the hollow where the owl was sitting than she pounced upon him and ate him up."[1]

Reflection: As the above fable of "The Grasshopper and the Owl" illustrates, the owl represents wisdom. This hooting bird of prey is traditionally described as wise because of its fixed gaze, as if it were considering something very carefully. Aesop's fable above not only displays the owl's pondering, but portrays her as a trickster. The owl is a predatory, usually nocturnal, bird with a large head, two large front-facing eyes, hooked and feathered talons, a small beak, a short neck, and a distinctive hooting call.

Other than the story above, *Aesop's Fables* contains only one other tale about an owl, and this one begins, "The owl is a very wise bird."[2] In "The

1. Aesop, 124.
2. Ibid., 50.

Owl and the Birds," the owl calls together all the other birds to warn them about three things. The first is that they should destroy the tiny oak tree to keep mistletoe from growing upon it, "from which birdlime will be prepared for [the birds'] destruction."[3] The second warning concerns the sowing of flax. "Go and eat up that seed," says the owl, "for it is the seed of the flax, out of which men will one day make nets to catch [the birds]."[4] After seeing the first archer, the owl warns the birds that he will be their deadly enemy, who will "wing his arrows with their own feathers and shoot them."[5] The birds heed none of the owl's warnings. "When, however, everything turned out as she had foretold, they changed their minds and conceived a great respect for wisdom."[6] Thus, when the owl appears, the birds wait upon her in the hope of hearing something that may be for their good. The owl, however, gives no advice; she sits moping and pondering on the folly of her kind. Thus, the owl is wisely prophetic.

Grimm's Complete Fairy Tales contains one story about an owl which illustrates fear.

> By some mischance one of the great owls, called horned owls, had come from the neighboring woods into the barn of one of the townsfolk in the nighttime, and when day broke did not dare to venture forth again from her retreat, for fear of the other birds, which raised a terrible outcry whenever she appeared.[7]

That line from "The Owl" illustrates both the fear the owl has of people and the fear the other birds have of the owl. However, the next morning

> when the manservant went into the barn to fetch some straw, he was so mightily alarmed at the sight of the owl sitting . . . in a corner, that he ran away and announced to his master that a monster, the like of which he had never set eyes on in his life, and which could devour a man without the slightest difficulty, was sitting in the barn, rolling its eyes about in its head.[8]

The master goes to the barn to slay the monster.

> When, however, he saw the strange grim creature with his own eyes, he was no less terrified than the servant had been. With

---

3. Ibid.
4. Ibid.
5. Ibid.
6. Ibid.
7. Grimm, 121.
8. Ibid.

two bounds he sprang out, ran to his neighbors, and begged them imploringly to lend him assistance against an unknown and dangerous beast, or else the whole town might be in danger if it were to break loose out of the barn, where it was shut up.[9]

The townspeople arrive with spears, hayforks, scythes, and axes. They march to the barn, surrounding it on all sides. One of the most courageous townsfolk "stepped forth and entered with his spear lowered, but came running out immediately afterwards with a shriek, and as pale as death, and could not utter a single word."[10] Two more followed in the same way. Finally, a great strong man stepped forward, put on armor, and put a sword in one hand and a spear in the other hand. His fellow townspeople praised his courage, but they feared for his life.

The barn doors were opened; the owl was seen perched in the middle of a crossbeam. The armed man got a ladder, raised it, and prepared to climb to the owl. "When he had just got to the top, and the owl perceived that he had designs on her, . . . she rolled her eyes, ruffled her feathers, flapped her wings, snapped her beak, and cried, 'Tuwhit, tuwhoo,' in a harsh voice."[11] The armed man backed down the ladder. The townsfolk said, "The monster has poisoned and mortally wounded the very strongest man among us, by snapping at him and just breathing on him. Are we, too, to risk our lives?"[12] After discussing the matter for a while, they decided to pay the master for his barn, corn, and straw, and then they burned the barn with "the terrible beast with it."[13] So, after setting fire to the four corners of the barn, the owl was destroyed.

The Rig Veda echoes Grimm's "The Owl," in a hymn against demons. In book 7, hymn 104, fiends are described as those "who wander like an owl at nighttime" (*RV* 7:104:17). Later in the same hymn, the fiend is "shaped like an owl or owlet" (*RV* 7:104:22). In book 10, hymn 165, an ill-omened dove appears, and "the screeching of the owl is ineffective" to drive it away (*RV* 10:165:4).

The Israelites are forbidden to eat the little owl, the great owl, or the desert owl (cf. Lev 11:17, 18; Deut 14:16, 17), according to the HB (OT). The fact that the owl is unclean and cannot be eaten gives rise to Isaiah's description of God's day of vengeance on Edom, after which the land shall be possessed by the owl, among other unclean creatures (cf. Isa 34:11). "There

---

9. Ibid., 122.
10. Ibid.
11. Ibid.
12. Ibid., 122–23.
13. Ibid., 123.

shall the owl nest and lay and hatch and brood in its shadow," writes the prophet (Isa 34:15). Likewise, the prophet Zephaniah predicts the destruction of Nineveh, the capital of Assyria, stating that wild animals, like the desert owl and the screech owl shall lodge on its capitals; the owl shall hoot at the window (cf. Zeph 2:14bc).

The Second Book of Nephi in *Mormon* echoes Zephaniah. In this book, however, the description is of "Babylon, the glory of kingdoms, the beauty of the Chaldees's excellency" which "shall be as when God overthrew Sodom and Gomorrah" (2 Ne 23:19). Babylon will never be inhabited again, and, among other wild beasts that take up residence, "owls shall dwell there" (2 Ne 24:21).

The distress of the singer of Psalm 102 leads him to compare his groaning to the hooting and screeching of the owl. He proclaims, "I am like an owl of the wilderness, like a little owl of the waste places" (Ps 102:6). Thus, biblically, the owl represents solitude in the midst of desolation.

While the owl represents wisdom, vision, and insight, this predatory bird can be understood as prophetic. It instills fear in others, and it is sometimes understood to be demonic. Because it is an unclean animal, it is a metaphor for desolation, destruction, and desert. Its unique hooting is considered equivalent to human groaning. Like the owl, people do well to spend time in solitude and to ponder or contemplate the spiritual experiences of their lives.

Journal/Meditation: When you read the word "owl," what meanings—both positive and negative—do you associate with it? What do these tell you about your spirituality?

Prayer: Holy One, source of all wisdom, send your Holy Spirit to make me wise. Grant that the insight you give me into your ways may enable me to recognize your presence in all the experiences of my day. Grant me this grace through your Son, Jesus Christ, who lives and reigns with you, Father, and the Holy Spirit, one God, forever and ever. Amen.

Partridge

Text: "On the first day of Christmas my true love sent (gave) to me a partridge in a pear tree." ("The Twelve Days of Christmas")

Reflection: Most people have heard and/or sung the song known as "The Twelve Days of Christmas," an English Christmas carol that enumerates in the manner of a cumulative song—that is, each verse is built on top of the previous verses—a series of increasingly grand gifts given on each of the twelve days of Christmas (December 25 through January 6). The song was first published in 1780; the arrangement used most today dates from 1909. As indicated in the text above, there are variations in the lyrics. The concern here is the bird named "partridge," the gift given on the first day of Christmas.

    A partridge is a medium-sized game bird that nests on the ground. It is not as large as a pheasant, and it is not as small as a quail. This bird, native to Europe, Asia, Africa, and the Middle East, displays variegated plumage and feeds primarily on seeds.

    Bulfinch's Mythology records the Greek mythology concerning the origin of the partridge. Daedalus, a skilful artificer and famous for making wings for himself and his son, was given his nephew, Perdix, to be taught the mechanical arts.

> Daedalus was so envious of his nephew's performances that he took an opportunity, when they were together one day on the top of a high tower, to push him off. But Minerva, who favors ingenuity, saw him falling, and arrested his fate by changing him into a bird called after his name, the Partridge. This bird does

not build his nest in the trees, nor take lofty flights, but nestles in the hedges, and mindful of his fall, avoids high places.[1]

In the HB (OT), David compares King Saul's pursuit of him to be "like one who hunts a partridge in the mountains" (1 Sam 26:20). The prophet Jeremiah employs a proverb about a partridge. He records the LORD saying, "Like the partridge hatching what it did not lay, so are all who amass wealth unjustly; in mid-life it will leave them, and at their end they will prove to be fools" (Jer 17:11). In other words, because the partridge makes its nest on the ground, other birds may lay eggs in it. Thus, the partridge hatches eggs it did not lay. Those who amass wealth unjustly are like the non-partridge eggs that are hatched by the partridge. Once the partridge recognizes that they are not hers, she leaves them, like wealth leaves those who have gotten it without working for it. In the end, both the partridge and those who have lost their wealth benefit nothing. In the OT (A) Book of Sirach, the wicked, who have many disguises, will never be true friends and will only cause ruin: "Like a decoy partridge in a cage, so is the mind of a proud man, and like a spy he observes [one's] weakness" (Sir 11:30).

Aesop narrates two fables featuring a partridge. In one the partridge is a decoy, but also a trickster. A fowler sits down to a scanty supper of herbs and bread, when a friend drops in. He goes out and catches "a tame partridge, which he kept as a decoy."[2] Just as he was about to kill the bird, the partridge said, "Surely you won't kill me? Why, what will you do without me next time you go fowling? How will you get the birds to come to your nets?"[3] The fowler decided she was right, and he let her go. Then, he went into the chicken house, found a plump young rooster, and proceeded to kill him and prepare him for his friend to eat. While the partridge tricked the fowler to spare her life, the rooster was not able to do the same, even when he asked the fowler: ". . . [H]ow will you know the time of night? And who will wake you up in the morning when it is time to get to work?"[4]

In "The Partridge and the Fowler," the bird is caught in the fowler's net. Just as the fowler was about to kill the partridge, it asked him to spare its life and promised to repay him "by decoying other partridges into [his] nets."[5] The fowler refuses to spare the bird.

Thus, the medium-size game bird known as a partridge is made famous by a Christmas carol. Because it was hunted as food, it gave rise to

1. Bulfinch, *Mythology*, 157.
2. Aesop, 197.
3. Ibid.
4. Ibid.
5. Ibid., 215.

the simile of King Saul hunting David, a metaphor about obtaining riches unjustly, and its function as a decoy to lure other birds into the fowler's net. After exploring the use of the partridge in literature, the reader will notice that "a partridge in a pear tree" is an extraordinary gift, since partridges tend to stay on the ground!

Journal/Meditation: Other than the Christmas carol, what is your experience of a partridge? If you have no experience of a partridge, think of a pheasant, grouse, prairie chicken, or ptarmigan.

Prayer: Holy Father, like a fowler hunting the partridge, you seek your people, gathering them like a bird calls her brood to take refuge under her wings. Guide me with your Holy Spirit that I am not decoyed by wealth, fame, or position on my journey to you. Hear my prayer in the name of your Son, Jesus Christ, who is Lord forever and ever. Amen.

Quarter Horse

Text: "[The city of] Troy ... held out, and the Greeks began to despair of ever subduing it by force, and by advice of Ulysses resolved to resort to stratagem. They pretended to be making preparations to abandon the siege, and a portion of the ships were withdrawn and lay hid behind a neighboring island. The Greeks then constructed an immense wooden horse, which they gave out was intended as a propitiatory offering to Minerva, but in fact was filled with armed men. The remaining Greeks then betook themselves to their ships and sailed away, as if for a final departure. The Trojans, seeing the encampment broken up and the fleet gone, concluded the enemy to have abandoned the siege. The gates were thrown open, and the whole population issued forth rejoicing at the long-prohibited liberty of passing freely over the scene of the late encampment. The great horse was the chief object of curiosity. All wondered what it could be for. Some recommended [taking] it into the city as a trophy; others felt afraid of it."

"... With regard to the wooden horse [a Greek named Sinon] told them that it was a propitiatory offering to Minerva, and made so huge for the express purpose of preventing it being carried within the city; for [a] ... prophet had told them that if the Trojans took possession of it, they would assuredly triumph over the Greeks. This language turned the tide of the people's feelings and they began to think how they might best secure the monstrous horse and the favorable auguries connected with it...."

"[The people] ... prepared to introduce [the wooden horse] with due solemnity into the city. This was done with songs and triumphal acclamations, and the day closed with festivity. In the night the armed men who were enclosed in the body of the horse, being let out by ... Sinon, opened the gates of the city to their friends, who had returned under cover of the night. The city was set on fire; the people, overcome with feasting and sleep, put to the sword, and Troy completely subdued."[1]

Reflection: The Greek wooden horse, which brings about the fall of Troy, illustrates ingenuity and trickery. While the monstrous horse was manufactured of wood, it also represents the Greek army's strength. In this latter regard, it is like the quarter horse, a strong animal bred for speed, particularly bred to run short races over a quarter mile. The focus here is the "horse" of quarter horse, that is, the strength represented by the animal.

The Rig Veda often refers to the horse's strength in its many hymns. For example, the god Agni is described as being decked "like a horse, the swift prize-winner" (*RV* 1:60:5), that is, the god is made to shine as one grooms a race horse. In hymn 7 of book 4, Agni "drives the swift horse onward" (*RV* 4:7:11); he "stirs all people, like a noble horse, like a fleet steed" (*RV* 8:43:25). Hymn 117 of book 1 mentions "the hoof of [the] strong horse" (*RV* 1:117:6), and hymn 117 of book 1 mentions "the hoof of [the Asvins's] strong horse" used to shower "a hundred jars of honey for the people" (*RV* 1:116:6b). The Asvins are twin horsemen gods, representing sunrise and sunset; they are depicted as humans having horse heads. The honey they bestow is the result of sunshine bringing forth blossoms from whose nectar bees make honey; the mead that is made from the honey is considered the drink of the gods. The Asvins help "the young man's horse to swiftness in the race; wherewith they bring delicious honey to the bees" (*RV* 1:112:21). "Like a strong horse with a fair back" is an altar in hymn 70 of book 7 (*RV* 7:70:1). Even the sacred drink called soma, when it is pressed from an unknown plant, "runs on like some victorious warrior's steed, hastening onward through the fleece [filter] like a swift horse [which] wins the prize" (*RV* 9:100:4).

The person who is aware, the one who is wide awake, "the one with great wisdom moves on, as a racehorse who leaves behind a nag," according to *The Dhammapada* (*Dhp* 2:29). In other words, the person who is endowed with mindfulness is like a noble horse, swift of speed, which overtakes a lame-legged, weak horse which has lost its swiftness.

War Horse

In the HB (OT), God is credited with the horse's strength. In the Book of Job, God asks Job, "Do you give the horse its might?" (Job 39:19a) Then God asks, "Do you clothe its neck with mane? Do you make it leap like the locust?" (Job 39:19b–20) After this follows God's description of the horse:

---

1. Bulfinch, *Mythology*, 229–231.

> Its majestic snorting is terrible. It paws violently, exults mightily; it goes out to meet the weapons. It laughs at fear, and is not dismayed; it does not turn back from the sword. Upon it rattle the quiver, the flashing spear, and the javelin. With fierceness and rage it swallows the ground; it cannot stand still at the sound of the trumpet. When the trumpet sounds, it says, "Aha!" From a distance it smells the battle, the thunder of the captains, and the shouting. (Job 39:20b–25)

According to MacKenzie, "The horse was reserved for warfare or hunting, at first (in pairs) to draw a chariot, then, after about the eighth century BCE, as a cavalry mount."[2] God admires the war horse; "[t]he animal's excitement and eagerness for the battle, its reaction to the trumpet call, its disregard of danger, have deeply impressed him."[3]

To Job God is describing the war horse, which, according to Psalm 33 is a vain hope for victory, because by its great might it cannot save (cf. Ps 33:17). As Psalm 147 makes clear, God's "delight is not in the strength of the horse" (Ps 147:10). While "the horse is made ready for the day of battle, . . . the victory belongs to the LORD" (Prov 21:31). Jeremiah describes the unrepentant inhabitants of Judah as being like a horse lunging headlong into battle (cf. Jer 8:6c). And the Second Book of Nephi in *Mormon* states that those who will punish God's people will ride horses whose "hoofs shall be counted like flint, and their [chariot] wheels like a whirlwind" (2 Ne 15:28). Doniger states "the horse . . . made possible conquest in war; the horse also came to symbolize conquest in war because of its own natural imperialism."[4] According to Blenkinsopp, "The horse was a symbol of pride, the war engine *par excellence*."[5]

God's power is often shown to be greater than that of a horse in the Bible. After the Israelites have passed through the Sea of Reeds, Moses and the Israelites sing a song about the LORD's triumph, stating that he has thrown horse and rider into the sea (cf. Exod 15:1, 21). Psalm 76 reminisces Moses' song when it declares that at God's rebuke "both rider and horse lay stunned" (Ps 76:6), as does Jeremiah when foretelling the destruction of Babylon when God will use his chosen people to smash the horse and its rider (cf. Jer 51:21). The prophet Isaiah records God declaring, "I am the LORD . . . who brings out chariot and horse . . .; they lie down, they cannot rise, they are extinguished, quenched like a wick" (Isa 43:15a, 17). In

---

2. McKenzie, *Dictionary*, 487.
3. Ibid.
4. Doniger, "Symbol," 336.
5. Blenkinsopp, "Deuteronomy," 103.

another place, echoing the exodus, Isaiah adds, "Like a horse in the desert, they did not stumble" (Isa 63:13b). However, the LORD promises to make the house of Judah like his proud war horse (cf. Zech 10:3). The horses of the enemy will be struck with panic and blindness, but God will be the strength of his people (cf. Zech 12:4–5).

Chariot Pullers

Closely associated with the war horse in strength is the chariot pulled by a horse or horses. *The Rig Veda* mentions the chariot pulled by a horse several times. For example, to gain the mercy of Varuna, the Hindu god of water, particularly the oceans, the singer hopes to bind the god's heart to his, "as binds the charioteer to his tethered horse" (*RV* 1:25:3). Hymn 161 in book 1 is dedicated to the Ribhus, three mortal beings who attained godhood by their austere practices, and who "out of a horse . . . formed a horse; a chariot they equipped, and went unto the gods" (*RV* 1:161:7b). The Maruts, Hindu storm gods, do not ride in a chariot pulled by a horse (cf. *RV* 7:66:7), but '[t]hey lead, as 'twere, the strong horse forth," that is, the cloud, "that it may rain" (*RV* 1:64:6). However, the god of wind, Vayu, comes from heaven with "noble steeds" in a mighty chariot (*RV* 8:26:23).

Biblically, God uses his people to smash the chariot and the charioteer of the Babylonians (Jer 51:21), while in Nineveh there is "[t]he crack of whip and rumble of wheel, galloping horse and bounding chariot, horsemen charging, flashing sword and glittering spear," which God promises to destroy (Nah 3:2–3a).

Mormon mentions "horses and chariots" a number of times (cf. Alma 18:9, 12; 20:6). In the Second Book of Nephi the author describes the land of Judah as being "full of horses" and chariots (2 Ne12:7). However in the Third Book of Nephi, God declares that the Gentiles need to repent "for it shall come to pass, says the Father, that [he] will cut off [their] horses out of the midst of them, and [he] will destroy [their] chariots" (3 Ne 21:14). In the *Book of Doctrine and Covenants*, however, God promises blessing to those who "ride upon horses or in chariots" (*D&C* 62:3).

Bit, Bridle, Whip, Reins

Because the horse is strong, it needs to be controlled. The psalmist sings to his listeners, "Do not be like a horse, without understanding, whose temper must be curbed with bit and bridle, else it will not stay near you" (Ps 32:9). Likewise, the HB (OT) Book of Proverbs states, that a whip for the horse for control is like a rod for the back of fools (cf. Prov 26:3). *The Dhammapada* echoes that sentiment when it states that like a good horse which makes a better attempt at obeying its master because of the whip, so does a person awakened by shame perform religious functions with mindfulness: "Like a good horse struck by a whip, be ardent and deeply moved. With faith and virtue and enterprise, with concentration and *dhamma*-discernment, with understanding and conduct endowed, mindful, [one] will leave behind ... weighty misery" (*Dhp* 10:144). The OT (A) Book of Sirach echoes that sentiment: "An unbroken horse turns out stubborn, and an unchecked son turns out headstrong" (Sir 30:8).

Horse discipline is also a topic of *The Rig Veda*. For example, hymn 28 of book 1 mentions the "reins to guide a horse" (*RV* 1:28:4), as does hymn 144 states that "he who drives the car[t] holds fast the horse's reins" (*RV* 1:144:3b). Agni, the god of fire, is "like an able steed," "like a young horse that runs astray" (*RV* 6:2:8), and "like a horse ... led forth to the sacrifice" (*RV* 3:2:7b). "Fierce is his gait and vast his wondrous body," states another hymn; "he champ[s] like a horse with bit and bridle" (*RV* 6:3:4a). Another hymn begins this way: "This day with praises, Agni, we bring you that which you love: right judgment, like a horse, with our devotions" (*RV* 4:10:1). In honoring Agni, people bring fire from their home to light the sacrificial fire. Thus, "Agni the herald, like a horse, is led forth at [the] solemn rite, god among gods adorable" (*RV* 4:15:1). Agni "stirs all people, like a noble horse, like a fleet steed" (*RV* 8:43:25). Even the refined, sacred soma juice is "like a good horse ... led out, when on the path that shines with light the mettled steeds exert their strength" (*RV* 9:15:3). It is also "like a horse for love of glory" (*RV* 9:96:16b) or like "a horse through love of glory" (*RV* 1:61:5). "Enamored are the people of ... well-bred horses ... ," adds *The Quran* (*Quran* 3:14).

However, if the horse is not broken, it is of no use to people. Aesop tells the fable of "The Horse and His Rider," a story about "a young man, who fancied himself something of a horseman."[6] He mounted "a horse which had not been properly broken in, and was exceedingly difficult to control."[7] The horse bolted immediately. When a friend met the horseman on the road, he asked where he was off to in such a hurry. The supposed horseman pointed to the horse and told his friend to ask him, because he had no idea.

---

6. Aesop, 98.
7. Ibid.

Valuable Horse

The horse represents wealth and value in various texts. In the First Book of Kings in the HB (OT), the writer identifies King Solomon's wealth; he had twelve thousand horses (cf. 1 Kgs 10:26; 2 Chr 1:17). Each horse cost 150 shekels (cf. 1 Kgs 10:29; 2 Chr 1:17). McKenzie states, "Wealth in horses was both a sign of a strong military posture and a display of the magnificence of the monarch . . . ."[8] *The Quran* alludes to this, portraying Allah saying that when "fleet-footed chargers" were brought to Solomon, he said, "'The love of horses is worthy of desire to me for the remembrance of my Lord;' and when they were out of sight, (he said), 'Bring them back to me,' and he began to rub and stroke their shanks and necks" (*Quran* 38:31–33). God "created horses . . . for riding and for splendor," states *The Quran* (*Quran* 16:8).

The Analects of Confucius considers horses to be a means of counting wealth. In one of the analects Confucius asks his dialogue partners to name something for which they wish. One of them states that he "should like to have carriages and horses" among other things (*Analects* 5:25). Another of the analects mentions "sleek horses" (*Analects* 6:3). And still another mentions "a thousand teams of horses" (*Analects* 16:11, 12).

Mormon lists horses among the creatures useful to man and counted as wealth by those who possessed them (cf. Ether 9:19; 3 Ne 6:1; Enos 1:21). In the *Book of Doctrine and Covenants*, "oats for the horse" is named as the appropriate food for this important animal (*D&C* 86:3). Aesop narrates a tale about a groom who spent "long hours clipping and combing the horse of which he had charge, but who daily stole a portion of his allowance of oats, and sold it for his own profit."[9] After suffering hunger, the horse told the groom, "If you really want me to look sleek and well, you must comb me less and feed me more."[10]

The Rig Veda portrays Indra, the chief god of Hinduism, as receiving "a ruddy horse, . . . filling his girth and rousing wealth" (*RV* 8:3:22). "Lead on the wild horse Indra with his vigorous grasp forward to drink the soma juice," states hymn 17 of book 8 (*RV* 8:17:15). And in another hymn the singer compares himself to that "of a costly horse grown old and feeble" (*RV* 10:34:3b). Quoting Leshnik, Doniger states that in South Indian village life a few landowners "still keep a few horses as symbols of prestige."[11] The

---

8. McKenzie, *Dictionary*, 372.
9. Aesop, 6.
10. Ibid.
11. Doniger, "Symbol," 338.

HB (OT) Book of Esther illustrates prestige. Haman, the villain of the story, tells King Ahasuerus that the man whom the king wishes to honor should be seated on a horse that the king has ridden. Then, one of the king's most noble officials should conduct the man on horseback through the open square of the city (cf. Esth 6:7–9).

Other characteristics of the horse are mentioned in *The Rig Veda*. For example, Indra, Hinduism's chief god, is roused by sacrifice, "eager as a horse to meet the mare" (*RV* 1:56:1). In another hymn, Indra is like "a vigorous horse when he comes near the mare" (*RV* 2:43:2b), as is Indu, the moon deity, like "a vigorous horse, [who] has neighed together steeds" (*RV* 9:64:3). In another hymn, the lyrics mention "the horse neigh" (*RV* 1:173:3). Vaisvanara, an epithet for the god Agni, is described as "neighing like a horse" (*RV* 3:26:3), as is Mithra, a solar deity, described as "neighing like an impatient horse amid the herd" (*RV* 9:77:5). Finally, Indra "has whinnied like a horse for food" (*RV* 10:96:10).

Horse Sense

When some people see a horse, they think of freedom. Aesop narrates "The Horse and the Stag" fable about "a horse who used to graze in a meadow which he had all to himself,"[12] until a stag came. The horse went to a man and asked for help to get rid of the deer. The man was more than willing to help the horse, but he told the horse, ". . . I can only do so if you let me put a bridle in your mouth and mount on your back."[13] The horse agreed. Together they drove the stag out of the field. However, the horse discovered that he had given away his freedom and now had a master. Likewise in *The Rig Veda*, Atri, a bard or seer, is made "free as a horse" by the Asvins, the twin gods of sunrise and sunset (*RV* 10:143:1; cf. 10:143:2).

The Quran reminds its readers that if they "fear (war or danger)," they are to "pray while standing or on horseback" (*Quran* 2:239). In *The Rig Veda*, various deities have "generated prayer" with "the horse," among other animals and things (*RV* 10:65:11). *The Analects of Confucius* echoes these words when the master says, "The [famous] horse Chi was not famed for its strength, but for its inner qualities" (*Analects* 14:35). "Inner qualities" refer to the horse's character, prestige, or virtue, as demonstrated in Aesop's fable of "The Man, the Horse, the Ox, and the Dog." On a winter's day, a horse, an ox, and a dog seek shelter in the house of a man, who readily admits them, lights a fire to warm them, and feeds them. More specifically for this

---

12. Aesop, 211.
13. Ibid.

context, the man "puts oats before the horse."[14] The animals showed their gratitude by endowing the man with the qualities peculiar to each. "The horse took youth, and hence young men are high-mettled and impatient of restraint...."[15] However, in another fable, "The Horse and the Ass," "a horse, proud of his fine harness... cried out impatiently that he could hardly resist kicking [the ass] to make him move faster."[16] The horse "became broken-winded, and was sold by his owner to a farmer."[17] While pulling a dung-cart, the ass met him, reminded him of his pride, and asked him what happened to his fine harness.

Flying Horse

In Greek mythology, "[w]hen Perseus [, the legendary founder of Mycenae and the first hero,] cut off Medusa's head, the blood sinking into the earth produced the winged horse Pegasus. Minerva [, the Roman goddess of wisdom,] caught him and tamed him...."[18] A gallant young warrior, named Bellerophon, agreed to fight a monster if he could ride Pegasus. Bellerophon passed the night before the battle

> in the temple of Minerva.... [A]s he slept Minerva came to him and gave him a golden bridle.... [A]t sight of the bridle the winged steed came willingly and suffered himself to be taken. Bellerophon mounted him, rose with him into the air, soon found [the monster], and gained an easy victory over the monster.[19]

Later, Bellerophon becomes proud and attempts "to fly up into heaven on his winged steed, but Jupiter sent a gadfly which stings Pegasus and makes him throw his rider, who became lame and blind in consequence."[20] Bulfinch narrates, "Pegasus ... has always been at the service of the poets," one of whom sold the horse to a farmer. However, "a youth stepped forth and asked leave to try him. As soon as he was seated on his back, the horse,

---

14. Ibid., 189.
15. Ibid.
16. Ibid., 218.
17. Ibid.
18. Bulfinch, *Mythology*, 124.
19. Ibid., 125.
20. Ibid.

which had appeared at first vicious, and afterwards spirit-broken, rose kingly, a spirit, a god, unfolded the splendor of his wings, and soared towards heaven."[21]

While *The Rig Veda* does mention that the horse has wings—"horses brown of hue that flew with swift wings" (*RV* 1:117:14b)—one hymn states that the creation of the natural horse descends from the original heavenly horse: "Here was the horse's birth; his was the sunlight" (*RV* 2:35:6a). In other words, the horse is born of Agni's fire, sunshine, which is "indestructible, dwelling at a distance in forts unwrought" (*RV* 2:35:6b). Likewise, the OT (A) Second Book of Maccabees records a vision had by Heliodorus, an officer of the emperor Seleucus IV, at the treasury: Heliodorus saw "a magnificently caparisoned horse, with a rider of frightening mien; it rushed furiously at Heliodorus and struck at him with its front hoofs" (2 Macc 3:25).

Skinner records a Pawnee Indian tale about a poor woman and her grandson, who "found browsing among the refuse of the village a sorry old horse, half-blind, lame, and sway-backed."[22] Skinner continues, "The horse certainly did not look like much, but there was something, just something, about him that inspired the young boy to bring him to his grandmother."[23] When the tribe was ready to move its camp, the boy, taking care not to push the old horse too hard, used him to carry their few possessions. When they arrived at the new camp, the chief announced that a spotted buffalo calf had been seen not far away, and he would give his daughter in marriage to the brave who returned with the spotted buffalo hide. Skinner narrates:

> The boy took his handful of crooked arrows, his cracked bow, and stood and looked at his poor excuse for a horse, thinking that the poor old thing would just collapse if he ever tried to run to keep up with the other hunters. But the horse looked him straight in the eye. "Drive me to the river and plaster me with mud," he said. The boy almost fainted, hearing the human voice coming from the horse. But, collecting his wits, he did just as the horse instructed. "Now," continued the horse, "climb on my back, and, when the word is given, let me have free reigns, let me fly!"[24]

The boy on the horse entered the race to retrieve the spotted buffalo skin. All the other young bucks laughed at him and his mud-covered horse. However, the other bucks gave a cry of astonishment "as the old dun horse

---

21. Ibid., 126.
22. Skinner, "Horse," 19.
23. Ibid.
24. Ibid., 19–20.

and his young rider passed them with such ease that he seemed not to be running at all, but flying across the earth."[25] The flying horse took the boy to the spotted calf, which the boy killed with one arrow and skinned while "his horse pranced in circles around him. . . . His age, lameness, and blindness had disappeared."[26] The boy took the meat and the skin on his flying horse to his grandmother, who prepared a feast. Meanwhile, the horse spoke again to the boy while he was grooming him: "The Sioux are coming. When they attack tomorrow, mount me, gallop straight against the chief, kill him, and ride back. Do this four times, killing a Sioux at each charge. Do not go a fifth time, for you may lose me or be killed yourself."[27] The next day everything happened as the horse had predicted.

However, the boy decided to go for a fifth strike. "His brave horse fell under a Sioux arrow, and the enemy cut him into pieces so that he might never bear another Pawnee on his back."[28] The boy had fled in safety, but was sad at the loss of his horse. After it got dark,

> he collected the bones of his horse, brought them back to camp, and pieced them together. Then, with the spotted robe drawn over his head, he mourned his steed. A great wind arose, bringing a rain that washed away the blood and refreshed the grass. . . . After he had mourned for several hours he looked up to see that the severed limbs and head had arranged themselves in a life-like attitude. Then the tail flicked, the animal arose, walked to the boy and said, "The Great Spirit is kind. He has let me come back to life. You have had your lesson. Hereafter, remember to trust me." In the morning the horse was as sound as ever, and during the rest of his long life he was honored by the people, while the boy established his grandmother in comfort, married the chief's daughter, and in the end became chief himself.[29]

The story of the horse's resurrection echoes that found in the HB (OT) Book of the Prophet Ezekiel. The LORD brings the prophet out of the city of Babylon in the spirit and sets him down in the middle of a valley full of bones (cf. Ezek 37:1). God instructs Ezekiel to prophesy to the bones, saying, "O dry bones, hear the word of the LORD" (Ezek 37:4). The prophet does as he is told, and suddenly "there was a noise, a rattling, and the bones came

---

25. Ibid., 20.
26. Ibid.
27. Ibid., 21.
28. Ibid.
29. Ibid., 21–22.

together, bone to its bone" (Ezek 37:7). Next, God instructs the prophet to prophecy to the breath, and the breath comes into them, and they live.

Other characteristics of the horse are often named in literature. Indra destroyed his enemies like "a horse's tail" sweeps away the flies (*RV* 1:32:12). "[A] horse . . . sunk in water" refers to the practice of bathing a horse in a river (*RV* 1:117:4). "[T]he horse's stake" refers to the post to which a horse could be tethered (*RV* 1:162:6), and "[t]he robe . . . spread upon the horse to clothe him, the upper covering and the golden trappings, the halters which retrain the steed, the heel ropes" (*RV* 1:62:16)—all refer to things used in horsemanship. Sometimes the horse is described as being brave (cf. *RV* 1:116:6), and sometimes as being playful (cf. *RV* 9:86:44). The CB (NT) Book of Revelation uses the horse as a standard of measure when describing the wine press of God's wrath. "[B]lood flowed from the wine press," states the author of the book, "as high as a horse's bridle" (Rev 14:20).

Horse of a Different Color

Before leaving this reflection on the horse, the various colors of horses must be explored. First, the white horse, representing victory or conquest, is well attested in various texts. The HB (OT) prophet Zechariah mentions white horses (cf. Zech 9:10), as does the author of the CB (NT) Book of Revelation. The author of the latter book looks to see a white horse whose rider had a bow; he came out conquering and to conquer (cf. Rev 6:2). A few chapters later, the writer sees heaven opened and a white horse whose rider is called Faithful and True (cf. Rev 19:11). A beast and the kings of the earth make war against the rider on the horse (cf. Rev 19:19), but the rider on the horse kills his enemies with the sword that comes from his mouth (cf. Rev 19:21).

The Rig Veda often mentions or alludes to the "royal horse sacrifice," according to Doniger. She writes:

> [T]he king's men "set free" the consecrated white stallion to wander for a year before he was brought back to the king and killed. During that year, he was guarded by an army that "followed" him and claimed for the king any land on which he grazed. The king's army therefore drove the horse onward and guided him into the lands that the king intended to take over.[30]

The white horse is mentioned often in *The Rig Veda* (cf. *RV* 1:116:6; 1:118:9; 1:119:10; 10:39:10). The white horse is "to be renowned, who bore his friend at speed, . . . to be invoked of men" (*RV* 10:39:10b). The white horse also

30. Doniger, "Symbol," 336.

serves as a spirit guide in many stories, especially those involving *The Lone Ranger* (2013) and in the film *Winter's Tale* (2014).

Horses also come in the color red, representing bloodshed in war. The HB (OT) prophet Zechariah has a vision in the night of a red horse (cf. Zech 1:8) and a sorrel horse (cf. Zech 1:8); sorrel is a reddish brown color. John of Patmos also sees a bright red horse in the CB (NT) Book of Revelation (cf. Rev 6:4). In *The Rig Veda*, Indra rides in a "golden car[t], yoked with bay horses" (*RV* 1:56:1), and is depicted as "the bay steeds' Lord" who "has whinnied like a horse for food" (*RV* 10:96:10); a bay horse was a reddish brown creature. The Hindu scriptures also mention "the bright red mares" which the Maruts, that is, the storm gods, are to yoke to their chariot (*RV* 5:56:6). One verse later in the same hymn there is a "loudly-neighing bright red vigorous horse who has been stationed, fair to see" (*RV* 1:56:7).

Nicholas Black Elk, a North American Native Lakota, had a vision of a bay horse and a multitude of other horses. According to Grim, "The horse is the animal that mediates entry into the numinous world."[31] The animal takes on a generative ideal for Lakota men and affirms the male gender role, becoming "an archetypal expression of maleness."[32] As such, according to Grim, native hunters and warriors often spoke of becoming one body with their horses, making them "an image associated with masculinity."[33] Because of the unity of horse and rider, the horse became a bridge or guide to the spirit world.

The CB (NT) Book of Revelation mentions a black horse (cf. Rev 6:5) and a pale green horse (cf. Rev 6:8). Black, the color of dead vegetation, represents famine, and pale green, the color of rotting flesh, represents death. Skinner narrates a tale about a black horse in "How the Black Horse Was Beaten." Sam Hart, "a lover of swift horses, a fearless rider, . . . had one mare that he offered to pit against any piece of horseflesh in the country."[34] Hart was visited by a dignified stranger "whose glittering black eyes"[35] got the attention of the narrator of the story. The stranger met Hart and bragged about his black horse "that would beat anything on legs, as he wished to prove by racing him against Hart's mare."[36] The stranger offered odds of three to one, along with his own horse in the bargain, and a head start by the mare. Hart accepted the challenge.

31. Grim, "Knowing and Being Known," 375.
32. Ibid.
33. Ibid.
34. Skinner, "Black Horse," 134.
35. Ibid.
36. Ibid., 135.

As the race took place, the black horse's "breath seemed . . . to smoke."[37] Hart began to realize who the gentleman on the black horse might be, so he headed for a church, which he circled three times before steering his mare close enough "to the church door to be on holy ground. Fire sprang from the black horse's nostrils."[38] The devil said to Hart: "You have cheated one whose business is cheating, and I'm a decent enough fellow to own up when I'm beaten. Here's your money. Catch it, for you know I can't cross holy ground . . .; and here's my horse; he'll be tractable enough after I've gone home, and as safe as your mare. Good luck to you."[39] As a whiff of sulphur rose from the place, the devil disappeared. Hart kept the black horse, entering him into races and winning all he entered. His neighbors, however, "used to say that the black horse was still the devil's horse, and that money won by racing . . . would weigh the soul of its owner down to the warm place when he died."[40]

The four colors of horses might be best summarized by a saying in *The Analects of Confucius*: "[W]hen a gentleman has spoken, a team of four horses cannot overtake his words" (*Analects* 12:8). In other words, the common person can say what he or she likes, and no harm will be done. However, when a person in a position speaks, he or she will be quoted as an authority, as one with a team of four variously colored horses!

Such is the wisdom of "The Wolf and the Horse" in *Aesop's Fables*. After a wolf discovers a field of oats, which he cannot eat, he notices a horse. "Look," said the wolf, "here's a fine field of oats. For your sake I have left it untouched, and I shall greatly enjoy the sound of your teeth munching the ripe grain."[41] The horse replies, "If wolves could eat oats, my fine friend, you would hardly have indulged your ears at the cost of your belly."[42] The moral of the fable is this: "There is no virtue in giving to others what is useless to oneself."[43]

Horse Gate, Horse Gods

Several biblical texts mention the "Horse Gate" (2 Chr 23:15; Neh 3:28; Jer 31:40) of the royal palace in Jerusalem. However, this is more accurately

37. Ibid.
38. Ibid.
39. Ibid., 135–36.
40. Ibid., 136.
41. Aesop, 174.
42. Ibid.
43. Ibid.

described as a chariot gate. According to McKenzie, "[T]here was probably only one gate of sufficient width for chariots in the entire defenses,"[44] that is, there was probably only one gate in the city wall that opened wide enough to permit the passage of a chariot pulled by a horse or horses.

Doniger mentions the relationship of the horse to the Dalits, a group of people traditionally regarded as untouchable in the caste system in India. Since most Dalits are casteless and disadvantaged people, they cannot afford horses. So, they create "clay representations of horses."[45] Some worship "a deity called Ghoradeva (Horse God) or a stone horse."[46] Doniger notes that some people erect a clay horse on the sixth day after birth and make a child worship it, while others make terracotta horses to give to various gods and goddesses to cure illness or guard a village.[47] Some horses are offered sacrifices. "Gods called Spirit Riders," according to Doniger, ride without stirrups on saddled or unsaddled (invisible) horses, guarding villages all over India, and village potters make their equestrian images."[48] Thus, these "mythical horses . . . are not drawn from life; they are drawn from art and from the imagination of horses."[49]

Doniger also mentions another group in India known as the Bhils, who "have horse rituals but no horses."[50] Hence, these people "use the image of the horseman" as "that of a Spirit Rider."[51] Nearby the Bhils, another group of people have "real horses . . . used as . . . instrument[s] of social mobility." As Doniger explains, "[A] warrior who had his own horse to ride into battle grew in importance. Horses were valuable booty, given to the king."[52] Among other groups, the "sacrificial stallion . . . symbolized power and fertility."[53]

Thus, the quarter horse signifies strength in terms of ingenuity and swiftness. God is often described using horse metaphors. The horse represents conquest, pride, and dominance, yet it needs to be broken and controlled. As a sign of wealth, the quarter horse also stands for splendor and prestige. In mythology and visions, the horse can fly, be brave, and be

44. McKenzie, *Dictionary*, 372.
45. Doniger, "Symbol," 339.
46. Ibid.
47. Cf. Ibid., 339.
48. Ibid., 340.
49. Ibid.
50. Ibid., 341.
51. Ibid.
52. Ibid.
53. Ibid.

playful. And it comes in all colors: white, red, black, and green; each of those colors represent even more spiritual aspects of the horse.

Journal/Meditation: What part of the above reflection on the horse got most of your attention? What application can you make to your own life? to your own spirituality?

Prayer: Father, Lord of all creation, you gave strength and swiftness to the horse and taught that this means of transportation needs human control. Grant that your word may serve as my reins and that your power may serve as my bit and bridle. Hear my prayer in the name of Jesus Christ, your Son, who reigns with you and the Holy Spirit, one God, forever and ever. Amen.

Raven

Text: . . .
Open here I flung the shutter, when, with many a flirt and flutter,
In there stepped a stately raven of the saintly days of yore;
Not the least obeisance made he; not a minute stopped or stayed he;
But, with mien of lord or lady, perched above my chamber door—
Perched upon a bust of Pallas just above my chamber door—
      Perched, and sat, and nothing more.

Then this ebony bird beguiling my sad fancy into smiling,
By the grave and stern decorum of the countenance it wore,
"Though thy crest be shorn and shaven, thou," I said, "art sure no craven,
Ghastly grim and ancient raven wandering from the Nightly shore—
Tell me what thy lordly name is on the Night's Plutonian shore!"
      Quoth the raven, "Nevermore."

. . .
Then, me thought, the air grew denser, perfumed from an unseen censer
Swung by angels whose faint foot-falls tinkled on the tufted floor.
"Wretch," I cried, "thy God had lent thee—by these angels he hath sent thee
Respite—respite and nepenthe from thy memories of Lenore!
Quaff, oh Quaff this kind nepenthe and forget this lost Lenore!"
      Quoth the raven, "Nevermore."

"Prophet!" said I, "thing of evil—prophet still, if bird or devil!—
Whether Tempter sent, or whether tempest tossed thee here ashore,
Desolate, yet all undaunted, on this desert land enchanted—
On this home by Horror haunted,—tell me truly I implore—
Is there—is there balm in Gilead?—tell me—tell me, I implore."
      Quoth the raven, "Nevermore."

...
And the raven, never flitting, still is sitting, still is sitting
On the pallid bust of Pallas just above my chamber door;
And his eyes have all the seeming of a demon's that is dreaming,
And the lamp-light o'er him streaming throws his shadow on the floor;
And my soul from out that shadow that lies floating on the floor
      Shall be lifted—nevermore![1]

Reflection: Edgar Allan Poe's (1809–1849) poem "The Raven" (1845) best illustrates all the qualities associated with the raven, a large bird with glossy black plumage, a wedge-shaped tail, and a large beak. The raven, as Poe illustrates, is the subject of legend and folklore, being often perceived as a bad omen, such "as the black raven seen after King Arthur's death" in the Arthurian stories.[2] While only some of the stanzas of Poe's poem mentioning the raven are printed above, once the poem's narrator opens the window, the raven enters the room and becomes the focus of the storyteller for the rest of the work.

The ominous bird's origin is from the ancient days of yore. It is impossible to know if Poe actually had in mind the Norse mythology of Huginn (meaning "thought") and Muninn (meaning "memory" or "mind"), a pair of ravens that fly over the world, gathering information, and bringing it to the god Odin, who himself is often referred to as the Raven-God. Odin bestows the gift of speech upon the ravens so that after they are sent out at dawn and fly all over the world until they return at dusk, they are able to report to and keep Odin informed of the events occurring all over the world. In Norse iconography, Odin is often pictured sitting on his throne flanked by his ravens, which may be perched on his shoulders. Thus, as Mortensen states, "[r]avens, through their speech and behavior, serve as divinatory messengers...."[3]

Another account of two ravens as messengers is found in the martyrdom of St. Meinrad, a hermit monk who lived in Switzerland in the Dark or Black Forest, where he built a hermitage and chapel and cultivated a plot of ground. For almost thirty years he lived in solitude, giving alms to those who sought him. "Even two ravens learned to know his beneficent hand."[4] Two men, hearing about the hermit, set out to rob him of the treasure they presumed he kept. So, after walking to the hermitage, they found Meinrad

---

    1. Bradley, "Edgar Allen Poe," 796–798.
    2. Cavendish, *Legends*, 63.
    3. Mortensen, "Raven Augury," 423.
    4. Kleber, *History of St. Meinrad*, 4.

and clubbed him to death in order to steal his treasure. Just as they were leaving the hermitage,

> the two ravens, coming on their usual quest for food and a kind word from their benefactor, sensed the plight of their friend. With excited cries they took up the pursuit of the criminals and occasionally darted down upon their heads. Pursued by the ravens, the villains hastened to the village. The unusual behavior of the hermit's pets aroused the suspicions of the people. The two men were held till investigation at the hermitage and the subsequent confession of the two brought to light the murder.[5]

St. Meinrad's two ravens serve both as omens and as messengers of their benefactor's death. In Christian iconography, the saint is often depicted lying dead on the ground with two criminals holding clubs over him and two ravens in midair.

Poe considers the raven to be a messenger of God with respite and nepenthe, that is, a potion to drink to banish his sorrowful memories of Lenore, a name meaning "light." Poe is not sure if the raven is a good or an evil prophet. At one time divining he reflects that the raven may be telling him that Lenore is in heaven, a new Eden, with God and his angels, and at another time he reflects that the raven, a demonic fiend, may be telling him that Lenore is lost forever to the horrors of death or even hell, like a shadow on the floor. Incense and angels are contrasted with black plumes and tempests.

Omen

The raven reminds the reader that he or she cannot escape the ultimate fate of death. This is why the ebony raven, from night's Plutonian shore—that is, the infernal region or underworld ruled by Pluto—perches on a bust of Pallas, the goddess of wisdom. The narrator wants to know more than the croaking, fiery-eyed bird is telling him. Specifically, he wants to know if there is balm in Gilead, an obscure reference to the HB (OT) prophet Jeremiah, who asks, "Is there no balm in Gilead?" (cf. Jer 8:22) Balm in Gilead refers to a medicinal herb that grew in that area. Thus, all the negative aspects associated with death are presented. More specifically, and not quoted above, the poem is set at midnight in bleak December when the dying fire was casting ghost shadows upon the floor. The dark of midnight and the lack of light in December add more to the bleakness of death.

5. Ibid., 5–6

Poe's raven is like Odin's ravens in that it speaks and like St. Meinrad's ravens in that they are able to arouse the village. However, Poe's raven speaks but one word, namely, "Nevermore." Mortensen states that the raven ". . . appears to play the role of an active medium between the human and divine world, or the human and the 'spirit' world . . . ."[6] It relates "otherwise unknowable information, usually temporal in nature, to the humans who pointedly endeavor to understand" it.[7] Thus, this bird, which can live for fifty years and with a wide wing span, is known for its intelligence, bravery, and variety of sounds.[8] The narrator of Poe's poem employs augury, "divination through the interpretation of the flight and speech of birds,"[9] to determine what has happened to the light of his life. Many people believe "that the raven . . . could see the future, and could report this future to humans," according to Mortensen.[10] This makes the raven an oracle, a source of wisdom, for the narrator of the poem, as well as an omen.

After reading Poe's poem, one could ask, "Why doesn't the narrator just get rid of the raven sitting above his chamber door? And the answer is simple. Some people believe "that anyone who has killed a raven will, following his or her own death, encounter a malevolent rooster-headed demon impeding passage on a bridge, along the path to heaven."[11] Thus, the narrator is left with the raven's shadow on the floor and his own soul comingled with it.

Aesop tells a fable about "The Crow and the Raven." The crow becomes jealous because the raven is "regarded by men as a bird of omen which foretold the future, and was accordingly held in great respect by them."[12] Mrs. Crow wanted to have a reputation like that of the raven. So, one day she flew to a branch of a tree and cawed as loud as she could as a band of travelers passed. The travelers considered her cawing to be a bad omen, until one of them spied her on the branch. "It's all right," he said, "we can go on without fear, for it's only a crow, and that means nothing."[13]

In the HB (OT) story of Noah, the raven serves as a messenger; however, the raven does not speak. It's movement has to be interpreted by the narrator of the story: "At the end of forty days Noah opened the window

---

6. Mortensen, "Raven Augury," 425.
7. Ibid.
8. Cf. Ibid., 424.
9. Ibid., 425.
10. Ibid., 431.
11. Ibid., 428.
12. Aesop, 206.
13. Ibid.

of the ark that he had made and sent out the raven; and it went to and fro until the waters were dried up from the earth" (Gen 8:6–7). Even though the raven "tells" Noah that the flood waters have not yet dried, in later biblical literature it is considered unclean. Every kind of raven is considered detestable and forbidden as food (cf. Lev 11:15; Deut 14:14).

Food Bearer

And yet the raven is well known for its "association with food," which it acquires either through hunting or scavenging.[14] In the First Book of Kings, the prophet Elijah is told by God to camp near the Wadi Cherith. God says, ". . . I have commanded the ravens to feed you there" (1 Kgs 17:4). Elijah obeys God, and "[t]he ravens brought him bread and meat in the morning, and bread and meat in the evening . . ." (1 Kgs 17:6). This biblical story of ravens as protectors[15] stands in opposition to many other tales in which ravens are considered to be thieves. Mortensen narrates an experience of seeing a raven with a golden pendant tied around its neck. Upon inquiry he discovered that if "ravens . . . are caught stealing from crops [in the Himalayas, they] are captured (if possible) with a net. The family that caught the raven then invests a substantial sum of money to commission a golden pendant of a jeweler, then ties it around the neck of the bird securely, so that in the future the particular bird [can] be identified as a thief."[16] According to Mortensen, this demonstrates that "ravens are treated with respect (not killed), and that although some are thieves, they certainly are not all so mischievous as to warrant capture and bedecking with gold."[17]

Grimm narrates two tales about ravens that illustrate mischievousness and enchantment. "The Seven Ravens" is a fairy tale about a man with seven sons and one daughter. "I wish the youngsters were all turned into ravens,"[18] said the father in disappointment at his sons' irresponsibility. After the daughter grew up and found out that she had seven brothers who were ravens, she determined that she would find them "to break the enchantment in which her brothers were held."[19] After traveling to the end of the earth, she ran into the sun, the moon, and the stars. The morning star gave her the

---

14. Mortensen, "Raven Augury," 424.
15. Cf. Ibid., 426.
16. Ibid., 427.
17. Ibid.
18. Grimm, 429.
19. Ibid.

key "to unlock the iceberg in which [her] brothers [were] shut up," but she lost the key.[20]

A dwarf happened by the gate, and she told him that she was seeking her "brothers, the seven ravens."[21] He told her that they were not at home, but she was welcome to wait for them to return. "Then the little dwarf took the maiden to the room where supper was prepared for the seven ravens, on seven little plates, by which stood seven little cups of water."[22] The little girl ate a few crumbs from each plate and drank a little water from each cup. Into the last cup she dropped a ring she had brought with her from home. Then, she hid behind the door.

Once the ravens flew in, they immediately recognized that someone had eaten some of their food and drank from their cups. Finally, one noticed the ring in his cup and remembered that it had once belonged to his parents. The eldest raven said, "Oh, I remember that ring! Oh, if our sister would only come here, we should be free!"[23] At that moment their sister stepped from behind the door and "the seven ravens were freed from their enchantment, and became seven handsome young men."[24] Then, all of them headed home to their parents.

In the other Grimm tale, named "The Raven," a queen became impatient with her daughter, "and as the ravens were flying about the palace, she opened the window and said, 'I wish you were a raven and would fly away, and then I should have some rest.' Scarcely had she spoken the words, before the child was changed into a raven, and flew from her arms out of the window."[25] The raven flew into the forest, where a man heard the raven tell him that she was the king's daughter by birth and needed to be set free from the queen's spell. She gives detailed instructions to the man about going further into the forest and finding a house with an aged woman within who would offer him meat and drink. He is not to accept any of it; if he does, he will fall into a deep sleep and not be able to help the raven-child. He is instructed to wait for her behind the house every day at 2 p.m. for three consecutive days. On the first day she will appear in a carriage pulled by four white horses; on the second day the carriage will be pulled by four chestnut horses; and on the third day the carriage will be pulled by four black horses.

20. Ibid.
21. Ibid., 430.
22. Ibid.
23. Ibid.
24. Ibid.
25. Ibid., 475.

The man enters the house and the woman offers him food and drink, which he accepts. Then, he goes to the garden to await the raven and falls asleep. The raven is unable to awaken him. On the second day, the same thing happens. And on the third day, the same thing happens. However, on the third day, the raven left him bread, meat, and wine, much like the ravens in the story of the prophet Elijah. The woman puts a ring on his finger and gives him a sheet of instructions for him to go to a golden castle. After wandering for days in search of the golden castle and not being able to find it, the man comes upon the house of a giant, who decides to eat the man for his supper. The man, however, offers the bread, meat, and wine that have continued to nourish him on his journey to the giant, who accepts them.

The man asks the giant if he knows where the golden castle is, but the giant does not. When the giant's brother comes home, he, too, is asked, but does not know. Finally, looking on a map they discover that the golden castle is "many thousand miles away."[26] The giant agrees to take the man half of the way, and the man "went onwards day and night, until at length he came to the golden castle . . . . It stood on a glass mountain, and the bewitched maiden drove in her carriage round the castle, and then went inside it."[27] The man tried to climb into the castle, but he could not get to it. He ended up building a hut for himself at the bottom of the golden castle, and every day he saw the raven-daughter drive her carriage around it.

One day he met three robbers who were fighting with each other over "a stick . . . that when [it] struck a door . . . that door would spring open; . . . a mantle . . . that whenever [it was] put on, [made the wearer] invisible, . . . and a horse on which a man could ride everywhere, even up the glass mountain."[28] The man tricks the robbers: "They put him on the horse, threw the mantle round him, and gave him the stick in his hand, and when he had all these things they were no longer able to see him."[29]

The tale continues:

> He rode up the glass mountain; but when he came in front of the castle at the top, it was shut. The he struck the door with his stick, and it sprang open immediately. He went in and ascended the stairs until he came to the hall where the maiden was sitting with a golden cup full of wine before her. She, however, could not see him because he had the mantle on. And when he came up to her, he drew from his finger the ring which she had

26. Ibid., 477.
27. Ibid., 478.
28. Ibid.
29. Ibid.

given him and threw it into the cup so that it rang. Then she cried, "That is my ring, so the man who is to deliver me must be here."[30]

The castle is searched, but the searchers cannot find the man, who has left it and is outside sitting on his horse without the mantle. The king's daughter sees him; he dismounts and takes her in his arms. Once he kisses her, she is set free from the enchantment, and they decide to be married the next day.

Creator

Besides the raven's mischievousness or trickster quality, the bird is also understood to be a creator god: "For the peoples of the Pacific Northwest of North America, raven is a divinity *par extraordinaire*, capable of doing just about anything he wishes . . . ."[31] As a divinity, the raven is a creator as can be seen in a story from a tribe of native peoples of North America living in British Columbia. In this account, the raven brings light from heaven to illuminate the world below. The tale begins:

> When the earth was young and still shrouded in twilight, . . . the chief of the sky gave one of the youth of heaven the skin of a raven, which the boy donned in order to fly about the world. Skirting the earth, raven took pity on its people, whom he observed fumbling about in the twilight. He knew that there was light in heaven, and he made up his mind to bring it to the world.[32]

In order for the raven to steal daylight from the sky chief, he had to disguise himself as a cedar leaf dropped into a stream, from which the chief's daughter drank and swallowed him. She discovered herself pregnant and gave birth to raven-boy, who insisted on playing with the box that contained daylight for four days. When the chief was not looking, he put on his raven skin and flew to earth with the box of daylight under one wing. He discovered people fishing in the twilight and asked the fishermen to bring him some fish to eat. When they ignored him, he "smashed the box on the rocks that lay below the tree" where he was perched. "There was a blinding flash of light, and instantly, the world was transformed. Dawn arrived."[33]

30. Ibid., 478–79.
31. Mortensen, "Raven Augury," 428.
32. *Spirit*, 26.
33. Ibid., 27.

In other Native American tribes, the raven is instructed by his father so that he can better the world, and one way to better the world was to create light. In another story, a girl drinks water containing a speck of dirt, gets pregnant, and gives birth to raven, who, playing with a box of stars, lets them go up the smoke hole in the tent. The next day he took the box containing the sun and flew out of the tent, going to a well he could not get to in order to drink. So, disguising himself, he got into the tent where the well was located and drank all the water. When raven tried to escape, he got stuck in the smoke hole. When the owner of the tent came home, he made a fire under raven and the smoke turned his feathers from white to black, but raven finally escaped and flew over the world creating all the rivers from the water he had consumed. Later, he opened the box of the sun and let the light out. With the water and the light, forests and oceans were created with all kinds of animals in them. Thus, raven is both a creator god and a trickster figure.

Fed by God

Even though Native American tribes describe the raven as being white in color at one time, all other tales indicate that the raven has ebony or black feathers. The female in the HB (OT) Song of Songs (Song of Solomon) declares that her lover's locks are wavy, "black as a raven"(Song 5:10). Other biblical references to the raven include the question God poses to Job in the Book of Job: "Who provides for the raven its prey, when its young ones cry to God, and wander about for lack of food?" (Job 38:41) Psalm 147 answers God's question: The LORD "gives to the animals their food, and to the young ravens when they cry" (Ps 147:9). In the CB (NT), Luke's Gospel portrays Jesus instructing his disciples about trusting God to provide food for them. Jesus says, "Consider the ravens: they neither sow nor reap, they have neither storehouse nor barn, and yet God feeds them" (Luke 12:24).

Biblically, the raven is used to describe God's vengeance on Edom; after the LORD is finished with the land of Edom only the raven shall live in it (cf. Isa 34:11), among other animals that prefer desolate locations. Likewise, Nineveh in Assyria will see the raven croak on the threshold (cf. Zeph 2:14c), among other wild animals, when the city is laid waste like a desert.

The raven plays a variety of spiritual roles. Representing mystery and exploration of the unknown, the raven serves as a messenger from the gods or God to people; the raven is a medium between the spirit world and the human world, sometimes serving as a good omen and sometime serving as a bad omen. The raven is a source of wisdom and a creator of light. The bird is associated with food, both bringing it to others and stealing it from others. In this latter way, raven serves the role of trickster. In the film *The Shawshank Redemption* (1994), one of the prisoners has a pet raven, much like Odin and St. Meinrad, which serves as his spiritual guide until he is paroled and commits suicide. "Quoth the raven, 'Nevermore.'"

Journal/Meditation: What spiritual characteristic of the raven most grabs your attention? In what ways does that spiritual characteristic connect with you?

Prayer: Almighty Creator of heaven and earth, the raven is your medium between both of the worlds you have made. As a bearer of your message, the ebony bird becomes a source of wisdom and food for your people. Open my ears to hear you in the raven's croak, and open my eyes to see you in the raven's flight. I ask this in the name of your Son, Jesus Christ, who with you, Father, and the Holy Spirit, are one God, forever and ever. Amen.

Rooster (Cock)

Text: "Peter said to [Jesus], 'Even though all become deserters, I will not.' Jesus said to him, 'Truly I tell you, this day, this very night, before the cock crows twice, you will deny me three times.'" (Mark 14:29–30)

Reflection: In general, any adult male bird, especially a domestic fowl, is called a rooster, a term that originated in the United States. Specifically, an adult male chicken is called a cock, as seen in the text above from the CB (NT) Gospel According to Mark. A male chicken less than one year old is called a cockerel, and a castrated male chicken is called a capon. The focus here is the adult male chicken (rooster), often known in literature as a cock. Because of modern connotations associated with that word, rooster replaces it in much of contemporary literature.

The cock is distinguished by its large red comb and long wattles. Also, it may bear a colorful hackle, that is, neck feathers, long curved tail feathers, and long saddle feathers. While he is usually portrayed as crowing at the break of dawn to proclaim his territory, a rooster can and often does crow at any time of the day or night, as noted in the passage above from Mark's Gospel which takes place after sunset.

Gospel writers differ in their predictions about how many times the cock will crow before Peter denies Jesus. Mark states that he will do it before the cock crows twice (cf. Mark 14:30), whereas Matthew's Gospel states before the cock crows (cf. Matt 26:34), Luke's Gospel states the cock will not crow this day (cf. Luke 22:34), and John's Gospel states before the cock crows (cf. John 13:38). Thus, the fulfillment of the prediction portrays the rooster crowing one or two times after Peter has denied knowing Jesus (cf. Mark

14:68; Matt 26:74; Luke 22:60; John 18:27). In each scenario, except John, Peter remembers Jesus' prediction about the cock crowing (cf. Mark 14:72; Matt 26:75; Luke 22:61). Because of this biblical story, the cock became one of the two emblems associated with St. Peter (the other was the keys). It the Middle Ages a common practice developed of putting a weathervane (weathercock) with the emblem of a rooster on church steeples to indicate that the church was governed by the pope, a successor of St. Peter.

In "The Origin of The Book of Mormon," Joseph Smith narrates his experiences of God's messenger named Maroni. After Maroni's third visit and departure, Smith writes that he pondered the strangeness of the visit. He states, "[W]hen almost immediately after the heavenly messenger had ascended from me the third time, the cock crowed, and I found that day was approaching, so that our interviews must have occupied the whole of that night."[1] Here, the crowing of the rooster awakens Smith to reality and makes him aware that it is morning.

Aesop's Fables contains several stories about crowing cocks. In "The Thieves and the Cock," robbers break into a house and take the only valuable thing they can find: the cock. When they were about to wring his neck and prepare him for their dinner, the cock said: "Pray do not kill me; you will find me a most useful bird, for I rouse honest men to their work in the morning by my crowing."[2] However, the cock's words backfire, because the thieves state that the rooster's crowing will make it harder for them to get a livelihood.

After a cat caught a cock in "The Cat and the Cock," the cat says to the cock, "You make a great nuisance of yourself at night by crowing and keeping people awake; so I am going to make an end of you."[3] However, the cock defends himself saying "that he crowed in order that men might wake up and set about the day's work in good time, and that they really couldn't very well do without him."[4] Nevertheless, the cat kills him and eats him.

A cock "rising to his full height and flapping his wings vigorously, uttered a tremendous crow" in "The Ass, the Cock, and the Lion" that scares away a lion from the ass (donkey), which begins to think that if the lion is scared of the rooster, how much more will the lion be afraid of the donkey.[5] So, the ass pursues the lion. However, when both were well out of sight and earshot of the cock, the lion turns on the ass and eats him.

1. *Mormon*, xv.
2. Aesop, 47.
3. Ibid., 92.
4. Ibid.
5. Ibid., 127–28.

In "The Fowler, the Partridge, and the Cock," a hungry fowler prepares for a meal of herbs and bread when a friend drops in for supper. At first he decides to kill the partridge to feed his guest, but after the partridge explains how useful she is, the fowler decides to go to the chicken house, where he had "a plump young cock," who pleads for his life, saying, "If you kill me, how will you know the time of night? And who will wake you up in the morning when it is time to get to work?"[6] The fowler acknowledges the rightness of the cock's words, but the demands of hospitality require him to wring the neck of the cock and prepare him for his visitor's dinner!

The HB (OT) Book of Proverbs adds another characteristic of the rooster, namely strutting. The author identifies four animals which are stately in their gait (cf. Prov 30:29), one of which is "the strutting rooster" (Prov 30:31). The usual strutting in a half circle with one wing extended down is a type of dance in which the cock displays his dominance to hens. When the strut is done among other males, it serves to distinguish the dominant rooster of the group.

In one of the few fables in Aesop's collection in which the cock is not killed and eaten by someone, the rooster is portrayed as outsmarting a fox, one of his primary enemies. After a dog and cock become good friends and agree to take a trip together, upon nightfall "the cock flew up into the branches of a tree to roost, while the dog curled himself up inside the trunk, which was hollow."[7] At daybreak the cock woke up and crowed. A fox heard him and thought he would make a great breakfast. So, after finding him in the tree, the fox said, "I should so like to make the acquaintance of one who has such a beautiful voice."[8] So, the cock tells the fox to wake up the porter who is still asleep at the foot of the tree. The fox knocks on the tree trunk and out rushes the dog, which kills the fox in "The Dog, the Cock, and the Fox."

The wisdom of a cock is displayed in Aesop's "The Cock and the Jewel," a very short fable. While scratching the ground looking for something to eat, a rooster finds a jewel that had been dropped there. The cock acknowledges the value the jewel has to the person who lost it, and the joy its owner would have if it were found. But a jewel means nothing to a hungry cock. "Give me a single grain of corn before all the jewels in the world," states the cock.[9] This fable also illustrates alectryomancy, a form of divination involving the observance of a cock pecking at grain.

6. Ibid., 197.
7. Ibid., 29.
8. Ibid.
9. Ibid., 120.

In "The Eagle and the Cocks," another fable about a cock that is not eaten—however, one is eaten—Aesop narrates how two roosters in the same farmyard fight to decide who should be master; this a reference to the cock's strutting mentioned above. Once the fight is over, "the victor flew up on to the roof of the stables and crowed lustily."[10] However, an eagle spotted him, swooped down, grabbed him, and carried him off for the eagle's dinner. The losing rooster emerged from the corner he had stepped into after being defeated "and ruled the roost without a rival."[11]

The cock is considered a sacred animal in several cultures, especially when it is involved in a cockfight. When held at a funeral, the winning rooster represents the power to revive the dead. When held at a festival, the winning cock represents the power of humans over the gods. If the cock is offered as a sacrificial animal, its blood signifies the spirit being bestowed on those anointed with it. And the rooster can be sacrificed as a substitute for people; in this latter sense, it is like the biblical scapegoat carrying away people's sins.

In "The Death of the Hen," one of Grimm's fairy tales, a cock and hen make a trip to the nut mountain, agreeing beforehand that whichever found a nut first would divide it with the other. However, after finding a large nut, the hen swallowed it, and it got caught in her throat. Calling to the cock, she said, "Cock, run as fast as you can and fetch me some water, or I shall choke!"[12] So, the cock runs to the brook, which tells him to go to the bride and ask for some red silk. In what becomes a wild goose chase, the bride sends him to fetch her garland in the willow. Ultimately, the cock brings the garland to the bride, who gives him red silk, which he takes to the brook, which gives him water to take to the hen, which has died because she did not share the nut she found with the cock. "And the cock was so grieved that he cried aloud, and all the beasts came and lamented for the hen; and six mice built a little wagon on which to carry the poor hen to her grave, and when it was ready they harnessed themselves to it, and the cock drove."[13]

Once the funeral procession begins, it is joined by a fox, a wolf, a bear, a stag, a lion, and all other beasts in the wood. After coming to a brook, which they needed to cross, the mice fell in and were drowned after trying to cross on a piece of straw. Next, a piece of burning coal attempted to help, but hissed and died. Finally, a stone laid itself across the stream and drew the wagon with the dead hen across the water to the other side, but the

10. Ibid., 114.
11. Ibid.
12. Grimm, 109.
13. Ibid.

wagon turned over and all those following it were drowned. Thus, "the cock was left all alone with the dead hen, and he dug a grave and laid her in it, and he raised a mound above her, and sat himself down and lamented so sore that at last he died. And so they were all dead together."[14] Thus, ends the tale of the cock and the hen, a narrative that illustrates what happens to the selfish.

Cocatrice

Mormon three times mentions a cockatrice (2 Ne 21:8; 24:29; 30:14), "a fiery flying serpent" (2 Ne 24:29), which could kill with its evil stare. In mythology, the cockatrice or fearsome serpent was hatched from a cock egg, one that contained no yolk. Bulfinch notes that this creature was called the king of serpents with a comb or crown upon his head. In appearance he was a giant rooster with some lizard characteristics. "He was supposed to be produced from the egg of a cock hatched under toads or serpents."[15] There were several species of cockatrice, but all of them were considered

> kings of serpents because all other serpents and snakes, behaving like good subjects, and wisely not wishing to be burned up or struck dead, fled the moment they heard the distant hiss of their king, although they might be in full feed upon the most delicious prey, leaving the sole enjoyment of the banquet to the royal monster.[16]

The cockatrice has only two enemies. "[T]he cockatrice quailed before the weasel," states Bulfinch, and "as soon as he heard the cock crow he expired."[17] Its carcass could be hung in houses to deter spiders or other small creatures. A cockatrice is a mythological creature. An egg without a yolk is laid by a hen, not a rooster. Such an egg is usually a pullet's or young hen's first effort at egg-laying. It indicates that her laying mechanism is not fully developed.

Thus, the rooster or cock is a sacred animal. The spirit of the rooster represents the apostle Peter, who three times denied Jesus. Peter's denial is signaled by a cock's crow; the rooster becomes an emblem of the memory of Peter's deed. The cock's crowing is also one of its favorite characteristics in fables and tales followed by its strutting and its wisdom. As a spirit animal,

---

14. Ibid., 109–110.
15. Bulfinch, *Mythology*, 312.
16. Ibid., 313.
17. Ibid., 314.

it serves as a marker for all who have experienced another's denial or denied another.

Journal/Meditation: Just as the rooster's crow marks Peter's denial of Jesus, what animal marks someone you have denied? Explain.

Prayer: The morning sunrise is greeted by your cock's crowing, O LORD, reminding me of Peter's denial of your Son. Keep me safe under your wing, and bestow upon me the wisdom that will enable me to remain faithful to my Lord Jesus Christ, who lives and reigns with you, Father, and the Holy Spirit, one God, forever and ever. Amen.

Serpent (Snake)

Text: "... [T]he serpent was more crafty than any other wild animal that the LORD God had made. He said to the woman, 'Did God say, "You shall not eat from any tree in the garden?"' The woman said to the serpent, 'We may eat of the fruit of the trees in the garden; but God said, "You shall not eat of the fruit of the tree that is in the middle of the garden, nor shall you touch it, or you shall die."' But the serpent said to the woman, 'You will not die; for God knows that when you eat of it your eyes will be opened, and you will be like God, knowing good and evil.'" (Gen 3:1–5)

Reflection: The Bible contains three major stories about serpents or snakes and lots of cross references to those three accounts. The first tale features a talking snake, which is a very intelligent and crafty creature made by God to live in his garden. The complete account in the HB (OT), Genesis 3:1–24, serves as the foundation myth for the origin of evil. Once the woman and man, who are not yet named Eve and Adam in the narrative, eat the forbidden fruit and God discovers their trespass, the LORD curses, that is, wishes ill upon the snake, saying, "Because you have done this, cursed are you among all animals and among all wild creatures; upon your belly you shall go, and dust you shall eat all the days of your life. I will put enmity between you and the woman, and between your offspring and hers, he will strike your head, and you will strike his heel" (Gen 3:14–15). The curse serves to explain mythologically why snakes have no legs and why humans are afraid of them.

Garden Snake

The basic sin of the couple in the garden is not eating from the tree of the knowledge of good and evil; the basic sin of the couple is idolatry, which is the sin that has to be fought throughout biblical literature. The Baal, who took many different forms, was primarily a Canaanite fertility god, often taking the form of a snake or phallus. By listening to the talking snake, the man and woman abandon the LORD God in the garden and worship the false god, incurring the sin of idolatry. This understanding, however, does not keep subsequent readers from declaring the talking snake to be the devil!

The Second Book of Nephi in *Mormon* echoes this idea. Presuming that the serpent is the incarnation of a fallen angel, the author states that "he said unto Eve, yea, even that old serpent, who is the devil, who is the father of all lies, wherefore he said: Partake of the forbidden fruit, and you shall not die, but you shall be as God, knowing good and evil" (2 Ne 2:18). Likewise, in the *Book of Doctrine and Covenants*, Smith declares that he "beheld Satan, that old serpent, even the devil" (*D&C* 76:3; cf. 85:35). St. Paul, too, alludes to the biblical account in his Second Letter to the Corinthians in the CB (NT). The apostle asks his readers to bear with him because he is afraid that as the serpent deceived Eve by its cunning, their thoughts will lead them away from Christ (cf. 2 Cor 11:3).

While it has a different point, "The White Snake" in *Grimm's Complete Fairy Tales* also echoes the Genesis talking snake narrative. The tale begins with a king, who was known for his wisdom throughout his country; he had a dish brought to him every day by a servant "after the table had been cleared and every one gone away."[1] The dish was always covered, so that even the servant did not know what was on it. As in the Genesis account of the man, the woman, and the talking snake, there came a day when the servant could resist his curiosity any longer. After taking the dish away, he brought it to his own room, uncovered it, and "saw a white snake lying on the dish."[2] It was a temptation he could not resist. So, he cut off a piece and ate it, and he was suddenly able to hear the animals talking to each other. "The virtue of the snake had given him power to understand the speech of animals."[3]

One day the queen lost her precious ring, but the servant overheard the ducks talking and discovered that one of them had swallowed it. The

---

1. Grimm, 231.
2. Ibid.
3. Ibid.

servant caught the duck, took it to the kitchen, and instructed the cook to kill it and prepare it for a meal. When the cook was cleaning the duck, he found the queen's ring, and the servant returned it to her. Because of this, the king rewarded him with a horse and money for traveling. The next day the servant set out on a journey.

He came to a pond and saw three fishes entangled in the rushes. He dismounted, removed the rushes, and set the fishes free. "We will remember and reward you, because you have delivered us," he heard the fishes tell him.[4] Next, he heard a voice from the sand under his horse's feet; it was the ant king. The man turned his horse away from the ant hill, hearing the ant king say, "We will remember and reward you."[5] In the woods, he heard a father and mother raven urging their three young ones out of the nest. He heard the young ravens begging for food; so, he killed his horse and left it for food for the ravens.

Traveling on foot he came to a town, where he heard the king's proclamation that his daughter needed a husband, but he would have to perform a difficult task. If the potential husband failed, he would lose his life. Several had already tried and died. The pilgrim was undaunted, and he went to the king to see what he had to do to win the princess' hand.

The first task was to retrieve a gold ring tossed into the sea. Before he could jump in to attempt to retrieve the ring, three fishes came swimming by, and one of them had a mussel in its mouth. The man took the mussel, opened it, and found the ring. After presenting the ring to the king, his next task consisted of re-gathering ten sacks of millet seed which had been strewed over the grass. While contemplating how to fulfill this deed, he fell asleep. But when he awoke the next morning, he discovered that the ant-king and his thousands of subjects had arrived during the night and picked up every grain of millet and put it in one of the sacks. The third task was set by the princess; she said that the man would not be her bridegroom unless he brought her "an apple from the tree of life."[6] The reader will note the obvious parallel with the Genesis account above.

Not knowing where the tree of life might be located, the pilgrim resumed his journey. After traveling through three kingdoms, he came to a wood, seated himself under a tree, and "heard a rustling in the boughs, and a golden apple fell into his hand."[7] Then, three ravens flew towards him, perched on his knee, and identified themselves as the three ravens to which

4. Ibid., 232.
5. Ibid.
6. Ibid., 233.
7. Ibid., 234.

he had fed his horse. Taking the golden apple, he headed back to the king, who gave him his daughter in marriage. "... [T[hey divided the apple of life, and ate it together; and their hearts were filled with love, and they lived in undisturbed happiness to a great age."[8]

While all this was caused by eating a bite of white snake, the fairy tale reverses the Genesis fall story. Instead of bringing evil into the world by eating the fruit of the tree of the knowledge of good and evil at the urging of a talking snake, as in the HB (OT) Book of Genesis, eating the fruit of the tree of life in this story, as a result of eating a piece of white snake, brings about happiness and long life. The white snake bestows the wisdom of being able to understand the speech of animals. Once he acquires this wisdom, the servant begins a journey, another biblical theme.

Not to be missed are the four sets of three, indicating theophanies or appearances of the divine. There are three fishes, three ravens, three tasks to accomplish, and three kingdoms. These four sets of three represent universality. Furthermore, in exchange for his three kind deeds to the fishes, the ants, and the ravens, he becomes the recipient of three kind or divine deeds that enable him to win the hand of the king's daughter in marriage. Thus, the wisdom gained from the snake in this story reverses the wisdom gained from the talking snake in the Genesis story. Instead of using his knowledge to do evil, the pilgrim employs his wisdom to accomplish good. In other words, Grimm's tale is one featuring an Adam and an Eve who do not choose evil over good. It is the reverse of the Genesis myth.

Similar to Grimm's tale is that of "The Snake-Eater" from the country of Georgia. Mindia, a member of a mountain tribe, is taken prisoner by a demon and held in captivity for twelve years. He notices that his captors' favorite dish is "a cauldron full of snake-meat, which from eating they seem to derive much of their supernatural powers."[9] One day Mindia eats a piece of snake and, "[to] his amazement, he feels a surging stream of strange delight pulsing through his veins."[10] He can hear blades of grass speaking to each other and understand the rustling of leaves in the woods. He knows the languages of birds and other animals. He makes his escape and returns to his own people. After getting married, he is obliged to hunt and fish for food and cut trees to burn for warmth. "The plants and animals refuse to share their secrets with him any longer."[11] After his village is attacked by enemies, he falls in battle and dies.

8. Ibid.
9. Cavendish, *Legends*, 144.
10. Ibid.
11. Ibid., 145.

The association of snakes and wisdom is attested in other sacred texts, too. The Matthean Jesus uniquely instructs his disciples to be wise as serpents (cf. Matt 10:16). Likewise, in *The Rig Veda* there is a hymn dedicated to the Visvedevas, the Hindu gods taken together as a whole, which mentions that the gods "[b]orne on refulgent car[t]s, sinless, with serpents' powers" enrobed are for the singers' "welfare in the height of heaven" (*RV* 10:63:4). The "serpents' powers" refer to the unsurpassable wisdom of the gods.

Staff Snake

The second major biblical story about serpents or snakes is that which narrates Moses' burning bush experience (cf. Exod 3:1–22). Moses asks the LORD for a sign, and God gives him a staff on the ground that becomes a snake (cf. Exod 4:3). "Then the LORD said to Moses, 'Reach out your hand, and seize it by the tail'—so he reached out his hand and grasped it, and it became a staff in his hand . . ." (Exod 4:4). Later in the HB (OT) Book of Exodus, Aaron, Moses' brother, throws down the staff in the presence of Pharaoh and it becomes a snake. Pharaoh's magicians do the same with their staffs, however. But Moses' staff-turned-snake swallows theirs (cf. Exod 7:8–13).

The Quran loves this story, narrating it over and over again. For example, in *The Quran's* version of Moses' encounter with God, the text states that God asks Moses, "'What is that in your right hand, O Moses?' 'It's my staff,' he answered . . . . 'Throw it down, O Moses,' said (the voice). So he threw it down, and, lo, it became a running serpent. 'Catch it,' said he, 'and have no fear; we shall revert it to its former state.'" (*Quran* 20:17–21). Another account refers to the staff as "wriggling like a serpent" (*Quran* 27:10; 28:31). And in another account after Moses tells Pharaoh that he has a sign from the Lord and Pharaoh asks to see it, ". . . Moses threw down his staff, and, lo, it became a live serpent" (*Quran* 7:107; cf. 26:32). The narrator continues by telling the reader about the Egyptian magicians' staff-snakes being eaten by Moses' staff-snake (cf. *Quran* 7:108–123; 26:33–49). In *The Quran's* version of the story, the magicians come to believe in Moses and Aaron!

Serpent Snakes

The third major biblical story about serpents or snakes is that narrated in the HB (OT) Book of Numbers. While they are making their journey, the Israelites become impatient and speak against God and Moses.

> Then the LORD sent poisonous serpents among the people, and they bit the people, so that many Israelites died. The people came to Moses and said, "We have sinned by speaking against the LORD and against you; pray to the LORD to take away the serpents from us." So Moses prayed for the people. And the LORD said to Moses, "Make a poisonous serpent, and set it on a pole; and everyone who is bitten shall look at it and live." So Moses made a serpent of bronze, and put it upon a pole; and whenever a serpent bit someone, that person would look at the serpent of bronze and live. (Num 21:6–9)

In the Book of Deuteronomy, Moses reminds the Israelites that it was the LORD their God who led them through the wilderness with poisonous snakes (cf. Deut 8:15), and the OT (A) Book of Wisdom poetically reminds its readers that the people "were being destroyed by the bites of writhing serpents" when they "received a symbol of deliverance" (the bronze serpent) so that "the one who turned toward it was saved, not by the thing that was beheld, but by [the LORD], the Savior of all" (Wis 16:5–7). God's "children were not conquered even by the fangs of venomous serpents" (Wis 16:10a). *Mormon* also narrates the "poisonous serpents" story (Ether 9:31, 33) and how the Lord God "gave unto Moses power that he should heal the nations after they had been bitten by the poisonous serpents, if they would cast their eyes unto the serpent which he did raise up before them . . ." (2 Ne 25:20).

The author of John's Gospel in the CB (NT) remembers this story and portrays Jesus applying it to himself in a unique dialogue with Nicodemus. Jesus says, ". . . [J]ust as Moses lifted up the serpent in the wilderness, so must the Son of Man be lifted up, that whoever believe in him may have eternal life" (John 3:14–15). Similarly, the Book of Helaman in *Mormon* interprets Moses' words as applying to the Messiah and asks,

> Yes, did he not bear record that the Son of God should come? And as he lifted up the brazen serpent in the wilderness, even so shall he be lifted up who should come. And as many as should look upon that serpent should live, even so as many as should look upon the Son of God with faith, having a contrite spirit, might live, even unto that life which is eternal. (Hel 8:14–15)

Even St. Paul in his First Letter to the Corinthians in the CB (NT) warns his readers not to put Christ to the test as some of the Israelites put God to the test and were destroyed by serpents (cf. 1 Cor 10:9). The Second Book of Kings narrates that it was King Hezekiah who "broke in pieces the bronze serpent that Moses had made, for until those days the people of Israel had made offerings to it; it was called Nehushtan" (2 Kgs 18:4b).

Healing Snake

Grimm's Complete Fairy Tales contains a story about a snake that provides healing. In "The Three Snake Leaves," a young man leaves home, joins a great king's army, goes to war, and distinguishes himself on the battlefield as a leader. The king, of course, has a daughter, who "had made a vow that she would take no man for a husband who did not promise that if she should die, he would allow himself to be buried alive with her in the grave."[12] She also promised to be buried alive with her husband should he die before she did. Needless to say, the daughter's strange vow had frightened away many potential husbands. The brave soldier declared his love for the king's daughter, accepted the conditions of the vow, and married her.

After a few years of marital bliss, the princess died, and her husband remembered the vow. On the day of her funeral, he was led with her coffin to the vault where her body was placed, and he was locked in. "Near the coffin stood a table upon which were four lights, four loaves of bread, and four bottles of wine, and he knew that when these provisions came to an end, he must starve."[13] The astute reader will immediately recognize the sacred number four, representing the universe, and the sacred number three (sets of four), representing a theophany. Nevertheless, the soldier ate sparingly.

One day when he was just about out of supplies, he saw a white snake creep out of a corner of the vault. Thinking that the snake was going to attack the body of the princess, he drew his sword and cut the snake into three pieces. Again, the reader will note the scriptural number three. After a while a second snake appeared, saw the dead snake, turned around, went back, and then returned with three green leaves in its mouth. Then, taking the three parts of the dead snake and putting them together he placed a leaf on each wound, and "the snake raised himself as lively as ever"[14] and slithered off with his companion, leaving the three green leaves on the floor.

The snakes' coming into the tomb echo the mythology of the Kom, a group of people who live in northwest Cameroon. "Snakes are regarded as representatives of the ancestors by the Kom," states Opoku.[15] ". . . [S]erpents are regarded as intermediaries between the dead ancestors and the living."[16] In this Grimm story, the two snakes function as intermediaries between

---

12. Grimm, 227.
13. Ibid., 228.
14. Ibid.
15. Opoku, "African Mythology," 355.
16. Ibid.

those in the tomb and those outside it, not to mention between those in the tomb and the Divine.

As the man watched this take place, it occurred to him that if the leaves could restore a snake to life, then they might work on his princess-wife. So, he picked up the leaves and placed one on the mouth and one on each eye of his dead wife. "The blood began to circulate in the veins and blushed softly in the pale face and lips of his dead wife. She drew a deep breath, opened her closed eyes, and exclaimed faintly, 'Where am I?'"[17] He told her that she was with him and all that had occurred.

She ate a little of the bread and drank some of the wine that was left, got strong enough to rise from her bier and walk to the door of the vault with her husband, and knocked and called loudly until someone heard them and came and opened the door to the vault. The king was very pleased to see his daughter and son-in-law alive.

The young man kept the three leaves with him, entrusting their care to his faithful servant. Meanwhile, the princess' love for her husband dwindled. Thus, while they took a voyage across a sea, she made friends with the wicked captain. While her husband was asleep on the deck, she and the captain picked him up and threw him overboard. Then, they turned the ship around and headed back to her father, whom she thought would permit her to marry the captain and one day make him king.

However, the soldier's faithful servant, to whom he had entrusted the three leaves, jumped into the sea and rescued his master's body, placed it in a smaller boat, and rowed to shore. He took the three leaves and placed one on the mouth and one on each eye. The dead man very quickly showed signs of life and became strong enough to help row the boat. They arrived at the king's palace before the princess and the captain did. They informed the king of his daughter's wickedness; he hid them in a private room until the princess and the captain should arrive.

A few days later the princess and the captain of the ship made their way to the castle. The princess explained that her husband "was taken suddenly ill and died" and that the "good captain had . . . stood by [her] and conducted [her] home."[18] The king told her that he could restore her dead husband to life. So, throwing open the door of the private room, he called to his son-in-law and servant to come out. Seeing them, the daughter fell on her knees and begged mercy from her father. "I can show you no mercy," said the king. "Your husband was not only ready to be buried and die with you, but he used the means which restored you to life, and you have mur-

17. Grimm, 228.
18. Ibid., 230.

dered him while he slept, and shall receive the reward you so truly merit."[19] Consequently, the princess was put in a boat full of holes and driven out to sea, where the boat sank and she was drowned. Thus, even though the princess lost her life, her husband gained his life because of the three leaves brought by a snake. The husband was healed by the leaves, just as were the people healed by looking at the bronze serpent Moses erected in the desert.

Snake Venom

While those are the three major biblical stories about snakes, a great deal of writing is devoted to being bitten by and injected with venom from snakes. Psalm 58 states that wicked people "have venom like the venom of a serpent, like the deaf adder that stops its ear, so that it does not hear the voice of charmers or of the cunning enchanter" (Ps 58:4–5). The Book of Ecclesiastes echoes that sentiment, stating that if the snake bites before it is charmed, there is no advantage in being a charmer (cf. Eccl 10:11). Psalm 140 states the evildoers "make their tongue sharp as a snake's, and under their lips is the venom of vipers" (Ps 140:3). This leads the Matthean Jesus to call his opponents, the scribes and Pharisees, snakes and a brood of vipers (cf. Matt 23:33) because according to the OT (A) Book of Sirach, "There is no venom worse than a snake's venom" (Sir 25:15a). Even God refers to the punishment that is going to afflict his people as letting snakes loose among them; these snakes cannot be charmed, and they will bite them (cf. Jer 8:17).

The HB (OT) Book of Deuteronomy records a song of Moses which mentions the wine made in Sodom and Gomorrah as "the poison of serpents, the cruel venom of asps" (Deut 32:33), as does the Book of Proverbs, which states that mixed wine "bites like a serpent, and stings like an adder" (Prov 23:32).

It is the wish that "[t]hose who destroy . . . the simple, and with their evil natures harm the righteous," be given "over to the serpent" by drinking the sacred soma juice in *The Rig Veda* (*RV* 7:104:9). A hymn in a later book beseeches the god Agni, the god of fire, to heal, among other things, serpent bites on a deceased person whose body is being cremated on a funeral pyre (cf. *RV* 10:16:6). In an earlier hymn, the Maruts, the storm gods, are described as marching "in companies . . . with serpents' ire" and displaying "lightning visible as light" (*RV* 1:64:9). The Mormon *Book of Doctrine and Covenants* also mentions "the poison of a serpent" (*D&C* 83:11) and "the poisonous serpent" (*D&C* 107:30).

19. Ibid.

From Japan comes the story of "Yamato and the Serpent." Yamato Date, a wondering hero, possesses a sword named Cloud Cluster. After seeing an apparition of the Great Serpent, who had been killed by another warrior, and taking Cloud Cluster from the serpent's tail, "[t]he serpent demanded the return of the sword, but Yamato simply ignored the apparition and continued on his journey."[20] While journeying, Yamato falls in love with a girl, leaves the girl, saves himself from a conspiracy seeking his life, returns to the girl, and leaves the girl, hanging his sword on the branches of a mulberry tree as a memento.

Now, no longer protected by his sacred sword, "Yamato once more encountered the apparition of the evil serpent. Again he tried to ignore the monster and pass it by, but when he leaped over the serpent's body, his foot touched it, and he was struck by a fever which rapidly spread throughout his body."[21] His girlfriend, who had been secretly following him, embraced him as he died.

Aesop's Fables contain five stories about poisonous snakes that bite creatures and kill them. In "The Farmer and the Viper," after the farmer found a viper frozen and numb from the winter's cold, picked it up, warmed it in his bosom, and revived it, the viper "turned upon its benefactor and inflicted a fatal bite upon him."[22] In "The Laborer and the Snake," it is the worker's little son who is bitten and dies from the wound. The man gets an ax and stands close to the snake's hole, watching for a chance to kill it. When it emerges, he strikes it with the ax, but only cuts off a small portion of its tail. He tries to get it come out again, but the snake refuses.[23] After spying a snake asleep in a sunny spot, a crow captures it and carries it off to a place where he could eat it in "The Crow and the Snake." However, the snake bites the crow, and the crow dies.[24] In a similar fable, titled "The Serpent and the Eagle," an eagle captures a snake, but the serpent, who is too fast for the bird, coils itself around the eagle, intent on killing it. A countryman saw the encounter and helped free the eagle from the serpent, which "spat some of his poison into the man's drinking-horn."[25] The eagle saved the man by knocking the cup out of his hand.

Echoing the biblical narrative above about God's curse of the serpent, there is "The Snake and Jupiter." The fable begins, stating, "A snake suffered

---

20. Cavendish, *Legends*, 63.
21. Ibid.
22. Aesop, 126.
23. Cf. Ibid., 149.
24. Cf. Ibid., 187.
25. Ibid., 217.

a good deal from being constantly trodden upon by man and beast, owing partly to the length of his body and partly to his being unable to raise himself above the surface of the ground; so he went and complained to Jupiter about the risks to which he was exposed."[26] Jupiter had very little sympathy for the snake, saying, ". . . [I]f you had bitten the first that trod on you, the others would have taken more trouble to look where they put their feet."[27]

The psalmist declares that those who trust the Most High God will tread on the adder, and they will trample the serpent under foot (cf. Ps 91:13). Probably inspired by this verse, the Lukan Jesus tells the seventy(-two) disciples he sent out on mission that he gave them "authority to tread on snakes" (Luke 10:17) so that nothing would hurt them. Make no mistake about it, the hissing of snakes is fearful (cf. Wis 17:9b). Grimm says that "a snake cries, 'Huhu, huhu.'"[28] However, some snakes do flee from people in fear (cf. *RV* 10:95:8), while others merely bask in the sunshine on a rock (cf. Prov 30:19).

The OT (A) Book of Sirach makes it clear that people should flee from sin as from a snake; if one approaches sin, it will bite (cf. Sir 21:2). Sirach also asks, "Who pities a snake charmer when he is bitten . . . ? (Sir 12:13) The HB (OT) prophet Isaiah declares to the Philistines that "from the root of the snake will come forth an adder, and its fruit will be a lying fiery serpent" (Isa 14:29; cf. 30:6). In other words, a dead king's successor will be worse than the king. In *Mormon*, it is "out of the serpent's root [that there comes] forth a cockatrice, and his fruit shall be a fiery flying serpent" (2 Ne 24:29). For information on the cockatrice, the reader should see the "Cock (Rooster)" entry.

Snakes glide. Jeremiah shames Egypt, writing that he makes a sound like a snake gliding away (cf. Jer 46:22), while the prophet Micah asks God to shame the nations so that they lick dust like a snake (cf. Mic 7:17a). *The Rig Veda* describes the god of fire, Agni, as "a raging serpent" (*RV* 1:79:1), hard to grasp, "like offspring of the wriggling snakes" (*RV* 5:19:4), when he consumes wood. The Asvins, divine twin horsemen, "who glide like serpents" (*RV* 2:38:3), symbolizing the shining of sunrise and sunset, give to Pedu a horse "who killed the brood of serpents" (*RV* 9:187:4b); thus Pedu is known as "the serpent slayer" (*RV* 1:117:9). However, the Asvins themselves change shape "like serpents, fearless, void of guile" (*RV* 1:3:9) and are described as "shining like a serpent mid trees" (*RV* 1:180:3).

---

26. Ibid., 190.
27. Ibid.
28. Grimm, 576.

Even "those first, freshest drops of soma juice" are said to be "beauteous as serpents" (*RV* 9:77:3). Likewise, "the juice . . . flowing onward like a mighty stream" also "glides like a serpent from his ancient skin" (*RV* 9:86:44). The Maruts, the storm gods, are compared to the "serpents' fury through their might" (*RV* 1:64:8), "who gleam as serpents gleam" (*RV* 1:172:1), that is, the thunder accompanying lightning strikes.

"The Fox and the Snake" in *Aesop's Fables* describes a snake crossing a river and getting carried away by the current but manages "to wriggle on to a bundle of thorns which was floating by, and was thus carried at a great rate downstream."[29] On the river bank a fox sees the snake and thorns whirling along in the water and says, ". . . [T]he passenger fits the ship!"[30]

In Isaiah's depiction of a restored or ideal world, "[t]he nursing child . . . plays over the hole of the asp, and the weaned child . . . puts its hand on the adder's den" (Isa 11:8). *Grimm's Complete Fairy Tales* contains a three-part story, titled "Tales of Snakes," which also present this same idea. In part one, a little child is given a small bowl of milk and some bread every day which she takes to the yard and sits and eats. A snake comes out of a crevice in the wall, dips its head in the milk, and eats some of the bread. She composes a verse to call the snake: "Snake, snake, come swiftly, / Hither come, thou tiny thing, / Thou shalt have thy crumbs of bread, / Thou shalt refresh thyself with milk."[31] In gratitude, the snake brings the child pretty things from its hidden treasure. One day the little girl hit the snake on the head with her spoon. The child's mother heard her talking to the snake and went out to see what was going on. When her mother saw the snake, she took a log of wood and killed it. However, as was seen above, snakes represent life. So, after her mother killed the snake the little girl began to waste away, until she died.

In part three of "Tales of Snakes," an orphan child is sitting on a wall spinning, when she sees "a snake coming out of a hole low down in the wall."[32] The girl spreads a blue silk handkerchief for the snake to rest on, but the snake turns around, goes back into its hole, and then comes back with a small golden crown, which it lays on the handkerchief and then goes away. "The girl took up the crown; it glittered and was of delicate golden filigree work."[33] When the snake returns and it does not see the crown on the handkerchief, it begins to smite its head against the wall in grief until it

29. Aesop, 212.
30. Ibid.
31. Grimm, 576.
32. Ibid., 577.
33. Ibid.

kills itself. "If the girl had but left the crown where it was, the snake would certainly have brought still more of its treasures out of the hole."[34]

Wily Snake

The last characteristic of a snake or serpent is being wily, and this brings the reader back to the crafty snake in the Book of Genesis. The creature is skilled at using clever tricks to deceive people, as seen above in the biblical text narrating the temptation to eat the forbidden fruit. *The Rig Veda* also attests to "the wiles of serpents" (*RV* 6:20:7; 6:52:15). And in the patriarch Jacob's farewell address to his sons in the HB (OT) Book of Genesis, the small tribe of Dan was able to punish its enemies like "a snake by the roadside, a viper along the path, that bites the horse's heels so that its rider falls backward" (Gen 49:17). In other words, the small tribe of Dan was capable of winning skirmishes.

One of the most widely depicted snakes is the cobra, which appears on the uraeus, the headdress of Egyptian pharaohs. Representing the goddess Wadjet, who was depicted as a snake, the cobra became a sign of sovereignty, royalty, deity, and divine authority in ancient Egypt. "Coiled before striking, the cobra represents latent energy, the source of spiritual endeavor and advancement, ready for action," according to Kemmerer.[35] Vargas adds that snakes are also linked "with rebirth and fertility;"[36] Cavendish adds that "snakes shed their skins and . . . that in doing so they rejuvenate themselves."[37] He also narrates a story about an old woman, who kept a pet snake which copulated with her.[38] This latter detail is woven into the tale surrounding the conception of Alexander the Great. His mother, Olympias, wife of Philip II of Macedon, is promised a son "through the intervention of the god Zeus Ammon, [who] visits her by night in the form of a serpent . . . until Alexander is conceived."[39]

The rebirth symbolism of the snake is echoed in Aesop's "The Wasp and the Snake." In this fable, a wasp landed on the head of a snake "and not only stung him several times, but clung obstinately to the head of his victim."[40] After trying to get rid of the wasp, the snake decides that the

---

34. Ibid.
35. Kemmerer, *Animals*, 71.
36. Vargas, "Snake-Kings," 226.
37. Cavendish, *Legends*, 366.
38. Cf. Ibid., 366.
39. Ibid., 283.
40. Aesop, 178.

only way to kill the wasp is to kill itself. So, the snake lays his head with the wasp still on it under the wheel of a passing wagon, and both of them die together. While Aesop attaches no moral to the story, it certainly echoes the idea presented above about the snake being able to rejuvenate itself in a type of resurrection and ties into the biblical story in the Book of Numbers about the bronze serpent on the pole, which ultimately gave rise to the caduceus, a winged staff with two intertwined serpents representing the Greek god of healing, Asclepius; the caduceus is still used by the medical profession today. It is often seen on ambulances, in hospitals, and in doctors' offices.

Thus, the crafty, wily, talking serpent represents deception and the origin of evil, often associated with the devil or Satan. However, the snake is also a sign of wisdom, sovereignty, royalty, deity, and divine authority. There is the association of the serpent with healing, fertility, rebirth, and resurrection. John's Gospel understands the account of Moses making a bronze serpent and lifting it up on a pole to be a foretelling of Jesus' death and resurrection. The snake's venom brings death, and so one should flee from gliding, slithering serpents, but simultaneously the snake's shedding of skin represents a restored world in which it is no longer to be feared.

Journal/Meditation: What spiritual qualities of the serpent (snake) grab your immediate attention? In what events of your life have you employed those spiritual qualities?

Prayer: In order to heal your people, LORD God, you instructed your servant Moses to make a bronze serpent and mount it on a pole in the desert so that the instrument of death became the instrument of life. Trace in me the death to selfishness represented by the lifting up of your Son on the cross so that I may also experience his resurrection to new life. I ask this in the name of Jesus Christ, who lives and reigns with you, Father, and the Holy Spirit, one God, forever and ever. Amen.

Sheep (Ram, Ewe, Lamb)

Text: "The LORD said to Moses and Aaron in the land of Egypt: Tell the whole congregation of Israel that on the tenth of this month they are to take a lamb for each family, a lamb for each household. Your lamb shall be without blemish a year-old-male; you may take it from the sheep or the goats. You shall keep it until the fourteenth day of this month; then the whole assembled congregation of Israel shall slaughter it at twilight. They shall take some of the blood and put it on the two doorposts and the lintel of the houses in which they eat it. They shall eat the lamb that same night; they shall eat it roasted over the fire with unleavened bread and bitter herbs. . . . [Y]ou shall eat it hurriedly. It is the Passover of the LORD." (Exod 12:1, 3, 5–8, 11)

Reflection: This entry on the stocky, hooved mammal with ribbed horns that is raised for its meat and wool, known as the sheep, will also cover the male sheep, known as a ram; the female sheep, known as a ewe; and the young sheep, usually under one-year-old, known as a lamb. The passage above from the HB (OT) Book of Exodus serves as the foundation text for the annual Jewish celebration of Passover, an eight-day remembrance of the exodus of the Hebrews from slavery in Egypt.

Sheep

The sheep is a sacrificial animal. In order to fulfill the LORD's instruction that the firstborn of the Israelites' livestock that are males belong to him, a firstborn donkey is redeemed with a sheep (cf. Exod 13:12–13) or with a lamb (cf. Exod 34:19). The sheep is sacrificed on an altar of earth (cf. Exod

20:24). The HB (OT) Book of Leviticus gives detailed directions about a burnt offering from the flock of sheep, namely, it shall be a male without blemish (cf. Lev 1:10). A sacrifice of well-being consists of a sheep, male or female, upon which the offerer has laid his hands on its head. Then, it is slaughtered, its blood is dashed against the sides of the altar, and the rest of it is burned on the altar (cf. Lev 3:6–11). A sin offering consists of a female sheep without blemish that is treated in exactly the same way as a sacrifice of well-being (cf. Lev 4:32–35). For perjury, uncleanness, or oath-taking, a female sheep is offered; however, if one cannot afford a sheep, two turtledoves or pigeons can serve as a substitute (cf. Lev 5:1–10). A male sheep without blemish is offered in fulfillment of a vow or as a freewill offering (cf. Lev 22:21).

God instructs Moses to divide the booty of war so that he gets one out of every five hundred sheep given to warriors, and the Levities get one out of every fifty sheep given to the Israelites (cf. Num 31:28–30). After Adonijah, one of David's sons, proclaims himself to be king while his father is still alive, he celebrates his coronation by sacrificing sheep (cf. 1 Kgs 1:9, 19, 25); he is, of course, deposed by his brother Solomon, who builds the temple and brings the ark of the LORD from the tent his father, David, had prepared for it, all the while "sacrificing so many sheep . . . that they could not be counted or numbered" (1 Kgs 8:5; 2 Chr 5:6). Later, Solomon offers 120,000 sheep as sacrifices of well-being (cf. 1 Kgs 8:63; 2 Chr 7:5). Other sheep-booty offered to God include seven thousand sheep (cf. 2 Chr 15:11). Under King Hezekiah's reforms, burnt offerings included two hundred lambs, and consecrated offerings included three thousand sheep (cf. 2 Chr 29:32–33). For the festival of unleavened bread, the chronicler records that King Hezekiah gave the assembly seven thousand sheep, and the officials gave the assembly ten thousand sheep (cf. 2 Chr 30:24).

The Analects of Confucius also mention the sheep as a sacrificial animal. In book 3, "Tzu-kung wanted to do away with the presentation of a sacrificial sheep at the announcement of each new moon. The Master said, Ssu! You grudge sheep, but I grudge ritual" (*Analects* 3:17). Tzu-kung wants to do away with the ritual that announces to the ancestors the beginning of each new month; the announcement is accompanied by a sacrificial sheep. Tzu-kung does not think the sacrifice of a sheep is necessary. Confucius, the Master, teaches that the ritual code prevails. According to Taylor, "Since the basis of ritual is to be found in the practices of the sages of antiquity, and since these sages represent the ultimate paradigm of moral reflection and activity, the details of ritual encapsulate their informed moral guidance and must be viewed as authoritative."[1] Thus, if the ritual code requires the sacrifice of a sheep, it is to be made.

Biblically, the firstborn of sheep belongs to God (cf. Lev 27:26; 18:17). However, after a sheep is born, it stays with its mother for seven days; on the eighth day it is given to God (cf. Exod 22:30) as an offering by fire (cf. Lev 22:27). No sheep that has any kind of a defect can serve as a sacrifice (cf. Deut 17:1); it must be without blemish.

Besides serving as a sacrifice, sheep, including mountain sheep, were considered as clean animals and could be eaten by the Israelites (cf. Deut 14:4). So, for example, Abigail brings "five sheep ready dressed" (1 Sam 25:18), among other foodstuffs, to feed David and his men. King Solomon's royal provisions included one hundred sheep every day (cf. 1 Kgs 4:23), while Nehemiah states that six choice sheep (cf. Neh 5:18) were prepared, among other foods, to feed those who ate at his table. Even *The Quran* declares that specific parts of sheep are acceptable as food (cf. *Quran* 6:143, 146), and *Mormon* states that sheep are used for food (cf. Ether 9:18).

Before a sheep could be eaten it had to be slaughtered. The prophet Isaiah mentions slaughtering sheep (cf. Isa 22:13), as does the prophet Jeremiah, when he asks God to take revenge on his enemies: "Pull them out like sheep for the slaughter, and set them apart for the day of slaughter" (Jer 12:3b). God tells the prophet Ezekiel to tell Israel's shepherds that they clothe themselves with the wool of the sheep they slaughter, but they do not feed the flock (cf. Ezek 34:3). Isaiah's words about a suffering servant of God are applied in the Acts of the Apostles; Philip explains to an Ethiopian eunuch that the words "Like a sheep he was led to the slaughter, and like a lamb silent before its shearer, so he does not open his mouth" (Acts 8:32) aptly describe Jesus. Quoting Psalm 44:22 in his Letter to the Romans, Paul writes that followers of Jesus are accounted as sheep to be slaughtered (cf. Rom 8:36).

Besides being a source of food, sheep are also a source of clothing. Once they are sheared the fleece can be turned into wool, and the wool can be woven into cloth. Sheepshearers are mentioned in the HB (OT) (cf. Gen 38:13; 1 Sam 25:2, 4). Usually, as Isaiah states, the sheep before its shearers is silent (cf. Isa 53:7b). The levitical priests are given, among other things, "the first of the fleece of [the] sheep" as part of their support by the Israelites (Deut 18:4). In one of his speeches, Job states he has never seen a poor person without clothing who was not warmed with the fleece of his sheep (cf. Job 31:20).

---

1. Taylor, "Of Animals and Humans," 295.

Sheep (Ram, Ewe, Lamb)

In the CB (NT), Jesus warns his disciples about false prophets, "who come . . . in sheep's clothing but inwardly are ravenous wolves" (Matt 7:15), as does the Third Book of Nephi in *Mormon* (cf. 3 Ne 14:15).

Aesop narrates a fable about "The Pig and the Sheep." After a pig wanders into a meadow where a flock of sheep are grazing, the shepherd catches him and carries him off to the butcher shop while he squeals and struggles to get away. The sheep rebuke him for making such a scene, saying, "The shepherd catches us regularly and drags us off just like that, and we don't make any fuss."[2] The pig points out that his case and the sheep's case are quite different. "He only wants you for wool, but he wants me for bacon," states the pig.[3]

Sheep's fleece is also mentioned in many of the hymns in *The Rig Veda*, usually serving as a type of primitive strainer or sieve for the sacred soma juice. For example, hymn 69 of book 9 states that the "soma passed through the sheep's fair bright fleece, and has, as 'twere, endued a garment newly washed" (*RV* 9:69:4). In the same book, the next hymn portrays soma as a royal official seated on a throne with "the sheepskin [as] his ornament" (*RV* 9:70:7). Later, the soma is said to flow "through the long wool of the sheep" (*RV* 9:74:9), that is, through "the fine fleece of the sheep [the soma is] cleansed" (*RV* 9:86:47). Repeatedly the phrase "long wool of the sheep" appears in these Hindu hymns (cf. *RV* 9:103:2–3; 9:106:10; 9:107:9; 9:108:5, etc.). One hymn also mentions "weaving the raiment of the sheep and making raiment beautiful," that is, making woolen cloth (*RV* 10:26:6).

Sheep need a shepherd. The Bible names Abel as a keeper of sheep (cf. Gen 4:2); he is followed by other shepherds. The narrator of the Book of Exodus states that "Moses was keeping the flock of his father-in-law Jethro; he led his flock beyond the wilderness, and came to Horeb, the mountain of God" (Exod 3:1). David, before he became king of Israel and Judah, was a keeper of sheep (cf. 1 Sam 16:11, 19; 17:15, 20; 2 Sam 7:8; 1 Chr 17:7). The prophet Isaiah says that God "will feed his flock like a shepherd; he will gather the lambs in his arms, and carry them in his bosom, and gently lead the mother sheep" (Isa 40:11). Ezekiel adds to the image of God as a shepherd, writing that "as shepherds seek out their flocks when they are among their scattered sheep, so [God] will seek out [his] sheep. [He] will rescue them from all the places to where they have been scattered . . ." (Ezek 34:12). In the CB (NT) the author of John's Gospel describes Jesus as being the good shepherd (cf. John 10:11, 15). The Letter to the Hebrews calls Jesus "the great shepherd of the sheep" (Heb 13:20).

---

2. Aesop, 171.
3. Ibid.

One aspect of the shepherd that is found only in John's Gospel is how sheep respond to the shepherd, who is usually considered a man but may be a woman (cf. Gen 29:6, 9). The Johannine Jesus tells his disciples that "the sheep hear [the shepherd's] voice" (John 10:3). He continues, "He calls his own sheep by name, and leads them out. When he has brought out all his own, he goes ahead of them, and the sheep follow him because they know his voice. They will not follow a stranger, but they will run from him because they do not know the voice of strangers" (John 10:3–5). Later, Jesus adds, "My sheep hear my voice. I know them, and they follow me" (John 10:27). Likewise, in *Mormon*, Jesus says, ". . . You have . . . heard my voice, . . . and you are my sheep . . ." (3 Ne 15:24). Also, God tells his servant Alma to gather together his sheep. "And he that will hear my voice shall be my sheep" (Mosiah 26:21).

Only John's Gospel in the CB (NT) mentions a sheepfold (cf. John 10:1), an enclosure or shelter for sheep, like a cave. Comparable to what most people think of as a pen attached to a shed, folds for sheep (cf. Num 32:36) are some of the first things built by the Israelites once they conquered the promised land. The prophet Micah portrays God telling the Jewish exiles returning from Babylon that he "will gather the survivors of Israel; [he] will set them together like sheep in a fold, like a flock in its pasture" (Mic 2:12). Also, in *Mormon*, mention is made of the sheepfold (cf. 1 Ne 22:25; 3 Ne 15:17), as there is in the *Book of Doctrine and Covenants* (cf. D&C 3:14).

A shepherd is responsible for separating sheep when they are driven into the sheepfold. Sometimes rams are separated from ewes, the sick are separated from the healthy, the ewes nearing the birth of a lamb are separated from the rest of flock. The prophet Ezekiel uses this image to portray God as judge. "As for you, my flock, thus says the Lord GOD: I shall judge between sheep and sheep, between rams and goats. I myself will judge between the fat sheep and the lean sheep" (Ezek 34:17, 20; cf. 34:22). This application is employed by the author of Matthew's Gospel in the CB (NT) in an analogy about judgment. "When the Son of Man comes in his glory, . . . he will separate people one from another as a shepherd separates the sheep from the goats, and he will put the sheep at his right hand and the goats at his left" (Matt 25:31, 32b–33).

If there is no sheepfold, the sheep wander, stray, or scatter. The HB (OT) mentions repeatedly what happens to sheep without a shepherd: they stray. Before his own death, Moses asks the LORD to "appoint someone over the congregation [of Israel] who shall go out before them and bring them in, so that the congregation of the LORD may not be like sheep without a shepherd" (Num 27:17–18). One of the commandments in the Book of Deuteronomy states that a person shall not watch his neighbor's sheep straying away and ignore it; he shall take it back to its owner (cf. Deut 22:1). Even though one psalmist considers the LORD to be his shepherd (cf. Ps 23:1), another states that God has made his people like sheep for slaughter, and God has scattered them among the nations (cf. Ps 44:11, 22), and still another psalmist declares that he has "gone astray like a lost sheep" (Ps 119:176). The prophets Isaiah, Jeremiah, and Ezekiel echo the psalmists (cf. Isa 53:6; Jer 23:1, 50:6; Ezek 34:6, 8, 10–12) as does Mosiah 14:6 in *Mormon*. The prophet Zechariah declares that the people wander like sheep, and they suffer for lack of a shepherd (cf. Zech 10:2).

In the CB (NT) the Matthean Jesus says that he is the shepherd "sent only to the lost sheep of the house of Israel" (Matt 15:24; cf. Matt 10:6). Also, Matthew's Gospel, like Luke's Gospel, contains the Q (for Quelle meaning "source") parable of the lost sheep. Jesus says, "If a shepherd has a hundred sheep, and one of them has gone astray, does he not leave the ninety-nine on the mountains and go in search of the one that went astray? And if he finds it, truly I tell you, he rejoices over it more than over the ninety-nine that never went astray" (Matt 18:12–13; cf. Luke 15:4–6). In Mark's Gospel, Jesus tells his disciples, "You will all become deserters; for it is written, 'I will strike the shepherd, and the sheep will be scattered'" (Mark 14:27; cf. Matt 26:31). The quotation, from the prophet Zechariah, is God's judgment on the leaders of Judah, the shepherds of God's people: "Strike the shepherd, that the sheep may be scattered" (Zech 13:7b). The author of Mark's Gospel is equating Jesus' death with the shepherd who is struck in Zechariah. The First Letter of Peter makes this clear, writing, that people were going astray like sheep, but now they have returned to the shepherd and guardian of their souls (cf. 1 Pet 2:25).

Sheep have enemies. When David was serving Saul, he mentions that as a shepherd he had to defend the sheep "whenever a lion or a bear came, and took a lamb from the flock" (1 Sam 17:34). He would track the animal and kill it, thus rescuing the lamb from its mouth. The prophet Micah describes the remnant of the Jews taken to Babylon as "like a lion among the animals of the forest, like a young lion among the flocks of sheep, which, when it goes through, treads down and tears in pieces, with no one to deliver" (Mic 5:8). Jeremiah declares, "Israel is a hunted sheep driven away by lions" (Jer 50:17a). Besides lions and bears, wolves also were enemies of the sheep. The Matthean Jesus tells his disciples that he is sending them "like sheep into the midst of wolves" (Matt 10:16). The author of John's Gospel even describes how the hired hand, who is not the shepherd, "sees the wolf coming and leaves the sheep and runs away—and the wolf snatches them and scatters them" (John 10:12). *The Rig Veda*, too, mentions "the wolf, the savage beast that rends the sheep" (*RV* 8:55:8).

Aesop's Fables contains two stories about enemies of sheep. In "The Wolf and the Sheep," a wolf that had been bitten by dogs, called to a passing sheep, asking for water and telling the sheep that he can get by without meat. "But this sheep was no fool. 'I can quite understand,' said he, 'that if I brought you the water, you would have no difficulty about the meat.'"[4] Thus, the sheep did not bring the wolf any water and continued on his way. In "The Sheep and the Dog," the sheep complain to their shepherd about the unfair treatment they receive in comparison to the dog. "We provide you with wool and lambs and milk and you give us nothing but grass, . . . but you get nothing at all from the dog . . . ,"[5] said the sheep. The dog addressed the sheep, explaining how he keeps them from being stolen by thieves, how he keeps them from being eaten by wolves, and how he keeps them from being terrified so they can graze. The sheep acknowledge the dog's truth and never again make a grievance against their master.

While most people think the sheep are white, the Bible mentions speckled and spotted sheep and black lambs (cf. Gen 30:32). In terms of the sound that sheep make, only the First Book of Samuel mentions the "bleating of sheep" (1 Sam 15:14). The Book of Nehemiah mentions the Sheep Gate in the walls around Jerusalem three times (cf. Neh 3:1; 3:32; 12:39), as does John's Gospel (cf. John 5:2). Presumably, this gate was used to bring sheep into the city. It may have also given rise to the Johannine Jesus' statement that he is the gate for the sheep (cf. John 10:7).

All of these aspects of sheep lead to the comparison of people to sheep, as has already been hinted at above. King David refers to the people he rules as sheep (cf. 2 Sam 24:17; 1 Chr 21:17). The prophet Micaiah tells King Jehoshaphat that he sees "all Israel scattered over the mountains, like sheep that have no shepherd" (1 Kgs 22:17; 2 Chr 18:16). Likewise, in the OT (A) Judith tricks Holofernes, telling him that he will drive the Israelite army like sheep that have no shepherd (cf. Jdt 11:19), before he lures her into his tent and she beheads him. The lamenter in Psalm 44 declares that God has made him and his people "like sheep for slaughter, and [has] scattered [them] among the nations" (Ps 44:11), even though, according to Psalm 78, the same God once led "his people like sheep" out of Egypt "and guided them in the wilderness like a flock" (Ps 78:52). The phrase "sheep of [God's] pasture" (Ps 74:1; cf. Ps 100:3) or "people of his pasture" (Ps 95:7; cf. Ezek 34:31) are used frequently, and, of course, Isaiah writes that the people of Babylon will be "like sheep with no one to gather them" on the day of God's anger (Isa 13:14).

---

4. Ibid., 109.
5. Ibid., 169.

Sheep (Ram, Ewe, Lamb)

The narrator of Mark's Gospel in the CB (NT) employs this comparison, noting that the crowds that followed Jesus "were like sheep without a shepherd" (Mark 6:34). The author of Matthew's Gospel kept that comparison (cf. Matt 9:36) when he copied Mark's Gospel, but the author of John's Gospel used it in a second ending, called the epilogue, to portray Jesus giving Peter the opportunity to undo his three-fold denial by making a three-fold profession of love. After Jesus asks Peter if he loves him and Peter makes his response, Jesus tells him to feed his lambs (cf. John 21:15), to tend his sheep (cf. John 21:16), and to feed his sheep (cf. John 21:17). The three commands compare people to sheep and serve to undo Peter's three-fold denial of Jesus (cf. John 18:17–27).

Sheep represent wealth. One way ancient people calculated their wealth was by the number of sheep they owned (cf. Gen 12:16; 20:14; 21:27). Jacob, son of Isaac, grandson of Abraham, and noted for his genetic engineering, grew exceedingly rich, and had large flocks, according to the Book of Genesis (cf. Gen 30:43). The Book of Numbers calculates that the booty after a battle with the Midianites included 675,000 sheep of which the warriors got 337,500 sheep and the Israelites got 337,500 sheep; the LORD got 675 sheep from the warriors' allotment (cf. Num 31:32–43). King Saul decides to spare the best of the sheep from the LORD's command to kill all of King Agag's sheep (cf. 1 Sam 15:9, 15); however, God is not pleased with Saul's disobedience. After waging war on the Philistines, David took away the sheep (cf. 1 Sam 27:9) because they were valuable to his men. The Second Book of Kings mentions sheep as payment of tribute by King Mesha of Moab to King Ahab of Israel. The narrator states that King Mesha "was a sheep breeder, who used to deliver to the king of Israel one hundred thousand lambs, and the wool of one hundred thousand rams" (2 Kgs 3:4). The First Book of Chronicles states that after a battle the tribes of Israel took 250,000 sheep from their enemy (cf. 1 Chr 5:21).

Job's wealth was measured in sheep, among other animals. He possessed seven thousand sheep (cf. Job 1:3) before he was tested, and once he was restored, he owned fourteen thousand sheep (cf. Job 42:12). The singer of Psalm 144 asks God to let his "sheep increase by thousands, by tens of thousands in [the] fields" (Ps 144:13b). Even so, Jesus reminds his listeners that a human being is much more valuable than a sheep (cf. Matt 12:12).

Because sheep are valuable, the Book of Exodus stipulates the penalties for sheep-stealing. For example, the person who steals and then sells or slaughters a sheep is to make restitution of four sheep (cf. Exod 22:1). If the stolen sheep is found alive, then the restitution is only two sheep (cf. Exod 22:4). If a dispute arises over the ownership of a sheep, God in the person of a judge decides who owns the sheep, and the other claimant pays two sheep to the determined owner (cf. Exod 22:9). Other restitution laws concerning sheep can be found in other books of the Torah.

In *The Analects of Confucius* there is a story that illustrates how sheep represent wealth.

> The "Duke" of She addressed Master Kung saying, In my country there was a man called Upright Kung. His father appropriated a sheep, and Kung bore witness against him. Master Kung said, In my country the upright men are of quite another sort. A father will screen his son, and a son his father—which incidentally does involve a sort of uprightness. (*Analects* 13:18)

Upright Kung was a legendary paragon of honesty. After his father stole a sheep, his son turned him in to the authorities because a sheep was of considerable value. Confucius argues that both father and son should keep each other upright; then there would be no sheep-stealing. In other words, there should be reciprocity among those who are righteous.

The Rig Veda, too, considers sheep a sign of wealth. One hymn asks the god Agni to assure that his devotees will be "rich in . . . sheep" (*RV* 4:2:5). Another hymn mentions "hundreds of sheep" (*RV* 5:61:5), and another mentions "a hundred head of fleecy sheep" (*RV* 8:100:3/Valakhilya 8:3).

Aesop narrates a fable about a smart sheep in "The Sheep, the Wolf, and the Stag." After a stag asks a sheep to lend him a measure of wheat, telling her that his friend the wolf would be his surety, the sheep, being afraid, denied his request, saying, "The wolf is in the habit of seizing what he wants and running off it with it without paying, and you, too can run much faster than I. So how shall I be able to come up with either of you when the debt falls due?"[6] The smartness of the sheep in the fable is contrasted sharply with that of the usual stereotype of sheep as dumb.

Ram

The generic noun "sheep" gets specified in some texts. One of those specifications is the ram, a male sheep. "[A] ram three years old" (Gen 15:9) is specified in the covenant-making ceremony between God and Abraham. The ram represents the power of generation, fertility, Abraham's future. The fact that it is to be three years old indicates that it, along with the other two three-year-old animals, signifies a theophany, an appearance of God as fire. Likewise, when Abraham was ready to sacrifice his son, Isaac, he spies a ram, caught in bushes by its horns, and he takes the ram and offers it to God

---

6. Ibid., 97.

as a burnt sacrifice instead of his son (cf. Gen 22:13). In both accounts, the sacrifice of the ram indicates Abraham's submission to God in terms of his future.

The two rams featured in the account of the consecration of Aaron and his sons as priests represent the submission to God of the power to generate. On the head of one ram Aaron and his sons lay their hands, after which the ram is slaughtered, its blood is dashed on all sides of the altar, and its carcass is turned into a burnt offering to the LORD (cf. Exod 29:15-18). The second ram suffers the same fate as the first, except its blood is put on the right lobe of the ear of Aaron and his sons, on the thumb of their right hand, and the big toe on their right foot. Because the right side is the position of power and the ram represents power, when Aaron and his sons are anointed with the blood on their right ears, thumbs, and feet, they are given the power to be priests of the LORD (cf. Exod 29:19-20; Lev 8:18-25).

The power of the ram is further emphasized in the story about Balaam who is brought by Balak to curse the Israelites, and, instead, he ends up blessing them. Before doing anything, Balaam instructs Balak that seven altars are to be erected and seven rams are to be prepared (cf. Num 23:1). After the seven rams are offered, Balaam consults God, who tells him not to curse the Israelites. Two more times this ritual of slaughtering a ram on seven altars is repeated, and each time God tells Balaam that he is to bless Israel instead of cursing his people (cf. Num 23:1-24:1). Thus, the offering of the seven rams secures Israel's future.

The HB (OT) Book of Leviticus makes clear that a sacrificed ram without blemish serves as a guilt offering (cf. Lev 5:15-16), that a ram without blemish serves to remove the guilt associated with a trespass against the LORD (cf. Lev 56:1-7), that a ram serves as a burnt offering (cf. Lev 9:2), that a ram serves as a sacrifice of well-being (cf. Lev 9:18-19), that a ram for a burnt offering must be brought by Aaron when he enters the sanctuary (cf. Lev 16:3, 5), and that a man who has sexual relations with a slave must present a guilt offering of a ram to the LORD (cf. Lev 19:21, 22). In all these scenarios, the ram represents the sacrifice of power and generativity and submission to God.

The HB (OT) Book of Numbers also lists a ram among the other sheep to be offered when nazirites, men and women who offered themselves in service to God for a specific time, are to be consecrated. Standing at the entrance of the tent of meeting, "they ... offer their gift to the LORD, one male lamb a year old without blemish as a burnt offering, one ewe lamb a year old without blemish as a sin offering, [and] one ram without blemish as an offering of well-being" (Num 6:14, cf. 6:17). The offering of the lambs and the ram indicate the total submission of their future lives from this point forward as servants of God.

According to the Book of Numbers on each day of the twelve-day celebration of the dedication of the tabernacle "one ram [and] one male lamb a year old for a burnt offering" and "for the sacrifice of well-being, . . . five rams, . . . and five male lambs a year old" are presented by each of the tribes of Israel (Num 7:15, 17, 21, 23, 27, 29, 33, 35, 39, 41, 45, 47, 51, 53, 57, 59, 63, 65, 69, 71, 75, 77, 81, 83). Thus, the livestock for the dedication consisted of twelve rams and twelve male lambs a year old for the burnt offering (cf. Num 7:87) and sixty rams and sixty male lambs a year old for the sacrifice of well being (cf. Num 7:88). Every month of the Israelite year was also dedicated with a burnt offering of a ram and seven male lambs a year old without blemish (cf. Num 28:11). There are other biblical references indicating when a ram was to be sacrificed (cf. Ezra 10:19; Ezek 43:23, 25; 45:23; 46:4–6).

Besides serving as sacrifices, rams also served as food. It could be boiled (cf. Exod 29:31; Num 6:19) or roasted (cf. Tob7:9). Only the HB (OT) Book of Joshua mentions "seven priests bearing seven trumpets of rams' horns" (Josh 6:4), each one making "a long blast with the ram's horn" (Josh 6:5), until the walls of Jericho fell. Today this musical instrument used for religious purposes is known as a shofar.

One of *Aesop's Fables* features a wise ram. In "The Wolves, the Sheep, and the Ram," the wolves send a deputation to the sheep with a proposal of lasting peace, if the sheep give up the sheep dogs to death. After the foolish sheep agree to the terms, "an old ram, whose years had brought him wisdom, interfered and said, 'How can we expect to live at peace with you? Why, even with the dogs at hand to protect us, we are never secure from your murderous attacks.'"[7]

Ewe

Besides the specific male sheep or ram, the generic noun "sheep" also gets specified as a ewe, a female sheep. The ewe has already been mentioned above in some texts; while the ram is usually the sacrificial animal, in some cases the ewe is mentioned as the sacrificial animal. For example, the HB (OT) Book of Leviticus stipulates that one ewe lamb in its first year without blemish (cf. Lev 14:10) serves as part of the offering by a cleansed leper on the eighth day after he becomes clean. For the consecration of a nazirite, one who has dedicated himself or herself to God for a special service, one ewe lamb a year old without blemish is offered as a sin offering (cf. Num 6:14).

7. Ibid., 189.

Ewe lambs were used in the covenant-making ceremony between Abraham and Abimelech, a Canaanite king, in the HB (OT) Book of Genesis. "Abraham set apart seven ewe lambs of the flock" (Gen 21:28) to give to Abimelech in exchange for his acknowledgment that Abraham had dug a certain well from which to draw water for his flocks (cf. Gen 21:29–30).

One of the more famous biblical stories employing a ewe lamb is the one narrated by Nathan, one of the King David's prophets. The LORD sends Nathan to David, and Nathan tells a story to David:

> There were two men in a certain city, the one rich and the other poor. The rich man had very many flocks and herds; but the poor man had nothing but one little ewe lamb, which he had bought. He brought it up, and it grew up with him and with his children; it used to eat of his meager fare, and drink from his cup, and lie in his bosom, and it was like a daughter to him. Now there came a traveler to the rich man, and he was loath to take one of his own flock or herd to prepare for the wayfarer who had come to him, but he took the poor man's lamb, and prepared that for the guest who had come to him. (2 Sam 12:1b–4)

As the narrator makes clear, the story is an analogy, which Nathan applies to David in light of the king's action of taking Uriah the Hittite's wife (Bathsheba) and having Uriah placed on the front line of battle so that he is killed (cf. 2 Sam 12:5–15) once David discovers that Bathsheba is pregnant.

The Quran presents another story about a ewe that illustrates David's wisdom and judgment in legal matters. Allah asks the reader,

> Have you heard of the litigants who jumped over the wall into [David's] chamber? When they came before David, he was frightened of them. "Do not be afraid," they said. "The two of us are disputing the wrong one has done the other. So judge between us with equity, and do not be unjust, and guide us to the right path. This man here is my brother. He has ninety and nine ewes while I have only one. He demands that I should give him my ewe, and wants to get the better of me in argument." (David) said: "He is unjust in demanding your ewe to add to his (many) ewes. Many partners are surely unjust to one another, except those who believe and do the right; but there are only a few of them." It occurred to David that he was being tried by us, and he begged his Lord to forgive him, and fell down in homage and repented. So we forgave him. He has surely a high rank with us and an excellent place of return. "O David, we have made you trustee on the earth. So judge between men equitably, and do

not follow your lust lest it should lead you astray from the way of God." (*Quran* 38:21–26b)

Thus, the story uses one ewe lamb to demonstrate both David's wisdom and the selfish wealth of the brother who owned ninety-nine ewe lambs.

Lamb

Besides the specific male sheep or ram and the female sheep or ewe, the generic noun "sheep" also gets specified as a generic lamb, which can refer to a young sheep, especially one under a year old. A lamb is gentle, innocent, and very vulnerable, and evokes emotions such as those illustrated in the two stories above about ewe lambs. Lambs have already been mentioned above in many texts, especially the one that appears at the beginning of this section in reference to Passover. However, before Passover is instituted, astute Isaac, before he is about to be tied and prepared for sacrifice, asks his father, Abraham, "The fire and the wood are here, but where is the lamb for a burnt offering?" (Gen 22:7) Abraham replies that God will provide the lamb for the burnt offering.

In the directions for dedicating the altar in the HB (OT) Book of Exodus, God instructs Moses to offer two lambs a year old (cf. Gen 29:38) every day, one in the morning and one in the evening (cf. Num 28:1–8). One-year-old lambs without blemish regularly serve as burnt offerings (cf. Lev 9:3; 12:6; 14:10; 23:12; Num 6:14; 7:15, 21, 27, 33, 39, 45, 51, 57, 63, 69, 75, 81; 15:5; 28:14; Ezek 46:13) and well-being sacrifices (cf. Num 7:17, 23, 29, 35, 41, 47, 53, 59, 65, 71, 77, 83). In fulfillment of the commandment to redeem the first born, a lamb redeems a first-born donkey (cf. Exod 34:20). Following in the path of Moses, the prophet Samuel is portrayed in the First Book of Samuel as an intercessor for the Israelites before God. When preparing for war with the Philistines, the people ask Samuel to cry out to the LORD, asking that he save them from their enemy. The narrator of the account states that "Samuel took a suckling lamb and offered it as a whole burnt offering to the Lord" (1 Sam 7:9a). This deed is remembered in the OT (A) Book of Sirach (cf. Sir 46:16).

Besides serving as sacrifices, lambs were slaughtered for food (cf. Isa 53:7; Jer 11:19; Acts 8:32). The institution of the feast of Passover begins with God telling Moses to explain to the Hebrews that they are to take a lamb for each family, a lamb for each household (cf. Exod 12:3). The lamb is to be without blemish, a year-old male (cf. Exod 12:5). It is to be slaughtered at twilight (cf. Exod 12:6) and to be eaten roasted over a fire (cf. Exod 12:8). This lamb for food is given another meaning, however. Its blood, sprinkled on doorposts and lintels, will mark the houses which God will pass over when he comes to destroy the firstborn of the Egyptians. Thus, the lamb not only serves as food, but its blood represents salvation. It becomes a yearly ritual for the Hebrews, Israelites, and Jews (cf. 2 Chr 30:15, 17; 35:1, 6, 11, 13; Ezra 6:19–20) until the destruction of the second Temple in 70 CE.

In Mark's Gospel (cf. Mark 14:12), Matthew's Gospel (cf. Matt 26:16), and Luke's Gospel (cf. Luke 22:7), Jesus of Nazareth eats the Passover lamb with his disciples. However, in John's Gospel, Jesus replaces the Passover lamb with himself. Twice he is referred to as the "Lamb of God" (John 1:29, 36), and he dies on the day of preparation for the Passover (cf. John 19:14, 31, 42), sometime between noon (cf. John 19:14) and before sunset when that Sabbath-Passover began. The Johannine narrator notes that Jesus' legs are not broken (as are those of the other two co-crucified criminals) because he is already dead. The narrator understands this to allude to several HB (OT) passages about not breaking the legs of the Passover lamb (cf. John 19:36; Exod 12:46; Num 9:12; Ps 34:21). Before this well-explained Johannine concept of Jesus replacing the Passover lamb with himself, Paul had declared that the "paschal lamb, Christ, [had] been sacrificed" (1 Cor 5:7). Later, the First Letter of Peter declares that people have been ransomed with the precious blood of Christ, like that of a lamb without defect or blemish (cf. 1 Pet 1:19).

Repeatedly, the author of the CB (NT) Book of Revelation refers to Jesus as "a Lamb standing as if it had been slaughtered" (Rev 5:6). In John of Patmos's visions, many are heard singing, "Worthy is the Lamb that was slaughtered . . ." (Rev 5:12), giving glory to the Lamb (cf. Rev 5:13). The Lamb opens the seals on the scroll held in the right hand of the one seated on the throne, that is, God (cf. Rev 6:1, 3, 5, 7, 9, 12; 8:1). Those who have been martyred for their faith are described as those who "have washed their robes and made them white in the blood of the Lamb" (Rev 7:14; cf. 12:11). It is "the Lamb at the center of the throne [who is] their shepherd" (Rev 7:17a). Those whose names are not "written . . . in the book of life of the Lamb that was slaughtered" (Rev 13:8) worship the beast; they are tormented "in the presence of the Lamb" (Rev 14:10). They "make war on the Lamb, and the Lamb will conquer them, for he is Lord of lords and King of kings" (Rev 17:14).

In another vision, John of Patmos sees "the Lamb standing on Mount Zion" (Rev 14:1). His warriors "follow the Lamb wherever he goes" (Rev 14:4). These are they who conquer the beast and sing "the song of the Lamb" (Rev 15:3). The Lamb marries them (cf. Rev 19:17b): "Blessed are those who are invited to the marriage supper of the Lamb" (Rev 19:9a). They are "the bride, the wife of the Lamb" (Rev 21:9b), living in the city whose walls have "twelve foundations, and on them are the twelve names of the twelve apostles of the Lamb" (Rev 21:14). The temple in the city is the Lamb, illumined by the lamp of the Lamb (cf. Rev 21:22–23). These citizens have their names "written in the Lamb's book of life" (Rev 21:27).

Mormon repeatedly refers to Jesus as the Lamb (cf. 1 Ne 13:29, 33, 35, 36), the Lamb of God (cf. 1 Ne 13:33, 34; 14:1, 2), the twelve apostles of the Lamb (cf. 1 Ne 13:24, 26, 39, 40), the gospel of the Lamb (cf. 1 Ne 13:26, 29, 32, 34), the book of the Lamb (cf. 1 Ne 13:28, 38), the power of the Lamb (1 Ne 13:35, 39), the kingdom of the Lamb (cf. 1 Ne 13:37), the mouth of the Lamb (cf. 1 Ne 13:41), the church of the Lamb (cf. 1 Ne 14:14), and the truth which is in the Lamb (cf. 1 Ne 14:26). According to *Mormon*, "the Lamb of God is the Son of the Eternal Father, and the Savior of the world" (1 Ne 13:40). There is but "one God and one Shepherd over all the earth" (1 Ne 13:41).

According to the *Book of Doctrine and Covenants*, at the end of the world when the graves of the saints are opened, they will "stand on the right hand of the Lamb" and "sing the song of the Lamb, day and night forever and ever" (*D&C* 108:15). The influence of the Book of Revelation from the CB (NT) is obvious. Further influence from Revelation can be found in references to "the supper of the Lamb" (*D&C* 65:1), "the marriage of the Lamb" (*D&C* 58:3), "the glory of the Lamb, who was slain" (*D&C* 76:4), the throne of the Lamb (cf. *D&C* 86:35), giving glory to God and the Lamb (cf. *D&C* 76:21; 124:8), and being "in the presence of the Lamb" (*D&C* 108:10).

Lambs have enemies. Before he became king, David explained to King Saul that lions and bears are enemies of lambs. If the lion or bear took a lamb from the flock, David says that he went after it and struck it down, rescuing the lamb from its mouth (cf. 1 Sam 17:34–35). The OT (A) Book of Sirach identifies the wolf as the enemy of the lamb (Sir 13:17). In Isaiah's ideal world of peace, the wolf would live with the lamb (cf. Isa 11:6a), and the wolf and the lamb would feed together (cf. Isa 65:25a).

Aesop narrates two fables about wolves and lambs. In "The Wolf and the Lamb," a wolf spies a lamb straying from the flock, but feels guilty "about taking a life of so helpless a creature without some plausible excuse."[8] So, the wolf tells the lamb that he was insulted by the lamb's remarks the previous year. The lamb bleats, "That is impossible, sir, for I wasn't born then."[9] So, the wolf tries again, telling the lamb that it feeds in his pastures, but the lamb replies that it has not yet tasted grass. So, for the third time, the wolf tells the lamb that it drinks from his spring. The lamb replies that all it drinks is its

---

8. Ibid., 9.
9. Ibid.

mother's milk. After his three-time attempt to find a reason to kill the lamb and not being able to do so, the wolf, nevertheless, decides not to go without dinner. He "sprang upon the lamb and devoured it without more ado."[10]

In "The Lamb Chased by a Wolf," the wolf is pursuing a lamb, which takes refuge in a temple. The wolf urges the lamb to come out of the temple, saying, "If you don't, the priest is sure to catch you and offer you up in sacrifice on the altar."[11] The lamb tells the wolf that he has better odds staying where he is and risking being sacrificed than emerging from the temple and risking being eaten by the wolf.

In most texts, the lamb is black (cf. Gen 30:32, 35), brown, or white. A white lamb is the epitome of innocence, as seen in "The Lambkin and the Little Fish," one of *Grimm's Fairy Tales*. As the story unfolds, a little boy and a little girl are not treated kindly by their step-mother, who bewitches them, changing the little boy into a fish and the little girl into a lamb. The fish swam sadly in a pond, while the "lambkin walked up and down the meadow, and was miserable, and could not eat or touch one blade of grass."[12] When visitors came to the castle where the evil step-mother lived, she told the cook to "fetch the lamb from the meadow and kill it."[13] The cook got the lamb, took it to the kitchen, and tied its feet. "When he had drawn out his knife and was whetting it on the doorstep to kill the lamb, he noticed a little fish swimming backwards and forward in the water in front of the kitchen sink and looking up at him."[14] The lamb addressed the fish, and the fish responded. "When the cook heard that the lambkin could speak and said such sad words to the fish down below, he was terrified and thought this could be no common lamb, but must be bewitched by the wicked woman in the house."[15] The cook promised to spare the lamb, and he got another sheep and prepared it for the guests. He took the lamb to a good peasant woman, who in turn took the lamb and the fish to a wise woman. The wise woman blessed the lambkin and the fish, and they regained their human form. They went to live in a little hut in a great forest where they were content and happy.

Thus, sheep—rams, ewes, and lambs—are used for sacrifices of all kinds. They are food for ancient people, as well as means for counting wealth. Their fleece is sheared, spun into wool, and used to make clothing and other goods. Sheep, no matter if they are rams, ewes, or lambs, need a

10. Ibid.
11. Ibid., 139.
12. Grimm, 267.
13. Ibid., 267.
14. Ibid., 267–68.
15. Ibid., 268.

shepherd, who leads them to a sheepfold both to keep them from straying or scattering and to protect them from enemies, such as the lion and the wolf. Because sheep are so plentiful, the terms used to describe them become metaphors for people, who are like sheep without a shepherd, that is, they need to be gathered, led, fed, and watered. Whereas God was shepherd of his sheep-people in the HB (OT), Jesus becomes the good shepherd and the Lamb of God in the CB (NT). He is the one who gave his life for the sheep, that is, the lamb which provides the perfect sacrifice or the perfect Passover.

Journal/Meditation: What sheep products do you enjoy: meat (mutton, leg of lamb, rack of lamb, etc), cheese, milk, butter, clothing (wool)? Which of the following metaphors, taken from sheep language, echoes within you: like a lamb led to the slaughter; like a sheep before the shearer; like sheep that scatter; like sheep without a shepherd, like a wolf in sheep's clothing?

Prayer: Eternal Shepherd-God, you made people to be the sheep of your pastoral world, and you sent them the Good Shepherd to bring back to the sheepfold those who stray. Keep me safe from all my enemies and clothe me in the wool of your grace. Lead me to the pastures of eternal life, where you live and reign with your Son, Jesus Christ, and the Holy Spirit, one God, forever and ever. Amen.

Tadpole (Frog)

Text: "Once upon a time the sun was about to take to himself a wife. The frogs in terror all raised their voices to the skies, and Jupiter, disturbed by the noise, asked them what they were croaking about. They replied, 'The sun is bad enough even while he is single, drying up our marshes with his heat as he does. But what will become of us if he marries and begets other suns?'"[1]

Reflection: The above tale, titled "The Frogs' Complaint against the Sun," from *Aesop's Fables* does not mention tadpoles, but certainly hints at it by suggesting that the sun dries up marshes, in which frogs lay their eggs and hatch into tadpoles. Such larvae usually have oval bodies and long, vertically flattened tails. At this stage of development, tadpoles are totally aquatic. They lack eyelids and have cartilaginous skeletons, lateral line systems, external gills that turn into internal gills for respiration, and vertically flattened tails used for swimming in the water in the marshes.

As soon as the frog's egg hatches and the tadpole emerges, it begins metamorphosis. Lungs begin to develop, and the gills begin to disappear. Front legs emerge. The internal parts change from that of a herbivore to that of a predator. Hearing and vision becomes more acute. The skin becomes thicker. Gradually the tail disappears, and rear legs emerge. It is not long until the aquatic creature also becomes a terrestrial creature. *The Rig Veda* states that "every limb [of the frog] seems to be growing larger" (*RV* 7:103:5b). The metamorphosis is complete in about twelve weeks; by sixteen weeks what had been a tadpole has become a croaking, adult frog, representative of life in the water (cf. *RV* 10:16:14). Kassam says that the frog, which is both aquatic and a land animal, is best suited constantly to sing God's praises.[2]

1. Aesop, 29.
2. Cf. Kassam, "Animals Versus Man," 165.

In Hinduism's *The Rig Veda*, book 7 contains an entire hymn dedicated to frogs. While it serves as a satire on Hindu priests, it adequately describes the croaking of frogs. "The frogs have lifted up their voice, the voice Parjanya has inspired," states verse 1 (*RV* 7:103:1b); Parjanya means "rain" or "raincloud." "The music of the frogs comes forth in concert," continues the hymn (*RV* 7:103:2b); they seem to "converse with eloquence on the waters" (*RV* 7:103:5b), "when one of these repeats the other's language" (*RV* 7:103:5a). The sound they make is described as "cow-bellow and goat-bleat" (*RV* 7:103:6a, 10a), when they "combine their voices" (*RV* 7:103:4b). While talking, they "modulate the voice diversely" (*RV* 7:103:6b), as they "gather round the pool to honor this day of the year, the first of rain-time" (*RV* 7:103:7b), "as frogs from out the water croak, as frogs from out the water croak" (*RV* 10:166:5).

The Rig Veda also refers to the mating of frogs. "One seeks another as he talks and greets him with cries of pleasure" (*RV* 7:103:3b). "Each of these twain receives the other kindly, while they are reveling in the flow of waters" (*RV* 7:103:4b). Likewise, "[t]he male desires his mate's approach; the frog is eager for the flood" (*RV* 9:112:4). During mating season, the male frog climbs on the back of the female, stimulating her to lay eggs. As she releases eggs in a jelly-like substance in the marsh or pool, the male releases sperm to fertilize them. If they are not eaten by birds or other animals, or if the sun does not dry them, as feared in Aesop's fable above, in seven to nine days they hatch into tadpoles.

This is why *The Rig Veda* states that on the "dry skin [of the frogs] lying in the pool's bed, the floods of heaven descended" (*RV* 7:103:2a), and continues, "[w]hen at the coming of the rains the water has poured upon them as they yearned and thirsted; . . . they are reveling in the flow of waters" (*RV* 7:103:3a, 4a). Not only does the frog's croaking indicate his joy when it rains, but the water also serves as the frog's protection from predators. In "The Hares and the Frogs," Aesop narrates how a group of hares "rushed in a body towards a neighboring pool, intending to drown themselves" in order to escape being prey.[3] "On the bank were sitting a number of frogs, who, when they heard the noise of the hares as they ran, with one accord leaped into the water and hid themselves in the depths."[4]

In "The Mouse, the Frog, and the Hawk," Aesop first reminds the reader that "the frog was equally at home on land or in the water,"[5] after a mouse and a frog agreed to be friends. The frog tied himself to the mouse

---

3. Aesop, 22.
4. Ibid.
5. Ibid., 57.

with thread. With the hawk pursuing them, they came "to the edge of a pool; the frog jumped in, taking the mouse with him, and began swimming about and croaking with pleasure."[6] The mouse drowned and floated on the surface of the pond with the frog tied to him. "The frog was unable to lose the knot which bound him to the mouse, and thus was carried off along with him and eaten by the hawk."[7]

Another of *Aesop's Fables*, "The Two Frogs," echoes the one above. The story begins: "One [frog] lived in a marsh, where there was plenty of water, which frogs love. The other [lived] in a lane some distance away, where all the water to be had was that which lay in the ruts after rain."[8] The frog in the marsh invited the frog in the ruts to come and live with him, but the frog in the ruts refused the invitation. One day a wagon came down the road; the frog in the ruts was crushed to death under the wheels.

"[T]he frog moistened by the rain springs forward," states *The Rig Veda* (*RV* 7:103:4b). As "[s]oon as the rain-time in the year returns," the frogs who had been burned and scorched by the hot weather "gain their freedom" (*RV* 7:103:9). In terms of color, frogs are "green and spotty" (*RV* 7:103:4b; cf. 7:103:10), "one frog is green and one of them is spotty" (*RV* 7:103:6a). The color of frogs' skin led Aesop to narrate a tale about "The Quack Frog." Coming forth from the marshes, a frog proclaimed that he was a physician, skilled in drugs and able to cure diseases. However, the fox asked, ". . . [H]ow can you set up to heal others when you cannot even cure your own lame legs and blotched and wrinkled skin?"[9]

Two stories are about leaping or jumping frogs. A myth from the Native American Lillooet people of the Northwest Coast explains how "three frog sisters refused the advances of Beaver and Snake who came to court them."[10] The story states, "Beaver's disappointed weeping brought on rain. Threatened with a flood, the sisters escaped to the house of the moon. When the moon invited them to warm themselves by the fire, they insisted on sitting on his head. Jumping onto the moon's face, they spoiled his then unblemished beauty, and are still there to this day."[11]

The other account, titled "The Notorious Jumping Frog of Calaveras County" by Mark Twain, begins with a lengthy explanation as to how the author got the story associated with Jim Smiley. Then Twain continues: "He

6. Ibid.
7. Ibid.
8. Ibid., 126.
9. Ibid., 56.
10. Littleton, *Anthology of World Myth*, 496.
11. Ibid.

ketched a frog one day, and took him home and said he cal'lated to educate him; and so he never done nothing for three months but set in his back yard and learn that frog to jump."[12] As the story unravels, Smiley is portrayed as giving the frog a punch from behind to make it jump, and also teaching it how to catch flies. Smiley named the frog Dan'l Webster. Smiley would say, "Flies, Dan'l, flies!" and Webster would "spring straight up and snake a fly off'n the counter there and flop down on the floor ag'in as solid as a gob of mud, and fall to scratching the side of his head with his hind foot as indifferent as if he hand't no idea he'd been doin' any more'n any frog might do."[13] As the tale continues, Twain narrates, "Jumping on a dead level was his strong suit, . . . and when it came to that, Smiley would ante up money on him as long as he had a red."[14]

Smiley kept the frog in a box, and one day a stranger came to town and asked to see the frog. After looking at him, Smiley bet the stranger "forty dollars that he [could] out jump any frog in Calaveras country."[15] The stranger acknowledged that he did not have a frog to take the bet, but Smiley agreed to get one for him. While Smiley was out looking for a frog, the stranger pried open its mouth "and took a teaspoon and filled him full of quail shot."[16] Once Smiley returned with the frog he found in the swamp, the two men set the frogs side by side, touching them from behind to make them jump. The swamp frog jumped high, but Smiley's frog was unable to get off the ground. "Smiley was a good deal surprised, and he was disgusted too, but he didn't have no idea what the matter was, of course."[17] As the stranger was getting ready to leave with the forty dollars, Smiley picked up his frog and discovered how much he weighed. The frog burped out the shot, and Smiley then knew that he had been tricked. The stranger, however, could run faster than Smiley, and Smiley never caught him.

Frogs, like tadpoles, have enemies. In addition to the sun, Aesop names three enemies of frogs and tells a tale about each. In "The Frogs Asking for a King," a group of discontented frogs seeks a king to rule over them. After sending a delegation to Jupiter to honor their request, Jupiter "cast a log into the pool where they lived, and said that that should be their king."[18] At first the frogs were afraid of the log, but gradually they became accustomed to

12. Twain, "Jumping Frog," 161.
13. Ibid., 162.
14. Ibid.
15. Ibid., 163.
16. Ibid.
17. Ibid., 164.
18. Aesop, 62.

it, even sitting upon it. Gradually the frogs began to think that the king was an insult to their dignity, so they asked Jupiter to give them a better king. Jupiter sent a stork to rule the frogs. However, the stork "no sooner arrived among them than he began to catch and eat the frogs as fast as he could."[19] So, the stork is the enemy of frogs.

Another enemy is the ox. In "The Ox and the Frog," an ox walking to the pool of water where little frogs were playing steps on one of them and kills it. When the little frogs get home, one of them tells their mother that "an enormous big creature with four legs came to [the] pool [that] morning and trampled him down in the mud."[20] In order to understand the size of the creature from the little frog, the mother frog puffs herself out three times, getting bigger each time. However, with the third time she bursts.

The third enemy of frogs is mischievous boys, according to Aesop. While playing on the edge of a pond, some boys catch sight "of some frogs swimming about in the shallow water" in "The Boys and the Frogs."[21] The boys "began to amuse themselves by pelting them with stones, and they killed several of them."[22] One frog asked the boys to stop, saying, "[W]hat is sport to you is death to us."[23]

Biblically, the frog is considered to be unclean by the Israelites and, consequently, cannot be eaten because it does not have fins and scales (cf. Lev 11:9–10). This explains the second plague of frogs in the HB (OT) Book of Exodus; it is considered a plague because it violates the boundary between creatures of the water and creatures of the dry land, as established on the day of creation (cf. Gen 1:1–2:3). The LORD tells Moses to tell Pharaoh that he "will plague [the] whole country with frogs. The river shall swarm with frogs; they shall come up into [Pharaoh's] palace, into [his] bedchamber and [his] bed, and into the houses of [his] officials and of [his] people, and into [their] ovens and [their] kneading bowls" (Exod 8:2–3). Aaron stretches out his hand over Egypt, and frogs cover the land. Pharaoh asks Moses to ask the LORD to take away the frogs. Moses asks God to take away the frogs, and the LORD did as Moses requested. The frogs died in the houses, the courtyards, and the fields. The Egyptians gathered them together in heaps (cf. Exod 8:13–14). While the common frog of Egypt mentioned in this account is an edible water frog, the point of the story is the uncleanness visited by God upon the land of Egypt from a Hebrew point of view. This

19. Ibid.
20. Ibid., 81.
21. Ibid., 17.
22. Ibid.
23. Ibid.

is confirmed by the passage in the CB (NT) Book of Revelation in which the narrator states that he "saw three foul spirits like frogs coming from the mouth of the dragon, from the mouth of the beast, and from the mouth of the false prophet" (Rev 16:13). The three foul spirits are part of God's wrath upon all that is unclean, especially ancient Pharaoh and any later, similar types of rulers.

The frog plague is recounted in two Psalms. In recounting tales of his ancestors, the psalmist remembers that the Most High God, the Holy One of Israel, sent among the Egyptians frogs, which destroyed them (cf. Ps 78:45). "Their land swarmed with frogs, even in the chambers of their kings," states Psalm 103 (Ps 103:30). The OT (A) Book of Wisdom also recounts the plague of frogs, namely, how instead of fish the river spewed out vast numbers of frogs (cf. Wis 19:10). Even *The Quran* reflects Allah explaining how he "let loose on [the Egyptians] floods and . . . frogs. But they still remained arrogant . . ." (*Quran* 7:133). Thus did the frogs help "Moses against the Pharaoh."[24]

The most popular account of the transformation of a frog is that found in *Grimm's Complete Fairy Tales* and known as "The Frog Prince." "Long ago, when wishes often came true, there lived a king whose daughters were all handsome, but the youngest was so beautiful that the sun himself, who had seen everything, was bemused every time he shone over her because of her beauty," begins the story.[25] On hot days, the princess would go into the dark wood and sit by a cool well, tossing a golden ball up and down to entertain herself. One day the ball rolled into the well. Not being able to retrieve the ball because the well was deep, she began to weep. But then she heard a voice coming from "a frog stretching his thick ugly head out of the water."[26] The frog agrees to fetch her ball if she would love him, have him for her companion, let him sit by her at table, let him drink from her cup, and let him sleep in her bed. While she agrees with his wishes, she thinks to herself that what he asks is nonsense; he cannot do anything "but sit in the water and croak with the other frogs."[27] So, after getting back her ball, she runs home quickly, not listening to the frog asking her to honor her promises to him.

The next day the frog makes it up the castle's stairs and knocks on the door. While the frog remained outside, the princess told her father what had happened the previous day. The king told his daughter that she must

---

24. Kassam, "Animals Versus Man," 165.
25. Grimm, 1.
26. Ibid.
27. Ibid., 2.

honor the promises she made. "So she went and opened the door, and the frog hopped in, following at her heels, till she reached her chair."[28] He asked her to pick him up and sit him next to her, but she refused until the king ordered her to do so. Once on the chair, the frog jumped onto the table and ate from her plate. When he was finished, he told her to carry him to her room where he would lie down for a nap on her silk bed. She refused, but the king ordered her to fulfill her promises.

After taking him to her room, she put him in a corner and lay on the bed to nap, but the frog told her to put him on the bed beside her or he would tell her father. She picked up the frog and "threw him with all her strength against the wall . . . . But as he fell, he ceased to be a frog, and became all at once a prince with beautiful kind eyes. And it came to pass that, with her father's consent, they became bride and bridegroom."[29] In time, the frog-become-prince told her how a witch had bound him with a spell. After a carriage drawn by eight white horses appeared, they set off for his father's kingdom.

Several notes by Tatar help to understand the story. For example, before the frog was a frog, it was a tadpole. "Frogs are . . . animals that undergo transformations, existing in one form when young, in another when mature," states Tatar.[30] Thus, it should come as no surprise that the prince has been transformed into a frog and needs to be transformed back into a prince. Likewise, the princess needs to be transformed from the self-absorbed, ungrateful, and cruel daughter she is to a modest, obedient, and charitable wife. The princess' father, the king, presents the moral backbone of the story—namely, if one makes a promise, one has to keep it—in order to spark his daughter's transformation. Thus, in a way of looking at the story, the princess is like a tadpole which is transfigured into a frog.

A similar tale appears in Tibetan folk literature. Because it is Buddhist, its focus is on the interpenetrability, that is, oneness and inter-being. The story begins with a frog asking a widow to adopt him as her son, which she does. "Eventually the frog hops away to secure the most beautiful young woman in the area, who happens to be an only child."[31] When the young woman's family balks at such an idea, the frog says, "Human beings, animals, birds, even frogs" are all "of the same spiritual force."[32] The parents try

---

28. Ibid., 3.
29. Ibid.
30. Tatar, *Annotated Fairy Tales*, 117.
31. Kemmerer, *Animals*, 116.
32. Ibid.

to dissuade the frog, but the frog again says, "Can you not see that all beings, human or animal, are the same?"[33]

The frog reverts to a series of deceptive events to demonstrate his powers and convince the parents to let him marry their daughter. The parents give in, but the daughter is still reluctant to enter into "this web-toed marital match."[34] However, "[u]nder her father's instruction, she makes three attempts on the frog's life as they travel from her home toward his. Each time the frog patiently returns her weapon, reminding her 'that we are all one.'"[35] Eventually, the frog wins her over, and "she discovers him to be a handsome young man."[36] Thus, the story not only emphasizes transformation, but also "the oneness of all beings encouraging interspecies compassion.... Whether we are born with frog skin or human skin, we are essentially one."[37] Thus, the frog changed into a handsome man is like a tadpole transformed into a frog with the additional note that the tadpole, the frog, and the man are one, sharing the same being.

Thus, the tadpole that undergoes metamorphosis into a frog represents spiritual transformation. What was swimming in a pool grows legs and crawls out to sit among the marshes and croak. When enemies appear, the frog can leap back into the water. Considered unclean by the Israelites, a lot of frogs represent God's wrath and the cleansing of evil. In many ways, the lifecycle of a frog is like that of the spiritual lifecycle of people, namely, life gives birth to death, which, in turn, gives birth to life. Such ongoing transformation also reminds humankind of the oneness of being of all that exists and of its many spiritual forms.

Journal/Meditation: What is it about the transformation of a tadpole into a frog that most interests you? How does the transformation illustrate the oneness of all being? What spiritual quality of the frog helps you to understand your own spiritual journey better?

Prayer: Holy One, when Pharaoh hardened his heart and would not let your people escape slavery, you sent the plague of frogs to Egypt to demonstrate your power of transformation. Send your Holy Spirit to change my tadpole-like spirituality into a frog-like maturity so that I may be kept safe from my enemies. Hear this prayer in the name of your Son, Jesus Christ, whom you

---

33. Ibid.
34. Ibid., 117.
35. Ibid.
36. Ibid.
37. Ibid.

transfigured from death to life. He lives and reigns with you, Father, and the Holy Spirit, one God, forever and ever. Amen.

Turtle (Tortoise)

Text: "A hare was one day making fun of a tortoise for being so slow upon his feet. 'Wait a bit,' said the tortoise; 'I'll run a race with you, and I'll wager that I win.' 'Oh, well,' replied the hare, who was much amused at the idea, 'let's try and see.' And it was soon agreed that the fox should set a course for them, and be the judge. When the time came, both started off together, but the hare was soon so far ahead that he thought he might as well have a rest. So down he lay and fell fast asleep. Meanwhile the tortoise kept plodding on, and in time reached the goal. At last the hare woke up with a start, and dashed on at his fastest, but only to find that the tortoise had already won the race."[1]

Reflection: Aesop appends a moral to the well-known fable of "The Hare and the Tortoise," namely, "Slow and steady wins the race."[2] However, there is more to the tale than that simple moral. The tortoise is a sign of wisdom; the creature, as illustrated by the fable, represents steadfastness and tranquility, not to mention cleverness. The hare's self-absorbed presumption and arrogance is his downfall, while the tortoise's humble determination is his success.

As if to balance the wisdom illustrated in "The Hare and the Tortoise," Aesop also narrates "The Tortoise and the Eagle." In this account a tortoise is discontented with his lowly life and envious of the eagle, which could fly. The tortoise asks the eagle to teach him to fly, but the eagle reminds the

1. Aesop, 92, 95.
2. Ibid., 95.

tortoise that "nature had not provided him with wings."[3] After promising the eagle treasure and insisting that it was only a question of learning the craft of flying, the eagle consented to teach the tortoise as best as he could. So, the eagle "picked him up in his talons. Soaring with him to a great height in the sky he then let him go, and the wretched tortoise fell headlong and was dashed to pieces on a rock."[4]

A tortoise is a slow-moving land reptile with a large dome-shaped shell into which it can retract its head and limbs. A turtle is a water- or land-dwelling reptile (including the tortoise and terrapin) with a body protected by its bony dome-shaped shell. Because the word "turtle" includes the category of "tortoise," these words will be used interchangeably in this entry. In a simplistic sense, a tortoise has feet with toes, while a turtle has feet with webbed toes. While the turtle appears infrequently in sacred texts, it is present in folklore and creation myths.

One of the best descriptions of the turtle comes from "The Heron and the Turtle," an ancient Sumerian tale that exists only in fragments but has been translated into English. The tale features a narrator, monologues given by the heron and the turtle, and dialogue between the heron and the turtle. It is in one monologue that turtle describes itself:

> [T]he quarrelsome turtle, he of the troublesome way, said: "I am going to pick a quarrel with the heron . . . ! I, whose eyes are snake's eyes, am going to pick a quarrel! I, whose mouth is a snake's mouth, am going to pick a quarrel! I, whose tongue is a snake's tongue, am going to pick a quarrel! I, whose bite is a puppy's bite, am going to pick a quarrel! With my slender hands and slender feet, I am going to pick a quarrel! . . . I, who live in the vegetable gardens, am going to pick a quarrel! I, who like a digging tool spend my time in the mud, am going to pick a quarrel! I, an unwashed refuse-basket, am going to pick a quarrel!" The turtle, the trapper of birds, the setter of nets, overthrew the heron's construction of reeds . . . , turned her nest upside down, and tipped her children into the water. The turtle scratched the dark-eyed bird's forehead with its claws, so that her breast was covered in blood from it.[5]

The appearance, that is, the look, of the turtle led to its starring role in creation stories. In "Jupiter and the Tortoise," Aesop presents a myth about the tortoise. After Jupiter invites all the animals to a banquet to celebrate his

3. Ibid., 67.
4. Ibid.
5. "Heron."

marriage, all of them come except the tortoise. "I don't care for going out," said the tortoise. "There's no place like home."[6] Jupiter was not pleased, so the god decreed "that from that time forth the tortoise should carry his house upon his back and never be able to get away from home even if he wished to."[7] Thus, the story mythologically explains why turtles have shells.

The dome-like shell of the turtle became associated with the heavens, and the square underside became associated with the earth in the same way that the biblical number four (square) represents the earth. Thus, the turtle's shell with the rounded top and flat underside came to represent the idea of the domed sky over the flat earth. The turtle was considered an animal which magically united the heavens and the earth. With such an understanding in place Native American Seneca declared that after a frog dove into the ocean to get dirt, it was spread on the carapace or shell of a turtle "where it expanded and deepened until it was able to accommodate all the creatures that were produced thereafter."[8] In the Iroquois creation account, once the frog surfaces in the water with a mouthful of mud, the animals take it and spread it on the back of a turtle. The mud begins to grow and grow until it becomes the size of North America, which is often known as "Turtle Island." Likewise, the Cheyenne state that the earth is supported by the sacred green turtle.[9] The Great Spirit Maheo kneads mud from a coot's beak until the old grandmother turtle can support the earth on her back. In other Native American tales, it is the turtle which swims to the bottom of the water and surfaces with the mud that the creator uses to make the earth. And the Mohawk explain the trembling of the earth as the old grandmother turtle stretching beneath the great weight of the earth she carries upon her back.

According to *The Spirit World*, "To many Native American peoples, the earth itself was thought to be . . . a giant turtle floating in a vast, endless sea."[10] As a sky woman plummeted to what was to become the earth, and the duck went deep enough into the water to bring up some dirt, the chief of the birds said, "Put the earth on the turtle's back!"[11] The beaver pounded the earth onto the turtle's back. ". . . [T]he whole world is thus understood

---

6. Aesop, 59.
7. Ibid.
8. *Spirit*, 26.
9. Ibid., 133.
10. Ibid., 51.
11. Littleton, *Mythology*, 488.

to be an island resting on the back of that original turtle, and surrounded by the original waters."[12]

Chinese mythology uses the turtle as a representative of enduring strength. In the Chinese creation story, Gong Gong, the water god, destroyed the mountain that held up the world. Nuwu, a goddess known for creating humankind, cut off the legs of a tortoise and used them to prevent the sky from falling. Thus, the turtle keeps the world from collapsing upon itself. This further helps to support the understanding that the world is flat and the sky is domed. The constellations are etched on the inside of the shell. Thus, the tortoise symbolizes the universe in miniature. According to Sterckx, the turtle was "a creature endowed with numinous powers" or "spirit powers"[13] because its shell resembled the vision of the cosmos. It also enjoyed the status of a spirit medium, through which writing was revealed to humankind.

According to *The Spirit World*, Native Americans thought that turtles could make humans tougher. "Among the Sioux, people who were facing ordeals sometimes fortified themselves by eating the heart of a turtle."[14] This would give them the endurance they needed in order to pass a test, much like the tortoise that beat the hare.

Furthermore, the turtle is one of four animals that possess spirit. Tortoise shells were used by the Chinese for divination. The turtle is also one of the four animals that govern the four points of the compass. The black tortoise, representing the element of water and the season of winter, is the ruler of the north, representing endurance and strength. In Tibet the black tortoise is a sign of creativity. Because it represents the element of water, it is associated with the rear of one's home, signifying support for the home, family life, and personal relationships. A figure of a tortoise placed at the back door or in the backyard near a pond brings good fortune.

Because it is an aquatic animal, the turtle was associated with the underworld in Egypt. Thus, royalty often speared turtles, and hunters copied their shells by making shields for protection. The Native American Iroquois made a rattle from a turtle shell and shook it to scare away sickness.[15] And in ancient Greece and Rome, the turtle became a fertility symbol because of all the eggs the females laid on beaches.

A turtle's long lifespan, slow movement, sturdiness, resistance to ageing, and wrinkled appearance make it an emblem of longevity, stability,

12. Ibid.
13. Sterckx, "Tawny Bull," 263.
14. *Spirit*, 58.
15. Cf. Ibid., 142.

and felicity. "Because of its longevity, it became a symbol linked to physical immortality . . . ."[16] Along with Sterckx's point, Kemmerer recounts that in Hinduism, Vishnu is reborn, among other animals, as a tortoise. Each reincarnation demonstrates interpenetrability, that is, all are one. "As a tortoise," states Kemmerer, "Vishnu helps the gods to churn the ocean in order to obtain the nectar of immortality, with which they defeat demons and restore order to the universe."[17] In many Native American tribes the "capacity to retreat into their shells when threatened" along with "their mythical association with the primordial earth rising up out of the water" led to the association of turtles with longevity.[18] A unique Native American custom to bless a baby with long life required that the child's umbilical cord be sewn into a small turtle made of deerskin. "Each time children touched this talisman, it was said, they would receive some of the turtle spirit's medicine for long life."[19]

The turtle is considered a spiritual animal. It reminds those who gaze upon it that the way to heaven is through the earth. Like the turtle, people crawl upon the earth, seeking food and shelter; the turtle has one advantage over people, namely, it carries its shelter with it. And just as the turtle cannot separate itself from its shell, neither can people separate themselves from what they do on the earth. *The Quran* states: "Glorify the name of your Lord, most high, who creates and proportions, who determines and directs . . ." (*Quran* 87:1–3). In Sufism, one of the branches of Islam, the hatching of baby turtles in the sand on the seashore and their eventual return to the sea represents the human person returning to God through the Holy One's guidance. Thus, the journey of the baby turtle is a good illustration of the three Quranic verses above. The Lord creates baby turtles from the eggs laid by their mothers, proportions them to be able to live in the sea and crawl on the land, determines when they live in the sea and when they crawl on the seashore, and directs their movement in the sea and on the land.

Thus, the creature bearing the eyes, mouth, and tongue of a snake represents how being slow and steady wins the race. As an icon of the earth, the turtle (tortoise) bears the dome of the heavens on its back while carrying the plate of the earth's surface on its feet under the dome, thus uniting heaven and earth. The turtle is associated primarily with spiritual strength and longevity as it begins its life in the sand on the seashore and journeys

16. Sterckx, "Tawny Bull," 263.
17. Kemmerer, *Animals*, 78.
18. *Spirit*, 58.
19. Ibid.

back to the waters from which its mother came. Thus, it becomes an image of the life and pilgrimage of humankind.

Journal/Meditation: Which of the spiritual aspects of the turtle (tortoise) captures your attention? How can you incorporate that spiritual aspect into your life?

Prayer: All-holy One, I glorify your name as I review how you create and proportion all things. I praise you for the way you determine and direct all that you have made. Guide my life with the Holy Spirit just as you guide your creation to union with you, Father, through your Son, Jesus Christ, who is Lord forever and ever. Amen.

Unicorn

Text: "... [M]y horn shall be exalted like that of the unicorn; and my old age in plentiful mercy." (*Holy Bible*, Ps 91:11)

Reflection: Before the days of modern biblical scholarship, the "wild ox" of the Bible was translated from the Hebrew as "unicorn." In the verse above from Psalm 91 found in a 1748 edition of the Bible in English (based on the 1609 English College at Douay translation), the psalmist, after singing about how God's works are recognized only by some, like the singer, declares that while evildoers may flourish briefly, the righteous will be exalted like the horn of a unicorn. The *King James Version* states that "my horn shalt thou [, O LORD,] exalt like the horn of an unicorn: I shall be anointed with fresh oil" (*Official KJB*, Ps 92:10).

In the 1748 edition of the Bible in English, Psalm 28, employing the image of thunder, declares: "The voice of the Lord breaketh the cedars: yea, the Lord shall break the cedars of Libanus. And shall reduce them to pieces, as a calf of Libanus, and as the beloved son of unicorns" (*Holy Bible*, Ps 28:5–6). In the *King James Bible*, Psalm 29:6 states that the LORD "maketh them also to skip like a calf; Lebanon and Sirion like a young unicorn" (*Official KJB*, Ps 29:6). While the reader could never be sure what the "beloved son of unicorns" might mean, the "young unicorn" skipping along better conveys the image of a lightning strike followed by thunder!

A unicorn, meaning "one horn" (from two words in Latin: *uni* [one] and *cornu* [horn]), is a mythological animal generally depicted with the body and head of a white horse, the hind legs of a stag, the tail of a lion, and a single, straight, spiraled, twenty-seven-inch horn in the middle of the forehead. Sometimes, the head is the color purple and the eyes are blue.

The single horn is often described as being red at the pointed tip, black in the middle, and white at the base. Bulfinch, quoting the Roman naturalist Pliny, states that the unicorn is "a very ferocious beast, similar in the rest of its body to a horse, with the head of a deer, the feet of an elephant, the tail of a boar, a deep, bellowing voice, and a single black horn, two cubits in length, standing out in the middle of its forehead."[1] The supposed strength of the unicorn may be what lead the translators of the *King James Bible* to declare that God had "the strength of an unicorn" (*Official KJB*, Num 23:22; Num 24:8). Likewise, when God questions Job, he asks, "Will the unicorn be willing to serve thee . . . ?" (*Official KJB*, Job 39:9) and "Canst thou bind the unicorn with his band in the furrow?" (*Official KJB*, Job 39:10) In other words, the unicorn is a very strong beast.

In common mythology, the unicorn could not be taken alive[2] because of its strength and its horn. According to Bulfinch:

> Some [hunters] described the horn as movable at the will of the animal, a kind of small sword, in short, with which no hunter who was not exceedingly cunning in fence could have a chance. Others maintained that all the animal's strength lay in its horn, and that when hard pressed in pursuit, it would throw itself from the pinnacle of the highest rocks horn foremost, so as to pitch upon it, and then quietly march off not a whit the worse for its fall.[3]

This mythological understanding may have led biblical translators to portray Moses declaring that Joseph's sons—Ephraim and Manasseh—each possessed glory "like the horns of unicorns" (*Official KJB*, Deut 33:17). Likewise, the psalmist sings about the LORD having heard him and rescued him "from the horns of the unicorns" (*Official KJB*, Ps 22:21b).

In the punishment that God is going to give to Edom, the prophet Isaiah states that "the unicorns shall come down . . . ; and [the] land shall be soaked with blood" (*Official KJB*, Isa 34:7). Isaiah is describing a slaughter of unicorns that will cover the ground with blood. While God might be able to kill unicorns, no one else was able to do so. Medieval people thought that the fierce unicorn, an extremely wild woodland creature and a sign of purity and grace, could be captured only if a virgin maiden was thrown before it. It was thought that the unicorn would leap into the virgin's lap, and she would suckle it and lead it into captivity. According to Bulfinch, those who sought unicorns

---

1. Bulfinch, *Mythology*, 315.
2. Ibid.
3. Ibid.

discovered that it was a great lover of purity and innocence, so they took the field with a young virgin, who was placed in the unsuspecting admirer's way. When the unicorn spied her, he approached with all reverence, couched beside her, and laying his head in her lap, fell asleep. The treacherous virgin then gave a signal, . . . the hunters made in, and captured the simple beast.[4]

During the Middle Ages, the maiden became the Virgin Mary, who in popular iconography was depicted with a unicorn lying in her lap. The pure white unicorn represented Jesus, born of the Virgin Mary; thus, the unicorn became an emblem of the Incarnation. In some paintings, the archangel Gabriel is depicted blowing a horn, as hounds chase the unicorn into the Virgin Mary's arms, and a little Christ Child descends on rays of light from God the Father. Furthermore, since no unicorn had ever been captured alive, another level of meaning was added, namely, that the unicorn also represented the death and resurrection of Christ.

While the horse-like unicorn is the usual description of the mythical animal today, the HB (OT) Book of Daniel illustrates the unusual description of a goat-like animal possessing a long horn, cloven hooves, and sometimes a beard. In one of his visions in the third year of the reign of King Belshazzar (cf. Dan 8:1), that is, 552 BCE, Daniel narrates: "As I was watching, a male goat appeared from the west coming across the face of the whole earth without touching the ground. The goat had a horn between its eyes" (Dan 8:5). Belshazzar is the last administrator—not king—of Babylon before the country is conquered by King Cyrus of Persia, whose own kingdom was ultimately conquered by Alexander the Great. Daniel's unicorn-goat represents Alexander's conquest of Persia in 333–330 BCE. With this historical background the rest of Daniel's vision becomes clear: The unicorn-goat came toward the ram with two horns, representing the Persian-Media Empire.

> I saw it approaching the ram. It was enraged against it and struck the ram, breaking its two horns. The ram did not have power to withstand it; it threw the ram down to the ground and trampled upon it, and there was no one who could rescue the ram from its power. Then the male goat grew exceedingly great; but at the height of its power, the great horn was broken . . . ." (Dan 8:7–8)

The narrator continues to tell of the division of Alexander's empire into separate kingdoms after his death.

---

4. Ibid.

Biblical translators used to presume that the unicorn existed. The one-horned horse or goat became a sign of exaltation, especially as it was imagined to gambol like a colt in a meadow. The ferocious strength of the unicorn was likened to God's power. Once the mythical beast was associated with the purity and innocence of virginity, it was seen as a sign of Christ in the hands of his Virgin Mother Mary. Thus, the spiritual qualities of strength, purity, and innocence are represented by the mythical beast known as the unicorn.

Journal/Meditation: What spiritual qualities does the mythological animal generally depicted with the body and head of a white horse, the hind legs of a stag, the tail of a lion, and a single, straight, spiraled, twenty-seven-inch horn in the middle of the forehead represent for you?

Prayer: With the strength of a unicorn, O LORD, you led your chosen people out of Egyptian slavery to the promised land, making them skip like a young unicorn. For that mighty deed and for many more, I exalt your name like the horn of a unicorn. Keep me pure and innocent; keep me safe from all that would harm me, Father. You live and reign with your Son, Jesus Christ, and the Holy Spirit, one God, forever and ever. Amen.

Vulture

Text: Jesus said to his disciples, "Where the corpse is, there the vultures will gather." (Luke 17:37)

Reflection: A vulture is a large bird of prey featuring dark plumage and broad wings; it usually feeds on carrion, which is rotting or decaying animal flesh. Such is the reference in the passage above from the CB (NT) Gospel According to Luke. The Lukan Jesus is explaining to his disciples the proper response they need to be ready to make when the Son of Man, Jesus, returns in glory. Contextually, the author of Luke's Gospel does not think that Jesus is returning anytime soon, but he thinks that he will come back one day. When he does return, the correct response for those on the housetop is to forfeit all personal belongings. Those in the field must not turn back, but must go toward the revelation of the Son of Man. They need only remember the destruction of Lot's wife in the HB (OT) Book of Genesis (cf. Gen 19:26); she looked back at the destruction of Sodom and Gomorrah and was turned into a pillar of salt (cf. Luke 17:30–37).

Any person who tries to save his or her life will end up losing it. In other words, destruction will abound for those who attempt to escape from the appearance of the Son of Man. Likewise, the person who loses his or her life will end up saving it; the Son of Man will rescue the faithful person sleeping beside the unfaithful one and the faithful woman grinding meal next to the unfaithful one. Jesus' disciples want to know the place where this separation will occur. So, Luke portrays Jesus giving them a cryptic answer about vultures gathering around a corpse (cf. Luke 17:37). The answer does not answer the question! The author of Luke's Gospel cannot portray Jesus answering the question, because no one knows when Jesus will return, neither the angels of heaven, nor the Son, but only the Father (cf. Matt 24:36).

On one level, Jesus' answer describes the usual behavior of vultures; they are found where the carrion, that is, rotting or decaying animal flesh, is found. This is made concrete by the author of Matthew's Gospel who records the same saying (cf. Matt 24:28). On another level, Jesus' cryptic answer alludes to the HB (OT) Book of Leviticus, which names "as detestable among the birds . . . the vulture" (Lev 11:13). The vulture cannot be eaten, because it is an abomination (cf. Lev 11:13; Deut 14:12). Sometimes the bird of prey is described as the carrion vulture (cf. Lev 11:18; Deut 14:17). In *Mormon*, the birds are called "vultures of the air" that devour flesh (Mosiah 12:2; Alma 2:38). Thus, the vulture—no matter how it is described—is a detestable abomination, but by Jesus it is made a visible sign of the public event of the coming of the Son of Man!

The HB (OT) Book of Proverbs employs the vulture as a sign of disgrace. "The eye that mocks a father and scorns to obey a mother," states an oracle, "will be pecked out by the ravens of the valley and eaten by the vultures" (Prov 30:17). The child who mocks his or her father and scorns his or her mother will be left unburied, the ultimate disgrace. However, if the body is eaten by the vultures, that will heap one disgrace upon another one. The prophet Hosea employs the vulture in a similar way, declaring that Israel's enemy is like a vulture over the house of the LORD (cf. Hos 8:1). So, the prophet wants the alarm to be sounded with the trumpet because the people have broken God's covenant and transgressed his law (cf. Hos 8:1). The enemy, like a vulture, is coming to disgrace even further those who have disgraced themselves by their own unfaithfulness.

Even in *The Rig Veda*, the vulture carries a negative connotation. The purified soma, the sacred Hindu drink, is declared to be a "falcon amid the vultures" in one hymn (*RV* 9:96:6). In the last hymn of book 7, dedicated to Indra, the chief Hindu god, and soma, the god is asked to "[d]estroy the fiend shaped like . . . a vulture" (*RV* 7:104:22). The singer continues, "Destroy him . . . as with a stone, O Indra; crush the demon" (*RV* 7:104:22). Finally, in hymn 123 of book 10, either a rainbow or a sunrise over the ocean is personified as "looking with a vulture's eye to heaven" (*RV* 10:123:8a). Again, the connotation is negative, because the word "vulture" implies that which is seeking carrion.

Thus, the reader must turn this bird of prey into a positive spiritual scavenger which gathers around practices that are dead or decaying and sees them as signs of disgrace to be removed, renewed, or reinvented. Instead of seeing the vulture as one who waits eagerly for opportunities to take advantage of someone else—especially a weak or helpless thing—in a negative way, why not gaze upon its image as one who will do what no one else will do? The vulture illustrates the spiritual quality of mess-cleaning, spiritual house cleaning, and the removal of all that is detestable or abominable.

Journal/Meditation: Are you able to see the negative behavior of the vulture in a positive light? How? What spiritual quality of the vulture might be worthy of your imitation?

Prayer: Father, source of all that is, even the vulture gives you praise by consuming carrion on your earth. Your Son, my Lord Jesus Christ, made this bird of prey a sign as to the place of his return in glory. Enable me to view your bird of prey as a positive spiritual scavenger which spurs me to remove practices that hinder me from eagerly awaiting the return of Christ in glory. He lives and reigns with you and the Holy Spirit, one God, forever and ever. Amen.

Wolf

Text: "In the story of Joseph and his brothers are lessons for those who inquire. (... [G]oing to their father [Jacob]) [Joseph's brothers] said: 'O father, why don't you trust us with Joseph? We are in fact his well-wishers. Let him go out with us tomorrow that he may enjoy and play. We shall take care of him.' He said: 'I am afraid of sending him with you lest a wolf should devour him when you are unmindful.' They replied: 'If a wolf should devour him when we are there, a well-knit band, we shall certainly be treacherous.' So, when they took him out they planned to throw him into an unused well. We revealed to Joseph: 'You will tell them (one day) of this deed when they will not apprehend it.' At nightfall they came to their father weeping. And said: 'We went racing with one another and left Joseph to guard our things when a wolf devoured him. But you will not believe us even though we tell the truth.'" (*Quran* 12:7, 11–17)

Reflection: The above verses from *The Quran* contain the three mentions of wolf in the entire book, and they are contained in a part of the lengthy story about Joseph, son of Jacob, son of Abraham. Unlike the biblical text, Islam's sacred text portrays Jacob as fearing that Joseph would be attacked by a wolf, presumably because he and his brothers watched sheep. After setting aside their father's fear, the brothers take Joseph with them, put him in a well, and return to their father with the tale that, indeed, a wolf has attacked and devoured their young brother.

It is important to note here that the wolf is presumed to be a negative creature—and rightly so by sheepherders. The wolf, resembling a dog in stature, is a predatory carnivore that hunts in packs. Usually gray in color, its fur also may be red, black, or white. In popular understanding, the big, bad wolf stereotype is influenced by fables from Aesop and tales from the

Grimm brothers. Neither the HB (OT) nor the CB (NT) helps to dislodge the negative popular image. And as seen above, *The Quran* maintains the negative stereotype, as does *The Rig Veda*. However, in Native American mythology and folklore, the wolf has a positive image and possesses traits worthy of such a sacred or mystic animal. After exploring the predominate, negative stereotype, the less dominate, positive stereotype will be examined.

Ravenous Wolf

The wolf is characterized as being ravenous. This is made clear by the patriarch Jacob in his farewell speech in the HB (OT) Book of Genesis. As Jacob decrees the fate of his sons/tribes, he tells his youngest son, Benjamin, that he "is a ravenous wolf, in the morning devouring the prey and in evening dividing the spoil" (Gen 49:27). In the prophet Ezekiel's oracle against Jerusalem, he records the LORD telling him to announce to the city that "[i]ts officials within it are like wolves tearing the prey, shedding blood, destroying lives to get dishonest gain" (Ezek 22:27). Picking up on the same theme, the prophet Zephaniah states that Jerusalem's "judges are evening wolves that leave nothing until the morning" (Zeph 3:3). And in the CB (NT), Paul tells the elders of the church in Ephesus that he knows that after he has gone "savage wolves will come in among [them] not sparing the flock" (Acts 20:29); here, savage wolves metaphorically represent false teachers who distort the truth that Paul has preached.

The same ravenous characteristic of wolves in found in *The Rig Veda*. In one hymn, the singer compares his "torturing cares" that consume him to how "the wolf assails the thirsty deer" (*RV* 1:105:7). In another hymn, the singer declares that the quail have been set free from the wolf's jaws (cf. *RV* 1:116:14), and that "the she-wolf slew a hundred wethers," that is, castrated male sheep (*RV* 1:116:16). In another hymn, the singer asks the gods not to give him "up to any evil creature, as spoil to wolf or she wolf" (*RV* 6:51:6). The Asvins, the Hindu gods of sunrise and sunset, are declared to deliver "even from the wolf's deep throat . . . the swallowed quail" (*RV* 10:39:13); poetically, the gods of light bring dawn (quail) out of the darkness (wolf). Hymn 95 of book 10 mentions "fierce rapacious wolves" and "evil-omened wolves" (*RV* 10:95:14b, 15a), while hymn 56 of book 8 mentions being rescued "from [the] mouth of ravening wolves" (*RV* 8:56:14).

Aesop narrates several fables about wolves that portray their ravenous quality. For example, "The Wolf, the Mother, and Her Child" is about "[a] hungry wolf . . . prowling about in search of food."[1] Hearing a child cry, the

---

1. Aesop, 89.

wolf crouches beneath the window of a cottage, listening as the mother tells the child, "Stop crying . . . or I'll throw you to the wolf."[2] The wolf thought that she meant what she said, but later the wolf heard her fondling the child and telling him that when his father would come home, he would kill the wolf. So, the wolf left. Another fable, "The Wolf and the Crane," features a wolf with a bone stuck in his throat which goes to a crane and begs her to put her long bill down his throat and pull out the bone. After doing what she was asked, the crane asked about getting paid for her service. "[B]aring his teeth as he spoke," the wolf said, "You can go about boasting that you once put your head into a wolf's mouth and didn't get it bitten off."[3] The ravenous quality of the wolf leads to the phrase "to keep the wolf from the door," indicating that one needs strength to prevent hunger or starvation from approaching.

Trickster Wolf

The wolf is portrayed as an unsuccessful trickster in "The Wolf and the Horse." After finding a field of oats, but not being able to eat them, the wolf tempts a horse to enter the field and enjoy the grain. But the horse recognizes the trick. The moral of the story is this: "There is no virtue in giving to others what is useless to oneself."[4] The wolf is tricked in "The Dog and the Wolf." The wolf pounces upon a dog to eat him when the dog tells the wolf to wait a few days until he has eaten of his master's feast and fattened up. When the wolf returns a few days later, he finds the dog on the stable roof. The wolf asks the dog to come down to honor their agreement, but the dog refuses, and the wolf is left hungry and tricked.[5]

A half-starved wolf appears in "The Plowman and the Wolf." After the plowman gives his oxen a break and leads them to water, a wolf finds the leather straps attached to the yoke and begins to chew them "in the hope of satisfying his craving for food."[6] However, he gets entangled in the harness. Just as he cannot escape, the plowman returns and sees the wolf in place of the oxen in front of the plow. "[Y]ou old rascal," says the plowman. "I wish you would give up thieving for good and take to honest work instead."[7]

2. Ibid.
3. Ibid., 106.
4. Ibid., 174.
5. Cf. Ibid., 177.
6. Ibid., 192.
7. Ibid.

Prowling Wolf

As indicated in the first of *Aesop's Fables* above, wolves prowl. While a prisoner in the jail at Liberty, Missouri, in 1839 Joseph Smith wrote to his Reorganized Church of Jesus Christ of Latter Day Saints about false accusations from enemies who tear members away from their spouses, parents, children, and others. He wrote about being dragged to prison by enemies who "prowl around . . . like wolves for the blood of the lamb" (*D&C* 122:6). *The Rig Veda*, too, portrays the prowling wolf. The Hindu god that protects roads and journeys, Pusan, is ask to "[d]rive . . . from [the] road the wolf, the wicked inauspicious wolf, who lies in wait to injure" those passing by (*RV* 1:42:2). In another hymn, the stars are said to drive the wolf back from the path (cf. *RV* 1:105:11). Later, the singer states, "A ruddy wolf beheld me once, as I was faring on my path. He, like a carpenter whose back is aching, crouched and slunk away" (*RV* 1:105:18). A hymn dedicated to the night, asks the darkness to "[k]eep off the she-wolf and the wolf; [t]o keep the thief away" so it is easy for the singer to pass on the road (*RV* 10:127:6). Finally, in a poem dedicated to the god of peace, Aditya Varuna, the singer asks the god to protect him while he sleeps from "any wolf . . . [who] would harm" him (*RV* 2:28:10).

The wolf prowls in order to harm and destroy. In the HB (OT) Book of the Prophet Jeremiah, the destructive characteristic of the wolf is applied to Jerusalem's enemies, who, like a wolf from the desert, shall destroy the city (cf. Jer 5:6b). Likewise, the prophet Habakkuk describes the Chaldeans (Babylonians), enemies of Judah, as being more menacing than wolves at dusk (cf. Hab 1:8a). The Hindu Asvins, the gods of sunrise and sunset, are told not to let "the wolf, . . . not [to let] the she-wolf harm" them in *The Rig Veda* (*RV* 1:183:4). In another hymn, the Vajiins, the horses pulling the chariots of the Hindu gods, are told to crush the wolf (cf. *RV* 7:38:7). And in another hymn dedicated to the Visvedevas, all the Hindu gods taken together as a whole, the singer prays, "Protect us, god; let not the wolf destroy us" (*RV* 2:29:6b).

Wicked Wolf

The ravenous, prowling wolf that destroys is characterized as wicked. In book 1 of *The Rig Veda*, hymn 120, the Vasus, attendant deities of Indra, Hinduism's chief god, are asked to guard well the singer of the song and to keep him safe "from the wicked wolf" (*RV* 1:120:7) and to save him "from the injurer, the mortal foe who makes [him] looked upon as wolves" (*RV*

2:34:9). In another hymn, the god Agni is praised for giving food "even to the wicked wolf when he is hungry" (*RV* 6:13:5).

However, the wolf's wickedness is best illustrated by "Little Red Riding Hood" in *Grimm's Complete Fairy Tales*. As the story unfolds, a little maid receives "a little red riding hood of red velvet"[8] from her grandmother, who "lived away in the wood, half an hour's walk from the village."[9] Little Red's mother sent her with cakes and wine to her grandmother's house. In the wood "she met the wolf; but as she did not know what a bad sort of animal he was, she did not feel frightened."[10] After the wolf questions Little Red and finds out where she is going, what she is carrying, and where her grandmother lives, he thinks to himself, "That tender young thing would be a delicious morsel, and would taste better than the old one; I must manage somehow to get both of them."[11] Then, the wolf tricks Little Red into stopping to pick a bouquet of flowers for her grandmother while he beats her to her grandmother's house, pretends to be Little Red, tricks the grandmother into opening the door, and "fell on the grandmother and ate her up without saying one word."[12] He dresses himself in grandmother's clothes and lies on her bed awaiting Little Red's arrival. When she shows up and marvels at her grandmother's large ears, great eyes, large hands, and large mouth, the wolf "made one bound from the bed, and swallowed up poor Little Red Riding Hood."[13]

A huntsman appears on the scene and finds the wolf asleep on the bed. Taking a pair of shears, he slits the wolf's body and out pops both Little Red and her grandmother. Then, the huntsman takes the wolf's skin home with him. A few days later, Little Red again makes a trip to visit her grandmother, and another wolf meets her. Upon arriving at her grandmother's house she tells her how "the wolf had met her and wished her good day, but had looked so wicked about the eyes that she thought if she had not been on the high road, he would have devoured her."[14] Shortly thereafter the wolf came knocking at the door, but they would not let him in. "After that the wolf slunk by the house, and got at last upon the roof to wait until Little Red Riding Hood should return home in the evening; then he meant to spring

---

8. Grimm, 140.
9. Ibid.
10. Ibid.
11. Ibid., 141.
12. Ibid.
13. Ibid., 142.
14. Ibid., 142–43.

down upon her and devour her in the darkness."[15] However, the grandmother—smart in all things wolf!—has her own plan. She instructs Little Red to fill a large trough with water from boiled sausages, which tempts the wolf on the roof. While sniffing the smell of the sausage water, he slips off the roof and falls into the trough, where he is drowned. Then, Little Red goes home without any harm coming her way.

Joseph Jacobs's "The Story of the Three Little Pigs" also illustrates the wickedness of the wolf. A sow gives birth to three offspring and sends the three piglets to seek their fortune. The first finds a man with a bundle of straw, which he uses to build a house. The wolf comes along and huffs and puffs and blows his house in "and ate up the little pig."[16] The second piglet finds a man with a bundle of furze, a spiny shrub, with which he builds a house. The wolf comes, wants in, huffs and puffs and blows down the house, and eats the second pig. The third pig finds a man with bricks, which he uses to build a house. When the wolf arrives, he huffs and puffs, and huffs and puffs, and huffs and puffs, but he cannot "with all his huffing and puffing blow the house down."[17]

So, the big, bad wolf turns into a trickster in order to get the third little pig to come out of his brick house. First, he tempts him with turnips, agreeing to meet at six o'clock in the morning to steal some from Mr. Smith's field. However, the pig gets up at five, gets "a nice pot full for dinner,"[18] and tricks the wolf! Second, the wolf tells the pig about an apple tree full of ripe fruit. They agree to meet at 5 a.m., but, again the pig goes at 4 a.m., "hoping to get back before the wolf came; but he had further to go, and had to climb the tree, so that just as he was coming down from it, he saw the wolf coming, which . . . frightened him very much."[19] Again, the pig tricks the wolf by tossing an apple far from the tree. While the wolf was running after it, the pig jumped down and ran home. The third trick by the wolf is to invite the pig to a fair. They agree on a time to meet, but again the pig leaves early, goes to the fair, buys a butter-churn, and is on his way home when the wolf appears. "So [the pig] got into the churn to hide, and by so doing turned it round, and it rolled down the hill with the pig in it, which frightened the wolf so much, that he ran home without going to the fair."[20] Later, the wolf appears at the pig's house, tells his story about being frightened by "a great

15. Ibid., 143.
16. Jacobs, "Three Little Pigs," 208.
17. Ibid., 209.
18. Ibid., 210.
19. Ibid., 210–11.
20. Ibid., 211.

round thing which came down the hill past him,"[21] and listens as the pig explains that it was he. Thus, all attempts by the wolf to trick the pig failed.

> Then the wolf was very angry indeed, and declared he would eat up the little pig, and that he would get down the chimney after him. When the little pig saw what he was about, he hung on the pot full of water, and made up a blazing fire, and, just as the wolf was coming down, took off the cover, and in fell the wolf; so the little pig put on the cover again in an instant, boiled him, and ate him for supper, and lived happily ever afterwards.[22]

Thus, the third little pig becomes a better trickster than the wolf. And what the wolf intended to do to the third little pig—eat him—the third little pig does to the wolf.

Jacobs's story is very similar to Grimm's account of "The Wolf and the Seven Little Kids." In sacred story-telling, the number three signals the divine, as seen above in the trickster-wisdom of the third little pig. If the number for the divine, three, is added to the number signaling the earth, four, then the total is seven. Thus, Grimm's tale features seven little goats, born of a mother goat who loved her offspring just as a mother loves her children. Before going into the forest to fetch food one day she called all seven kids and said to them: "Dear children, I have to go into the forest; be on your guard against the wolf; if he comes in, he will devour you all—skin, hair, and all. The wretch often disguises himself, but you will know him at once by his rough voice and his black feet."[23]

After the mother goat leaves, the wolf appears knocking on the door of the house, but the kids recognize his voice and do not let him in. The wolf turns into a trickster, buying chalk, eating it, and, thus, making his voice softer. However, this time the kids recognize him by seeing his black feet. So, the wolf goes to the town baker and asks him to rub dough on them, after which he goes to the miller and, after threatening to devour him, forces him to make his paws white with meal. His third attempt is successful; the kids think they recognize their mother's voice and feet, and they let in the wolf.

> They were terrified and wanted to hide themselves. One sprang under the table, the second into the bed, the third into the stove, the fourth into the kitchen, the fifth into the cupboard, the sixth under the washing-bowl, and the seventh into the clock case. But the wolf found them all, and used no great ceremony; one

21. Ibid.
22. Ibid.
23. Grimm, 134.

after the other he swallowed them down his throat. The youngest in the clock case was the only one he did not find.[24]

After he had finished devouring the six kids, the wolf went outside, lied down under a tree, and fell asleep. Meanwhile, the mother goat came home. After searching for her kids and not finding them, she heard the voice of the youngest in the clock case who came out and told her all about the trickery of the wolf and how he had eaten the other six kids. After locating the wolf asleep under the tree, the mother goat took scissors and cut open the monster's stomach, and her little kids began to emerge one after another. They were still alive because the wolf had only swallowed them. Then, while the wolf still slept, she instructed her kids to gather large stones and put them in the wolf's stomach; she sewed his stomach back together. Once the wolf awoke, he went to a well to drink. As he leaned over the edge of the well, the stones made him fall into the well, where he drowned. The seven kids cried, "The wolf is dead! The wolf is dead!" as they and their mother danced around the well.[25]

Aesop narrates two fables about smart goats that escape wicked wolves. In "The Wolf and the Goat," the wolf spies a goat browsing above him on a mountain ledge and attempts to trick the goat to come down to where there is better food while feigning concern for the goat's safety. "It's little you care whether I get good grass or bad," states the goat. "What you want is to eat me."[26] In "The Kid and the Wolf," a kid strays from the flock and is chased by a wolf. However, the kid, recognizing its fate to be eaten by the wolf, asks the wolf to play his pipe so they can dance before the wolf eats the kid. Seeing no problem with having a little music before dinner, the wolf begins to play and the kid to dance. "Before many minutes were passed the gods who guarded the flock heard the sound and came up to see what was going on. They no sooner clapped eyes on the wolf than they gave chase and drove him away."[27] The wolf recognizes that the kid has tricked him, and all he can do now is flee for his life.

Lambs and Wolves

As has been seen, the wolf and the goat or the goat's kids are natural enemies. This is also true of the wolf and the lamb and the wolf and the sheep.

24. Ibid., 135.
25. Ibid., 136.
26. Aesop, 140.
27. Ibid., 152.

In fact, the author of the OT (A) Book of Sirach asks, "What does a wolf have in common with a lamb?" (Sir 13:17a) The Lukan Jesus in the CB (NT) makes the animosity even clearer, telling the seventy(-two) whom he sends out in pairs, that he is sending them like lambs in the midst of wolves (cf. Luke 10:3).

The antithesis of wolf and lamb is narrated in "The Wolf and the Fox," one of Grimm's fairy tales. As the tale unfolds, the wolf and fox live together, but the fox does all the hard work. The wolf tells the red fox to get him something to eat or he will eat the fox. The fox tells the wolf that he knows where there are "a couple of nice young lambs."[28] The wolf agrees to go with the fox to get a lamb. After stealing the lamb and giving it to the wolf, the fox runs away. The wolf, not yet content, decides to steal the other lamb. However, "the old sheep saw him, and began to cry and bleat so horribly that the farmer's people came running to see what was the matter. Of course they found the wolf there, and beat him so unmercifully, that, howling and limping, he returned to the fox."[29] The fox merely asks the wolf why he is such a glutton.

The next day the wolf tells the fox to get him something to eat. This time the fox knows about a woman making pancakes. They go to the house, and the fox sneaks around until he spies the dish with pancakes on it, steals six of them, and brings them to the wolf before he leaves. Of course, the wolf wants more, finds the pancakes, breaks the dish, and alerts the farmer's wife to his presence. She raises an alarm, and people arrive with all types of weapons to beat the wolf which "barely escapes with his life . . . to the wood where the fox was."[30] Again, the fox merely asks the wolf why he is such a glutton.

As in all good stories, the wolf is hungry a third time and sends the fox to get him something to eat. This time the fox knows a man who has been butchering and has the salted meat in a tub in his cellar. The fox takes the wolf into the cellar through a hole. This time the fox remains with the wolf while he gorges himself on the meat. The wolf notices that the fox keeps looking at the hole, and the fox tells him that he is keeping watch. The wolf states that he intends to eat the whole tub of meat before leaving.

Meanwhile, the farmer hears the fox running around in the cellar and goes to see what is happening. The fox leaps through the hole and disappears. But when the wolf attempts to follow, he has so increased his size by his greediness that he cannot succeed. He is stuck in the hole, which enables

28. Grimm, 136.
29. Ibid., 137.
30. Ibid.

the farmer to kill him with his cudgel.[31] The fox makes his way back to his home in the woods, happy that he is now free from the gluttonous wolf.

Aesop narrates three fables about wolves and lambs. After stealing a lamb from the flock and carrying it to a place where he could eat it leisurely in "The Wolf and the Lion," the wolf meets a lion, who takes his prey away from him. The wolf complains to the lion about the injustice of what the lion has done. The lion merely laughs and asks if it justly belonged to the wolf. Then, taunting the wolf, the lion asks if it were a gift of a friend.[32] In "The Lamb Chased by a Wolf," the wolf chases a lamb into a temple, where the wolf attempts to trick the lamb to come out, telling it that the priest of the temple will catch it and offer it in sacrifice. The lamb replies that he will stay where he is. "I'd rather be sacrificed any day than be eaten by a wolf" states the lamb.[33] Finally, in "The Wolf and the Lamb," the wolf finds a lamb straying from the flock and feels some compassion for such a helpless creature. Looking for a grievance so he would have an excuse to devour the lamb, he first accuses the lamb of having insulted him the year before, but the lamb states that is impossible, since the lamb had not yet been born. Next, the wolf accuses the lamb of feeding in his pastures, but the lamb tells him that he has not yet tasted grass. The wolf accuses the lamb of drinking from his spring, but the lamp states that his only drink has been his mother's milk. After trying three excuses, the wolf decides that he is not going to abandon his dinner. So, he consumes the lamb with little ado.[34]

In the HB (OT) the prophet Isaiah reverses the enemy status of the wolf and the lamb to depict the new paradise he envisions. The wolf will live with the lamb, writes Isaiah (cf. Isa 11:6), and "The wolf and the lamb shall feed together" (Isa 65:25). Both of Isaiah's statements are repeated in *Mormon*. "The wolf also shall dwell with the lamb," states the Second Book of Nephi (2 Ne 21:6). "And then shall the wolf dwell with the lamb," states the same book nine chapters later (2 Ne 30:12).

In terms of the natural enemies of wolf and sheep, John's Gospel in the CB (NT) makes it explicit. Jesus says, "The hired hand, who is not the shepherd and does not own the sheep, sees the wolf coming and leaves the sheep and runs away—and the wolf snatches them and scatters them" (John 10:12). The Book of Alma in *Mormon* echoes John's Gospel. The author asks, "For what shepherd is there among you having many sheep does not watch over them, that the wolves enter not and devour his flock? And behold, if

---

31. Cf. Ibid., 138.
32. Cf. Aesop, 96.
33. Ibid., 139.
34. Cf. Ibid., 9.

a wolf enters his flock, does he not drive him out? Yes, and at the last, if he can, he will destroy him" (Alma 5:59). The good shepherd, according to the Book of Alma, brings believers into his fold because they "are his sheep; and he commands . . . that [they] suffer no ravenous wolf to enter among [them], that [they] may not be destroyed" (Alma 5:6). In Matthew's Gospel in the CB (NT), Jesus tells his disciples that he is sending them out like sheep into the midst of wolves (cf. Matt 10:16), indicating the difficulty of their mission. Kienzle states, "The wolf makes numerous appearances in Scripture, where rapacity and deceit mark its character . . . ."[35] Based on this characterization, she notes that during the twelfth and thirteenth centuries, the wolf became a type of heretic *par excellance*.[36] This concept also gives rise to the phrase "to throw someone to the wolves," indicating that one person abandons another one to the enemy in order to save one's self from destruction.

The Rig Veda mentions the natural animosity between the wolf and the sheep. One hymn compares the Hindu god Indra's love of the sacred soma juice to "a wolf worrying a sheep" (*RV* 8:34:3). And another hymn, addressed to Indra, states that "[e]ven the wolf, the savage beast that rends the sheep, follows the path of his decrees" (*RV* 8:55:8). Grimm narrates a tale about the "Gossip Wolf and the Fox" that illustrates how the wolf and the sheep are natural enemies.

After a wolf gives birth, she invites the fox to be the pup's godfather, and the fox is honored by Mrs. Gossip's request. After a feast celebrating the fox's honor, the fox tells Mrs. Gossip, "I know a sheepfold from which we might fetch a nice morsel."[37] The wolf was very pleased with the fox's plan and went with him to the farmyard. "He pointed out the fold from afar and said, 'You will be able to creep in there without being seen, and in the meantime I will look about on the other side to see if I can pick up a chicken.' He, however, did not go there, but sat down at the entrance to the forest, stretched his legs and rested."[38] As the wolf crept into the sheepfold, a dog lying there awakened and made such a noise that a group of peasants came running, "caught Gossip Wolf, and poured a strong burning mixture, which had been prepared for washing, over her skin. At last she escaped, and dragged herself outside."[39] She found the fox relaxing; he immediately began to lie to her about barely escaping the peasants who beat him. She

---

35. Kienzle, "Bestiary," 107.
36. Cf. Ibid., 106.
37. Grimm, 139.
38. Ibid.
39. Ibid., 140.

carried him to her house, where the fox laughed at her for the roasting she had received and left her.

Six of *Aesop's Fables* illustrate the natural enemies that wolves and sheep are. "The Blind Man and the Cub" presents a blind man who is able to tell what a creature is by touching it. When a wolf cub is put into his hands, he explains that he is not sure if it is a wolf or a fox, but he does know that "it would never do to trust it in a sheepfold."[40] There is "The Shepherd's Boy and the Wolf," one of the more famous of *Aesop's Fables*. The shepherd's son is tending his father's flock and decides to trick the villagers "by pretending that a wolf was attacking the sheep; so he shouted out, 'Wolf! Wolf!' and when the people came running up, he laughed at them for their pains."[41] He did the same thing a second time. Finally, a wolf really did arrive, but when the boy shouted, no one came because he had tricked them before, and they failed to believe him. "And so the wolf had it all his own way, and killed off sheep after sheep at his leisure."[42] This fable gives rise to the understanding that anyone who gives a false alarm or cries for help too many times so that when help is really needed no one will come is crying wolf.

In "The Sheep, the Wolf, and the Stag," a stag attempts to borrow a measure of wheat from a sheep, pledging the wolf as his surety. However, the sheep was afraid that the stag and wolf were out to cheat her, declaring, "The wolf is in the habit of seizing what he wants and running off with it without paying, and you, too, can run much faster than I. So how shall I be able to come up with either of you when the debt falls due?"[43] "The Wolf and the Sheep" is another trickster story about a wolf which had been bitten by dogs and looked dead. As a sheep was passing by, the wolf asked him to bring him some water; he had meat. However, the sheep did not fall for the wolf's trick, stating, "I can quite understand that if I brought you the water, you would have no difficulty about the meat."[44]

In "The Wolf and the Shepherd," a shepherd spied a wolf near his flock of sheep, but the wolf made no attempt to kill them. At first the shepherd kept a sharp eye on the wolf, but as time went on and the wolf did not meddle with the flock, the shepherd let down his guard and began to think of the wolf as a protector of the sheep. Thus, the wolf tricked him into thinking that he would not harm the sheep. However, when the shepherd was away

---

40. Aesop, 36.
41. Ibid., 41.
42. Ibid.
43. Ibid., 97.
44. Ibid., 109.

one day, "the wolf attacked [the sheep] and killed the greater number."[45] When the shepherd returned, he berated himself for trusting his flock to a wolf. In another trickster story, "The Wolves, the Sheep, and the Ram," the wolves propose a lasting peace to the sheep if the sheep give up the dogs that keep watch over them. The foolish sheep agree, but an old ram, full of wisdom, interfered, knowing that without the dogs, the sheep would be attacked.[46]

Wolf in Sheep's Clothing

In a trick to get either a lamb or a sheep, a wolf will often disguise itself in sheep's clothing. In his Sermon on the Mount in the CB (NT), the Matthean Jesus tells his listeners to beware of false prophets, who come to them in sheep's clothing but inwardly are ravenous wolves (cf. Matt 7:15). In the Third Book of Nephi in *Mormon*, Jesus states almost the same thing, saying, "Beware of false prophets, who come to you in sheep's clothing but inwardly are ravening wolves" (3 Ne 14:15). Kienzle points out that this presents the wolf as having "decidedly negative qualities."[47] She explains that "the wolf rarely represents anything good."[48] Even *The Rig Veda* contains a hymn requesting that the greedy Pani, a class of demon, be driven away, "for a wolf is he" (*RV* 6:51:14).

The idea of a wolf in sheep's clothing most likely comes from Aesop's "The Wolf in Sheep's Clothing." The story is about a trickster wolf who decides to disguise himself in order to prey upon a flock of sheep. "So he clothed himself in a sheepskin, and slipped among the sheep when they were out at pasture. He completely deceived the shepherd, and when the flock was penned for the night, he was shut in with the rest."[49] However, when the shepherd decided to have mutton for dinner that night, he went to the sheepfold and grabbed the wolf, mistaking him for a sheep, and killed him on the spot. Thus the trickster wolf tricked himself to death. This story also gives rise to the understanding that a wolf in sheep's clothing can be anyone who looks harmless or pleasant but is in fact dangerous or unpleasant.

In "The Shepherd and the Wolf," a shepherd finds a wolf pup in the pasture and takes him home to rear him with his dogs. After the pup grew, he would join the dogs in hunting down any wolf that stole a sheep from the

45. Ibid., 120.
46. Cf. Ibid., 189.
47. Kienzle, "Bestiary," 107.
48. Ibid.
49. Aesop, 24.

flock. Even if the dogs abandoned the pursuit, the wolf would continue it, find the culprit, and "stop and share the feast with him."[50] However, if some time passed without a sheep being stolen, he himself would take one and share his plunder with the dogs. One day the shepherd caught the trickster wolf in the act. After "fastening a rope around his neck, [he] hung him on the nearest tree."[51] The moral of the story is this: "What's bred in the bone is sure to come out in the flesh."[52]

Defeated Wolf

In most wolf stories, the trickster wolf is somehow defeated by a person. Grimm narrates such a tale, called "The Wolf and the Man." The story begins with a fox talking to a wolf about how strong men are. The wolf boasts that he would attack any man he saw. The next day the fox takes the wolf to a road that was traveled daily by a huntsman. The first person down the road was an old discharged soldier; the fox explains that he had been a man. The second person was a boy; the fox explained that he would be a man. The third person to pass on the road was the huntsman with his gun on his back and his knife at his side; the fox told the wolf that he was a man. The wolf attacked the man, who fired a charge at the wolf's face, fired a second charge at the wolf's face, and hit the wolf with his knife several times until the wolf ran back to the fox. The wolf says, "I never thought the strength of man would be what it is." Then, the wolf narrates what he thought he saw: "First, he took a stick from his shoulder, and blew into it, and something flew into my face, which tickled frightfully. Then he blew into it again, and it flew into my eyes and nose like lightning and hail. Then he drew a shining rib out of his body, and struck at me with it till I was more dead than alive."[53] The fox then criticizes the wolf for his bragging about being able to defeat the man, when the man had defeated him.

In Aesop's "The Wolf and the Boy," it is a boy who defeats the wolf, which, after enjoying a good meal, saw a boy lying flat on the ground in an attempt to hide from the wolf. This time the wolf presents a challenge to the boy: "[I]f you can say three things to me, the truth of which cannot be disputed, I will spare your life."[54] After thinking for a moment the boy states: "First, it is a pity you saw me; secondly, I was a fool to let myself

50. Ibid., 170.
51. Ibid.
52. Ibid.
53. Grimm, 139.
54. Aesop, 135.

be seen; and thirdly, we will hate wolves because they are always making unprovoked attacks upon our flocks."[55] The wolf has to acknowledge that what the boy said was true from his point of view. Thus, the wolf had to let the boy go. The wolf makes it clear that it is the dog's master that he fears in "The Dog Chasing a Wolf." As a dog is chasing a wolf, the dog admires his strong legs and speed, but pities the wolf who is no match for him. However, the wolf informs the dog that he is not running away from the dog, but from the dog's master.[56]

In three other fables, Aesop portrays the wolf as a trickster who is tricked. For example, in "The Ass and the Wolf," a donkey feeding in a meadow catches sight "of his enemy the wolf in the distance" and pretends "to be very lame" and hobbling "painfully along."[57] The donkey tells the wolf that he has a thorn in his paw, and asks the wolf to pull it out so that when he eats the donkey it would not stick in his throat and hurt him. When the ass lifts up his foot, the wolf gets close enough for the donkey to give him "a fearful kick in the mouth."[58] After he runs away, the wolf says to himself, ". . . [M]y father taught me to kill, and I ought to have stuck to that trade instead of attempting to cure."[59] Likewise, in "The Wolf and His Shadow," a wolf "roaming about on the plain when the sun was getting low in the sky was much impressed by the size of his shadow."[60] Thinking that he was much larger than he really was, the wolf decides that he has no reason to be afraid of a lion, which springs upon him and begins to devour him. The wolf has tricked himself and lost sight of the fact that he is smaller than a lion. And in "The Lion, the Wolf, and the Fox," a wolf attempts to trick a fox by telling a sickly lion that all the other animals care about the lion except the fox. The fox tells the lion that he has been seeking a cure for the lion. When the lion asks if he has found one, the fox replies, ". . . [Y]ou must flay a wolf and wrap yourself in his skin while it is still warm."[61] The lion immediately kills the wolf in order to try the fox's prescription, while the fox laughs. Thus, the trickster is tricked.

55. Ibid.
56. Cf. Ibid., 219.
57. Ibid., 130.
58. Ibid.
59. Ibid.
60. Ibid., 191.
61. Ibid., 204.

Mythological Wolves

In Mongolian mythology, the wolf's killing of sheep is explained by a creation story that removes some of the negativity associated with the wolf. According to the creation account about the wolf, God explains to the wolf what it should and should not eat. The wolf may eat one sheep out of every thousand. The wolf, however, misunderstood God and thought that God said to kill one thousand sheep and eat one of them. The wolf's misunderstanding gives him a little more positivity.

Three wolves appear in Norse mythology. First, there is Fenris, who had to be chained. After breaking his fetters repeatedly, the gods had the mountain spirits make a chain that could bind him. Once bound, "the wolf found that he could not break his fetters, and that the gods would not release him."[62] Second, there are "Geri and Freki, to whom Odin (one of three creator gods) gives all the meat that is set before him."[63] These two wolves are Odin's faithful pets, portrayed in iconography as sitting on either side of his throne and being good omens.

While the wolf is first portrayed as being fearful in one of the stories about the life of Francis of Assisi, the saint ends up taming the wild creature. The people of Gubbio know that there is a dangerous wolf attacking and eating their livestock. Francis decides to stop the killing by heading for the wolf's den, where he speaks to the wolf about killing other animals. Francis was able to make peace between the wolf and the townsfolk. "The wolf agreed never to hurt any animal or man. The people of the town granted that neither the dogs nor they would harass the wolf, and they would feed the wild canine so that he would not need to kill."[64] As a result of the peace made by St. Francis, the villagers fed the wolf for two years until he died.

According to legend, the twin founders of Rome—Romulus and Remus—"were suckled by a she-wolf."[65] The twins, sons of Mars and Rhea Silvia, were ordered to be killed by their uncle, Amulius. The servant, who was supposed to kill them, placed them on the bank of the Tiber River, where they were adopted by Lupa (meaning "wolf"), a she-wolf and an animal sacred to Mars. In a similar vein is the Turkic story about a she-wolf with a sky-blue mane which found a baby, nursed him, and gave birth to a half-wolf, half-human cub from whom the Turkic people were born. Thus, the wolf is thought to possess generative spiritual powers.

62. Bulfinch, *Mythology*, 330.
63. Ibid., 330.
64. Kemmerer, *Animals*, 229.
65. Bulfinch, *Mythology*, 942.

The most positive presentation of the wolf is found in the stories of Native Americans. The wolf is considered a medicine being associated with courage, strength, loyalty, and success at hunting. Being closely related to humans, some mythologies hold that the first ancestors were transformed from wolves into people. In other mythologies, the wolf is a creator god. As a sacred animal, the wolf represents the importance of family, since wolves live in packs and distribute among themselves responsibilities to hunt, to mate, and to care for pups. Pueblo tribes consider the wolf one of the six directional guardians, associated with the east and the color white. For the Plains tribes, the wolf was associated with the west, and for the Pawnee, with the southeast. Likewise, in the Pawnee creation myth, the wolf is the first creature to experience death.

Among the many stories about wolves, there is one mythology which explains how Native Americans obtained dogs. There are several variations of the tale, but the basic story entails a hunter who sees buffalo tracks in the snow but is not able to find and kill the animal for food. Before dawn he finds more tracks and a wolf runs up to him and asks, "My son, why are you weeping?" The hunter answers, "I am in sore need. My wife and child are starving." The wolf instructs the hunter to hide behind some bushes and to use the wolf's bow and arrows. The wolf will drive the buffalo toward the hunter. Once the wolf disappears, the hunter examines the bow and discovers it to be very small, but when the buffalo appear, he kills six. When the seventh appears, he uses his own bow and misses. It is important to note that six is an incomplete number, while seven is a complete number in mythology.

The wolf returns and asks about how successful the hunter is. The hunter tells him. The wolf reminds the hunter that he did not follow the wolf's directions. Nevertheless, they butchered the animals. The wolf requests two buffalo for his pups, and the hunter takes the rest to his family. After satisfying their hunger, the hunter and his family moved their tent to where the rest of the carcasses were, and the wolf and his family did the same. The hunter's wife fed the wolves, and they became tame, even being harnessed to a travois. Then, the wolves remained with the Native Americans. And that is how the Native Americans obtained dogs.[66]

Another Native American tale that exists in several versions uses the wolf as a metaphor. The story begins with an old Native American, whose grandson with anger on his face visited and asked many questions. Sitting on his grandfather's knee, the boy explains how he had gone with his father to trade furs and buy a knife. Some boys came while the boy was admiring

---

66. Cf. "How Indians Obtained Dogs."

the knife and began to bully the boy and steal the knife. The young man is very angry. This occasions the grandfather's story:

> Hate wears you down, and does not hurt your enemy. It is like taking poison and wishing your enemy would die. I have struggled with these feelings many times. It is as if there are two wolves inside me; one is white and one is black. The white wolf is good and does no harm. He lives in harmony with all around him and does not take offense when no offense was intended. He will only fight when it is right to do so, and in the right way. But the black wolf is full of anger. The littlest thing will set him into a fit of temper. He fights everyone, all the time, for no reason. He cannot think because his anger and hate are so great. It is helpless anger, for his anger will change nothing. Sometimes it is hard to live with these two wolves inside me, for both of them seek to dominate my spirit.[67]

The boy asks his grandfather, "Which one wins?" And the grandfather smiles and says, "The one I feed."[68]

Thus, the wolf is considered a creature with predominately negative characteristics. It is ravenous, prowling, destructive, and wicked. When it comes to lambs or sheep, it is the enemy, especially when it disguises itself in sheep's clothing. In fables, it is often portrayed as an evil trickster who gets tricked. From a positive point of view, the wolf can be a nurturer or tamed as a pet. Among Native Americans the wolf represents the spiritual virtues of guidance, loyalty, community, prudence, family, teamwork, and stamina. In the words of Berry, "The wolf and the human came to an intimacy with each other beyond description."[69]

Journal/Meditation: Is the wolf associated with negativity or positivity for you? Which negative quality gets most of your attention? What positive quality can you use to learn a spiritual quality from the wolf?

Prayer: Almighty Father, you made your servant the wolf one of the most ravenous of your creatures, but instilled hope that one day the wolf and the lamb would be able to coexist in peace. Through your Holy Spirit, help me to learn guidance, loyalty, prudence, discipline, and teamwork from the wolf even though I may have to travel like a lamb in the midst of wolves. Hear this prayer in the name of your Son, Jesus Christ, who is Lord forever and ever. Amen.

67. "Which One."
68. Cf. "Native American Culture," "Native American Legends."
69. Berry, "Prologue," 8.

Yak (Ox)

Text: "This young maid from the east has shined upon us; she harnesses her team of bright red oxen. She will beam forth, the light will hasten hither, and Agni will be present in each dwelling." (*RV* 1:124:11)

Reflection: In a very poetic manner, *The Rig Veda* describes the sunrise as a young maid in the east. Her bright red oxen are the rays piercing the morning sky. Agni, the Hindu god of fire, will be present in each house as the sun's rays enter through the windows. In another hymn dedicated to the dawn, the singer addresses the start of the day directly: "Dawn, bring me wealth; untroubled, with your oxen you bear riches at your will and pleasure" (*RV* 6:64:5). And in still another hymn, "dawn . . . has sent out her sheen with beauteous oxen. The sun with light has opened earth and heaven" (*RV* 7:79:1). The beautiful rays of the sun at dawn are like oxen bearing riches to the earth. Indeed, hymn 80 of book 5, also dedicated to dawn, states, "She, harnessing her car[t] with purple oxen, injuring none, has brought perpetual riches" (*RV* 5:80:3).

Specifically, oxen are adult (usually) castrated bulls, used for pulling carts, wagons, and plows. In other words, they are bovine draft animals. They are usually of larger breeds, and usually males because they are generally larger. However, sometimes cows are used. While a single ox may be employed as a draft animal, usually there are two yoked together for major tasks. Ancient people used oxen for plowing, draft, and to thresh grain by treading it.

A yak is a large, long-haired ox with long curved horns, both wild and domesticated. As a prominent animal in Tibetan culture—used both as a pack animal and a sacrificial animal like the ox—the yak is often thought of as a divine being. The word "yak" means "grunting ox." According to Vargas, the yak flourishes "at high altitudes in Tibet and Nepal."[1] Furthermore, as "[a] valuable pack animal and a source of dairy, the yak also has great significance in terms of the identity of the Tibetan peoples, especially in terms of royal succession and religious competition among different groups."[2] The first Tibetan king, knowing that he was not "equal in prudence to the yak, ... ritually killed a red yak, which was believed to have been a 'demon' creature that ruled Tibet before him."[3] However, one of his successors "failed in his ritual fight with the yak."[4] Vargas thinks that "the yak represents a rival religious and political entity."[5] A Tibetan story about the conversion of a yak illustrates religious competition. According to Vargas, "the ancestral spirits in theriomorphic [animal] form of the royal clan of Tibet and its sacred mountain" are represented by the converted white yak.[6] Thus, previous religious traditions are replaced with new ones.

Besides the yak, the buffalo, the bull, the bullock, and the water buffalo can be considered types of ox. Thus, the focus here will be on the ox, which is the name used most frequently in sacred texts. Most of the time the ox is domesticated; however, the Bible refers to it being wild (cf. Job 39:9; Isa 34:7), and *The Rig Veda* states that the god Agni wanders the earth, "free roaming like an ox without a herdsman" (*RV* 2:4:7). Even the HB (OT) psalmist declares that the LORD has given dominion over the works of his hands and put the oxen under the feet of human beings (cf. Ps 8:7). In the words of the prophet Isaiah, the ox knows its owner (cf. Isa 1:3a), but the people of Israel do not know their God. Isaiah's derogatory comment implies that the people are dumber than the ox. Or, as *The Dhammapada* puts it, the "unlearned person grows up like an ox. His bulk increases; his wisdom increases not" (*Dhp* 11:152).

Strength

The first characteristic of the ox is its strength. The HB (OT) Book of Proverbs makes this clear when it states, "Where there are no oxen, there is no grain; abundant crops come by the strength of the ox" (Prov 14:4). While preparing the bronze furnishings for the first temple, King Solomon had made a molten sea, representing the LORD's creation of order out of chaos.

1. Vargas, "Snake-Kings," 230.
2. Ibid., 230–31.
3. Ibid., 231.
4. Ibid.
5. Ibid.
6. Ibid.

"It stood on twelve oxen, three facing north, three facing west, three facing south, and three facing east" (1 Kgs 7:25; cf. 2 Chr 4:4). The three sets of four oxen represent strength—divine and animal—and fertility over all the earth. *The Rig Veda* describes the Hindu god Brahmanaspati, the personification of piety and religion and the chief offerer of prayers and sacrifices to the gods, as being as mighty "as a bull conquers oxen, overcom[ing] with strength" (*RV* 2:25:3). In a prayer found in another hymn, the singer says: "Strong be the pair of oxen, firm the axels, let not the pole slip nor the yoke be broken. May Indra keep the yoke-pins from decaying" (*RV* 3:53:7).

In "The Flea and the Ox," Aesop illustrates the strength of the ox. A flea asks an ox, "How comes it that a big strong fellow like you is content to serve mankind, and do all their hard work for them, while I, who am no bigger than you see, live on their bodies and drink my fill of their blood, and never do a stroke for it all?"[7] The ox answers that people are kind to him, and he is grateful for the feed he receives, the barn he lives in, and the occasional pat on the head and neck he gets. The flea remarks that if he let people pet him, he would be killed. And in "The Man, the Horse, the Ox, and the Dog," a horse, an ox, and a dog beg for shelter from a man during a severe winter's storm. The man admits them to his house and builds a fire to warm them. He puts hay before the ox. Before the three creatures leave they divide the life of man among them, and each endows one part of life with the qualities which were particularly his own. Thus, "the ox took middle age, and accordingly men in middle life are steady and hard-working."[8]

The ox's strength is also illustrated in the American creation story known as "Paul Bunyan." As a giant lumberjack and logger, Bunyan was assisted by "his equally gigantic blue ox named Babe."[9] Some of the lakes in the states of Minnesota and Washington "were formed from Babe's hoof prints, and she helped Paul Bunyan straighten a road by just pulling on it."[10] According to the tale, the blue ox had once been white, but because the ox was caught in a snow storm, the cold "turned Babe into America's only blue ox, which grew into American's biggest ox."[11] According to Rounds in "Babe the Mighty Blue Ox," "Babe was so strong that [s]he could pull mighty near anything that [s]he could be hitched to."[12] Rounds narrates a story about an eagle that had been roosting in Babe's right horn and decided

---

7. Aesop, 133.
8. Ibid., 189.
9. Carola, "Paul Bunyan," 185.
10. Ibid.
11. Ibid., 186.
12. Rounds, "Babe," 188.

to fly to the left one. It took the eagle from October of one year to March of the next to reach the other horn, having worn off the feathers of its head and making it bald. The story is not only mythological, explaining why eagles are bald, but it illustrates the hugeness of Babe and the strength of the ox.

The ox gets its strength from eating grass (cf. Ps 106:20; Dan 4:25, 32, 33, 5:21), licking up the grass of the field (cf. Num 22:4), eating straw (cf. Isa 11:7; 65:25; cf. 2 Ne 21:7, 30:13), eating corn (cf. D&C 86:3), or lowing over and eating its fodder (cf. Job 6:6; RV 8:26:9). Isaiah foresees a day when the oxen that till the ground will eat silage, which has been winnowed with shovel and fork (cf. Isa 30:24). Agni, the Hindu god of fire, is described as consuming "many woods like an ox" (RV 5:9:4) and "like a grazing ox" rending the woods (RV 6:2:9).

Horns

Because of the ox's strength, one must be careful of its horns. The psalmist tells the LORD, "From the horns of the wild oxen you have rescued me" (Ps 22:21b), and ". . . [Y]ou have exalted my horn like that of the wild ox" (Ps 92:10a). In a hymn dedicated to Vishnu, one of the three supreme deities of Hinduism, the singer states, "Fain would we go unto your dwelling place where there are many-horned and nimble oxen, for mightily there, shines down upon us the widely-striding bull's sublimest mansion" (RV 1:154:6). As the verse makes clear, the many-horned and nimble oxen refer to the many heavenly, twinkling stars above which the god lives. In the HB (OT) Book of Numbers, the prophet Balaam utters an oracle, a part of which declares that God is like the horns of a wild ox for Israel (cf. Num 23:22; 24:8). This point implies that God gores Israel's enemies, like an ox gores people.

Being gored by an ox must have been somewhat of a common occurrence. The HB (OT) Book of Exodus states: "When an ox gores a man or a woman to death, the ox shall be stoned, and its flesh shall not be eaten . . ." (Exod 21:28). Furthermore, "If the ox has been accustomed to gore in the past, and its owner has been warned but has not restrained it, and it kills a man or a woman, the ox shall be stoned, and its owner also shall be put to death" (Exod 21:29). The book continues, "If it gores a boy or a girl, the owner shall be dealt with according to this same rule. If the ox gores a male or female slave, the owner shall pay to the slave owner thirty shekels of silver, and the ox shall be stoned" (Exod 21:31–32). The best poetic explanation of the ox's goring is found in Moses' farewell speech before his death. Joseph, Jacob's son, is described as a firstborn bull whose horns are the horns of a wild ox; with them he gores the peoples, driving them to the ends of the earth (cf. Deut 33:17).

Yoked

In order to control this strong animal with horns, a yoke is fitted around its neck. The yoke, a wooden frame for harnessing two oxen, is designed to fit around their necks and against their shoulders to focus their strength and regulate it. Sometimes in the ancient world, oxen were sold as a pair. In one of his great feast parables, the Lukan Jesus states that one of the invited guests says to the host, "I have bought five yoke of oxen, and I am going to try them out; please accept my regrets" (Luke 14:19). Lesser Hindu deities bring "efficacious power . . . from lofty heaven . . . as to the pole an ox," states *The Rig Veda* (*RV* 1:151:4). Likewise, the storm deities "with mighty strength overthrow [the earth], like oxen difficult to yoke" (*RV* 5:56:4). *The Dhammapada* states that polluted perception, that is, tainted by impulses instead of being pure consciousness, leads to suffering "as a wheel the draft ox's foot" (*Dhp* 1:1). In other words, as a wheel on a cart follows the yoked oxen from which they cannot get away, so does suffering follow a person with a polluted mind. Similarly, Confucius addresses trust, stating, "I do not see what use a man can be put to whose word cannot be trusted. How can a wagon be made to go if it has no yoke-bar or a carriage, if it has no collar-bar?" (*Analects* 2:22)

Aesop narrates a fable about a pair of oxen "drawing a heavily loaded wagon along the highway, and, as they tugged and strained at the yoke, the axletrees creaked and groaned terribly."[13] Titled "The Oxen and the Axletrees," the fable states that the oxen ask the axletrees why they moan when the oxen do all the work. The moral, according to Aesop, is that "they complain most who suffer least."[14]

In "The Plowman, the Ass, and the Ox," a plowman "yoked his ox and his ass together, and set to work to plow his field."[15] At the end of the day when the yoke was removed from the ox and the ass, the donkey asks the ox, ". . . [W]hich of us is to carry the master home?" The ox, looking surprised, answers, "Why, you, to be sure, as usual."[16] Aesop was not aware of the biblical prohibition concerning mixtures, that is, one cannot plow with an ox and a donkey yoked together (cf. Deut 22:10). Likewise, the OT (A)

13. Aesop, 61.
14. Ibid.
15. Ibid., 183.
16. Ibid.

Book of Sirach states, "Happy the man . . . who does not plow with ox and ass together" (Sir 25:8).

Plowing and Carting

Strong oxen are yoked, as indicated above, to pull a plow. In the HB (OT) First Book of Samuel, there is a story about Saul, who had been anointed the first king of Israel by Samuel, coming from the field behind the oxen (cf. 1 Sam 11:5). Saul is attempting to unite the people, but first he must show them their disunity. So, "[h]e took a yoke of oxen, and cut them in pieces and sent them through all the territory of Israel by messengers, saying, 'Whoever does not come out after Saul and Samuel, so shall it be done to his oxen!' Then the dread of the LORD fell upon the people, and they came out as one" (1 Sam 11:7). The author of the Book of Sirach considers manual labor, like plowing, a noble task, but he prefers to honor those who seek wisdom. He asks, "How can one become wise who handles the plow, and who glories in the shaft of a goad, who drives oxen and is occupied with their work, and whose talk is about bulls?" (Sir 39:25) In one of his indictment speeches of Israel's leaders, the prophet Amos facetiously asks, "Does one plow the sea with oxen?" (Amos 6:12a) The answer is, of course, "No." Amos is using the question to point out to Israel's leaders how much they have perverted justice and righteousness.

The best biblical account of oxen being used to plow a field is found in the HB (OT) First Book of Kings. The prophet Elijah has been sent by the LORD to Elisha to anoint him as Elijah's successor. Elijah finds "Elisha son of Shaphat . . . plowing. There were twelve yoke of oxen ahead of him and he was with the twelfth" (1 Kgs 19:19). After leaving the oxen to catch Elijah, Elisha is appointed prophet, whereupon he takes "the yoke of oxen, and slaughtered them; [then] using the equipment from the oxen, he boiled their flesh, and gave it to the people, and they ate (1 Kgs 19:21). Then, freed from his plowing responsibilities, he follows Elijah.

While *Mormon* does not mention plowing specifically, it does consider the ox, among other animals, "for the use of men" (1 Ne 18:25), and the land "for the sending forth of oxen" (2 Ne 17:26). *The Rig Veda* rejoices at the commencement of plowing. In one hymn devoted to various agricultural personifications, the singer says: "Happily let the shares turn up the plowland, happily go the plowers with the oxen" (*RV* 4:57:8).

In "The Heifer and the Ox," Aesop narrates a fable about a heifer finding an ox straining hard at the plow "and sympathized with him in a rather

Yak (Ox)

patronizing sort of way on the necessity of his having to work so hard."[17] Not long afterward, there is a festival in the village and the ox was turned loose in the pasture, while the heifer was taken as a sacrifice. As the heifer is being led away, the ox says to the heifer, "I see now why you were allowed to have such an idle time: it was because you were always intended for the altar."[18]

Besides plowing, oxen are also used to pull carts or wagons. The Second Book of Samuel in the HB (OT) narrates the account of David bringing the ark of God from one town to Jerusalem on a new cart which was shaken by the oxen pulling it (cf. 2 Sam 6:6; 1 Chr 13:9). As part of the celebration, food was also brought on oxen (cf. 1 Chr 12:40). *The Rig Veda*, too, mentions "two oxen with a wagon" (*RV* 5:27:1) and "two wagon-teams, . . . [of] twenty oxen" (*RV* 6:27:8).

Edible Beef

As was indicated above in the account of Elisha slaughtering twelve yoke of oxen, that is, twenty-four beasts, cooking the food, and giving it to his people to eat, the ox was considered to be a clean animal by the Israelites, and so it could be eaten (cf. Deut 14:4; 28:31). Other peoples also considered it to be a food source (cf. Jdt 2:17). Nehemiah, governor of Judah under the Persian King Artaxerxes, explains that every day one ox was part of the food prepared for him (cf. Neh 5:18). McKenzie states that oxen were "the most esteemed animal flesh for food."[19] The HB (OT) Book of Proverbs states that a young man seduced by a woman is like an ox taken to the slaughter (cf. Prov 7:22). The prophet Isaiah condemns the killing of oxen and the eating of meat in festivity when the LORD has called for repentance (cf. Isa 22:13). Even Matthew's Gospel in the CB (NT) illustrates that for a wedding banquet oxen were slaughtered (cf. Matt 22:4). Likewise, *The Rig Veda* mentions "oxen slain" at a wedding (*RV* 10:85:13), "an ox dissevered" (*RV* 1:61:12), and that the god Agni feeds on the ox (cf. *RV* 8:43:11). The Book of Ether in *Mormon* also states that oxen, among other animals, "were useful for the food of man" (Ether 9:18).

Aesop narrates a fable about "oxen determined to be revenged upon the butchers for the havoc they wrought in their ranks" in "The Oxen and the Butchers."[20] The plan was to put to death the butchers. So, the oxen

---

17. Ibid., 144.
18. Ibid.
19. McKenzie, *Dictionary*, 629.
20. Aesop, 96.

gathered together to discuss how to get rid of the butchers. The more violent oxen sharpened their horns. However, an old, wise ox addressed the rest of them, saying:

> My brothers, you have good reason, I know, to hate these butchers, but, at any rate, they understand their trade and do what they have to do without causing unnecessary pain. But if we kill them, others, who have no experience, will be set to slaughter us, and we will by their bungling inflict great sufferings upon us. For you may be sure that, even though all the butchers perish, [human]kind will never go without their beef.[21]

Wealth

An ox is an animal of value. In other words, wealth can be tabulated in oxen. McKenzie states that a person who possessed "herds of oxen meant [he had] great wealth."[22] Thinking that Sarai is Abram's sister, the Egyptian Pharaoh gives oxen to Abram (cf. Gen 12:16). Likewise, Abimelech gives oxen to Abraham (cf. Gen 20:14), and Abraham gives oxen to Abimelech (cf. Gen 21:27). Before reconciling with his brother Jacob sends oxen to Esau (cf. Gen 32:5). If anyone steals an ox and slaughters it or sells it, the thief must pay five oxen for an ox, according to the HB (OT) Book of Exodus (cf. Exod 22:1). If the ox is found alive in the thief's possession, the thief shall pay double (cf. Exod 22:4). If one person disputes ownership of an ox with another person, God—or a judge—decides, and the one found guilty pays double to the other (cf. Exod 22:9). If someone is taking care of another person's ox and it dies, is injured, or is carried off, the caretaker swears an oath to God, and the owner receives no restitution. However, if the caretaker steals it, he makes restitution, and if it were attacked by wild beasts, the mangled corpse is produced as evidence and restitution is made (cf. Exod 22:10–13). The ox was of such value that the Book of Exodus makes clear that if a person came upon his enemy's ox straying, he was required to bring it back (cf. Exod 23:4; Deut 22:1). Likewise, if one sees a neighbor's ox fallen on the road, he cannot ignore it; he is obliged to help lift it up (cf. Deut 22:4).

In the HB (OT) Book of Numbers, the LORD instructs Moses to divide the booty captured in a battle into two parts: one part for the warriors and one part for the rest of the Israelites. Moses is told to set aside for God from the booty given to the warriors one ox out of every five hundred captured.

21. Ibid.
22. McKenzie, *Dictionary*, 629.

Yak (Ox)

From the booty given to the Israelites one ox out of every fifty is to be set aside for the LORD. Thus, God was offered seventy-two oxen from the warriors (cf. Num 31:33) and 720 from the Israelites (cf. Num 31:47). Thus, 792 oxen were offered to Israel's God. The sacrificing of oxen, representing wealth, is the act of giving back to God what belongs to him.

Oxen were considered valuable by David before he became king (cf. 1 Sam 27:9). Among King Solomon's daily provisions were ten fat oxen (cf. 1 Kgs 4:23). After King David's son, Solomon, built the first temple in Jerusalem and he brought the ark into it, he ordered the sacrifice of so many oxen that they could not be counted or numbered (cf. 2 Kgs 8:5; 2 Chr 5:6); however, the Second Book of Chronicles states that Solomon offered "as a sacrifice twenty-two thousand oxen" (2 Chr 7:5).

The Book of Job features a character who measures his wealth in oxen. As the story begins, Job owns five hundred yoke of oxen among other wealth (cf. Job 1:3). A messenger tells Job that "[t]he oxen were plowing ... and the Sabeans fell on them and carried them off" (Job 1:14–15), but after all his suffering, Job's wealth is restored to one thousand yoke of oxen (cf. Job 42:12). The prophet Isaiah portrays the LORD explaining the wealth that an ox represents: "Whoever slaughters an ox is like one who kills a human being" (Isa 66:3a). And *The Rig Veda* mentions "a hundred oxen, all of speckled hue" (*RV* 5:27:5), "ten bright-hued oxen" (*RV* 8:1:33), and "[a] hundred oxen white of hue" (*RV* 8:99:2), all of which represent value.

Even though the HB (OT) Book of Deuteronomy prohibited work on the Sabbath by the ox (cf. Exod 20: 9–10; Deut 5:13–14), even going so far as to explain that one's ox needs the relief (cf. Exod 23:12), the Lukan Jesus asks the leader of a synagogue and the others in attendance in which he has just cured an ill woman, "Does not each of you on the Sabbath untie his ox ... from the manger, and lead it away to give it water?" (Luke 13:15) Later, Jesus asks lawyers and Pharisees, "If one of you has ... an ox that has fallen into a well, will you not immediately pull it out on a Sabbath day?" (Luke 14:5) In asking both questions, the Lukan Jesus presumes the value of the ox and the appropriate response any sensible man would make when confronted with that value. In other words, the wealth represented by the ox would lead its owner to take it to water or pull it out of a well even if it were the Sabbath day.

The Rig Veda emphasizes the watering of the ox, asking the god Indra to drink the sacred soma juice "as an ox drinks the spring, a very thirsty bull the spring" (*RV* 1:130:2). Aesop narrates a fable about "The Ox and the Frog." Two little frogs were playing by a pool "when an ox came down to the water to drink, and by accident trod on one of them and crushed the life out of him."[23] The one little frog reported what happed to his mother, stating, "[A]n enormous big creature with four legs came to our pool this morning and trampled him down in the mud."[24] In order to ascertain the size of the creature, the mother frog kept puffing herself up larger and larger until she burst.

Besides its value as a food source and a means to count wealth, the ox was also considered valuable for its hide from which clothing and tents could be made. *The Rig Veda* mentions that an ox's hide is used to capture the pressed plant's juice and measure the sacred soma (cf. *RV* 9:79:5; 9:101:16; 10:94:9). In another hymn the many clouds in the sky are compared to a herd of oxen (cf. *RV* 8:46:30), while "tall oxen, a thousand heifers, numberless devices" are offered in sacrifice to Agni (*RV* 10:69:7).

Furthermore, the ox's value is noted by the biblical Book of Exodus' prohibition of coveting one's neighbor's ox (cf. Exod 20:17; Deut 5:21), which is repeated in the Book of Mosiah in *Mormon* (cf. Mosiah 13:24). The wealth which the ox represents makes it a fitting animal for sacrifice. This has been hinted at many times above, but it will be examined more specifically below.

Sacrificial Ox

God instructs Moses to build an altar of earth and sacrifice upon it burnt offerings and offerings of well-being, both of which include oxen (cf. Exod 20:24). All the fat that covers the entrails, the two kidneys with the fat that is on them, and the liver belong to God and is burned as a sacrifice; the rest of the ox is taken to the ash heap where it is burned (cf. Lev 4:8–12). The fat of the ox is considered to be sacred or holy; no person can eat it (cf. Lev 7:23; cf. *Quran* 6:146). After Moses erects the portable tent of meeting or tabernacle, the heads of the tribes present twelve oxen, one for each leader of the twelve tribes (cf. Lev 7:3). Then, for twelve days the dedication of the altar was held, and each leader on each day brought, among other animals, two oxen for a sacrifice of well-being (cf. Num 7:17, 23, 29, 35, 41, 47, 53, 59, 65, 71, 77, 83). Thus, a total of twenty-four oxen—representing wealth returned to God—were offered in sacrifice (cf. Lev 7:88). Except for the dedication of the altar, a sacrifice of well-being usually consisted of only one ox per tribe (cf. Exod 24:5; Lev 9:4, 18). However, after the first temple was built under King Solomon's reign, its dedication featured Solomon offering "twenty-two thousand oxen" as sacrifices of well-being (1 Kgs 8:63).

23. Aesop, 81.
24. Ibid.

Yak (Ox)

Deuteronomy prohibits the sacrifice of an ox that has a defect because such an animal has no value (cf. Deut 17:1). However, Leviticus permits the offering of an ox that has a limb too long or too short as a free-will offering (cf. Lev 22:23). King David made sure to sacrifice a perfect ox as the procession began with the ark of the covenant (cf. 2 Sam 6:13) and after he bought a threshing floor and oxen (cf. 2 Sam 24:22; 1 Chr 21:23). The Second Book of Chronicles also records a sacrifice of "seven hundred oxen" (2 Chr 15:11). Oxen were sacrificed well into the first century; the Acts of the Apostles in the CB (NT) records the incident of Paul healing a man in Lystra, where the crowd thinks that he is the god Hermes. A priest of the god brings oxen to sacrifice to Paul, but he does not allow it (cf. Acts 14:8–18). The psalmist seems to nullify the sacrifice of oxen, singing that he will praise the name of God with a song; he will magnify him with thanksgiving. This will please the LORD more than an ox (cf. Ps 69:30–31). Likewise, *The Rig Veda* in a hymn dedicated to the god Agni asks the god to accept the hymn as an oblation of the heart so that the verses can be like oxen sacrificed to him (cf. *RV* 6:16:47; 10:91:14).

In the HB (OT) the firstborn ox belongs to God. In the Book of Exodus, God tells Moses that the firstborn of an ox belongs to him; it may stay with its mother for seven days, the time it takes to become ritually clean, and then it is given to God (cf. Exod 22:30). In the Book of Leviticus, the LORD makes it clear that the ox that belongs to him is to become an offering by fire (cf. Lev 22:27; 27:26; Deut 15:19). According to McKenzie, "Oxen were the most precious animal for sacrifice."[25]

Finally, in the prophet Ezekiel's inaugural vision of God's throne there are four living creatures, each of which had four faces. One of the faces is that of an ox on the left side (cf. Ezek 1:10). The four creatures, representing the earth or four cardinal directions, guard the divine presence; the face of the ox represents God's strength. The prophet's vision is reworked by the author of the Book of Revelation. Instead of each living creature having four faces, Revelation presents four creatures, each having a different face. "[T]he second living creature [is] like an ox" (Rev 4:7). Later in Christianity, once the four canonical gospels were accepted, each of Revelation's living creatures was paired with a book. Thus, Luke's Gospel was represented by the ox with wings. Such figures can be found on pulpits, in stained glass windows, above cathedral entrances—especially those depicting Christ in glory—and in icons.

The yak, a type of ox, representing strength, is a sacred Tibetan animal. Every morning the ox pulls the rays of the sun over the horizon according

---

25. McKenzie, *Dictionary*, 629.

to Hindu thought. Furthermore, the ox is considered a steady, hard-working beast, despite its horns, as long as it is yoked to a plow, cart, or wagon. Its meat is food; its hide can be tanned and used for many purposes. Ancient people not only counted their wealth in oxen, but sacrificed them as a sign of their dependence upon one more powerful than the oxen, namely, God. Ultimately, in time the ox with wings, which had been a guardian of the divine presence, became an icon for Luke's Gospel.

Journal/Meditation: What spiritual quality of the yak (ox) most interests you? How is that quality confirmed in your life? How does that quality challenge you to adopt it in your life?

Prayer: O LORD, my God, how wonderful your name through all the earth! Your strength is like the sacred yak, one of the creatures you have given to your people to assist them in their stewardship of the earth. Accept the work of my hands this day as you once did the sacrifice of an ox, and grant that one day I may gaze upon your face. You are one God—Father, Son, and Holy Spirit—forever and ever. Amen.

Zebu
(Cattle, Bull, Cow, Steer, Heifer, Calf)

Text: "Drink soma, mighty one, for which, when lauded, you break through the cattle stall, O Indra. Render of kine stalls, car[t]-borne, thunder-wielding, so pierce your way to wondrous strength, O Indra. Make the sun visible, make food abundant, slaughter the foes, pierce through and free the cattle. The mighty rock that compassed in the cattle, never moved, you shook from its seat, O Indra. You with your wisdom, power, and works of wonder, have stored the ripe milk in the raw cows' utters. Unbar the firm doors for the kine of morning, and . . . set free the cattle." (*RV* 6:17:1a, 2b, 3b, 5b–6)

Reflection: The zebu is a species of cattle, characterized by a humped back, curving horns, floppy ears, and a large dewlap or loose fold of skin hanging from its neck. Even though the zebu is one of the smallest species of cattle in the world, it is used for dairy, beef, and draft, and provides the byproducts of hides for clothing and shelter, dung for fuel and manure, and bone for knife handles. In India, it represents Nandi, the sacred bull which serves as the mount for the god Shiva. *The Rig Veda* mentions cattle more than two hundred times in its hymns, and that is not counting the use of the word "kine," an archaic plural word for "cows." In this entry, the zebu will represent the generic word "cattle," found in most sacred texts, and the more specific words designating bull (male), cow (female), steer (male calf), heifer (female calf), and calf (offspring) will then follow. As one of *The Rig Veda's* hymns state, "I sing to cattle . . ." first (*RV* 8:27:12).

Cattle

Cattle are grouped together as a herd. The patriarch Jacob in the HB (OT) Book of Genesis mentions traveling at the pace of the cattle herd (cf. Gen 33:14) and his son, Joseph, acquires herds of cattle (cf. Gen 47:18) from the people of Egypt in exchange for food during a time of famine. Likewise, during a locust plague, the prophet Joel declares, "The herds of cattle wander about because there is no pasture for them . . ." (Joel 1:18). In the past, according to the prophet Isaiah, before the people of Israel rebelled against their God, "[T]he spirit of the LORD gave them rest, [l]ike cattle that go down into the valley" (Isa 63:14). In *The Rig Veda*, Indra, Hinduism's chief god, is depicted as driving cattle from his foes (cf. *RV* 1:33:3). Hymn 164 of book 1 mentions a herd of cattle (cf. *RV* 1:164:17b), and hymn 166 of the same book explains how lightning "crunches up the cattle like a well-aimed dart" (*RV* 1:166:6). Other hymns mention "herds of cattle in a food-filled pasture" (*RV* 4:2:18), "a herd of cattle" (*RV* 4:38:5; 4:58:10), and "troops of cattle" (*RV* 4:51:8; 4:52:5).

Because cattle are grouped as a herd, those who tend them are named cattle herders. The Book of Genesis mentions that Jacob's sons were with his cattle herders (cf. Gen 34:5). *The Dhammapada* compares a person who recites sacred texts but does not practice them to "a cowherd counting others' cows" (*Dhp* 1:19). In other words, reciting a text about virtue, but not practicing the virtue, is like a cowherd who looks after other people's cows all day and returns them all accounted for in the evening, but never gets to enjoy the milk foods the cows produce. In another place, Buddhism's sacred text compares old age and death that goad the life of the living to the "rod a cowherd" uses to goad cows to a pasture (*Dhp* 10:135). *The Rig Veda* declares that Indra "made paths easy to drive forth the cattle" (*RV* 3:30:10), "a herdsman drives forth his cattle" (*RV* 5:31:10), "the household herdsman guards the cattle" (*RV* 6:19:3), "the herdsman drives home his cattle" (*RV* 6:49:12), "a brisk herdsman moving round his cattle" (*RV* 7:13:3), and being "made the herdsman of . . . cattle" (*RV* 10:108:3). Kemmerer states that the god Krishna, an incarnation of Vishnu, is sometimes depicted suckling directly from a cow. "When little Krishna grows from babyhood to boyhood, he tends white, brown, and spotted cattle with the other boys of his village, keeping them from harm while they graze . . . ."[1] She adds that Krishna "takes his duties as a cowherd seriously."[2]

---

1. Kemmerer, *Animals*, 70.
2. Ibid.

As has already been hinted, a cattle herder moves a herd of cattle to pasture, where the cattle can find food, primarily grass, and water. In the HB (OT), God tells Moses to give to the Levites pasture lands for their cattle (cf. Num 35:3). Psalm 104 states that God causes "the grass to grow for the cattle" (Ps 104:14a), and the prophet Isaiah declares that the "cattle will graze in broad pastures" (Isa 30:23b). In *Mormon*, the hills are to be cleared for "the treading of lesser cattle" (2 Ne 17:23).

In *The Rig Veda*, the god of tempests, Rudra, is asked to let "it be well with all . . . cattle . . . that in [the] village all be healthy and well-fed" (*RV* 1:114:1). In another hymn, the god Tvastar, the first-born creator of the universe and the god invoked when desiring offspring, is declared to have made "all forms and all the cattle of the field"; then he is petitioned to "cause them to multiply" (*RV* 1:188:9). In a hymn dedicated to the gods Mitra-Varuna, Hindu deities connected with the sun, the gods are petitioned "with fatness [to] dew the pastures of [the] cattle" (*RV* 7:62:5). In another hymn, Indra is asked to find enjoyment in the hymns that are sung "like cattle [find enjoyment] in the pasture lands" (*RV* 8:81:12b). Other than cattle taking corn, as is mentioned in hymn 52 of book 8 (cf. *RV* 8:52:9) and water quenching the cattle's thirst (cf. *RV* 1:23:18), cattle seem to prefer "ample pasturage" (*RV* 9:87:5).

When the cattle are not in the pasture, they are at rest in a shelter of some kind (cf. Mosiah 13:18) because "cattle seek their home" (*RV* 6:41:1). The HB (OT) Second Book of Chronicles states that King Hezekiah of Judah made stalls for all kinds of cattle (cf. 2 Chr 32:28). And *The Rig Veda* repeatedly refers to the "stall of cattle" (*RV* 4:2:17; 4:16:6; 6:65:5; 7:27:1; 7:90:4; 10:108:8; cf. 10:97:8), the "firm built stall of cattle" (*RV* 3:32:16), "the firm-closed stall of cattle" (*RV* 6:62:11), "the stable full of cattle" (*RV* 4:1:15; cf. 4:20:8; 6:10:3; 10:45:11), "the great stalls filled with cattle" (*RV* 6:73:3), and "shelter for cattle" (*RV* 8:30:4).

When cattle are at rest, the sound they make is referred to as lowing or mooing. For example, when the prophet Samuel discovers that King Saul has not eliminated all the animals of his enemies after he has defeated them, he asks, "What then is . . . the lowing of cattle that I hear?" (1 Sam 15:14) When writing about the destruction of Jerusalem, the prophet Jeremiah states that the lowing of cattle is not heard (cf. Jer 9:10b). *The Rig Veda*, too, mentions this sound made by cattle as "the lowing cattle" (*RV* 10:68:7; cf. 10:108:11), "the lowing company of hidden cattle" (*RV* 1:121:4), and "the kine were lowing as they greeted morning" (*RV* 7:75:7). Sometimes, however, "the cattle loudly bellow" (*RV* 8:85:5).

The number of cattle in a herd is a means for the owner to assess his wealth. Specifically mentioned among Esau's (Jacob's brother's) possessions are his cattle (cf. Gen 36:6). The cattle taken by the Israelites in war from the Midianites are considered booty (cf. Num 31:9). Likewise, "the Reubenites and the Gadites owned a very great number of cattle . . . and the land of Jazer and the land of Gilead was a good place for cattle" (Num 32:1). So the tribe of Reuben and Gad petition Moses to give them the land for cattle because they had many (cf. Num 32:4). In the First Book of Chronicles, the reader learns that Reuben's descendants had moved "east as far as the beginning of desert this side of the Euphrates, because their cattle had multiplied in the land of Gilead" (1 Chr 5:9). Moses tells the people that if they heed the LORD's ordinances, their cattle will increase (cf. Deut 7:13; 28:4), as did those of the tribe of Reuben. In his attempt to dissuade the Israelites from having a king, Samuel tells them that a king will take the best of their cattle (cf. 1 Sam 8:16). Their first king, Saul, disobeys the LORD's command to destroy not only his enemies, but his enemies' possessions, such as cattle, because of their value (cf. 1 Sam 15:9). Solomon, Israel's third king, needed twenty pasture-fed cattle (cf. 1 Kgs 4:23), among many other animals, as a daily provision for his court.

The value of cattle led the people of Gath to attack the tribe of Ephraim in order to raid their cattle (cf. 1 Chr 7:21; Ezek 38:12, 13). The chronicler also notes that cattle were so valuable that King David appointed stewards for the king's cattle (cf. 1 Chr 28:1). Even the psalmist sings to God asking that the "cattle be heavy with young" (Ps 144:14a). The OT (A) wisdom Book of Sirach states very clearly that cattle make one prosperous (cf. Sir 40:19). However, as *The Dhammapada* notes, the "man of entangled mind, inebriated by . . . cattle, death carries away like a great flood . . ." (*Dhp* 20:287). In other words, the wealth of cattle causes the non-enlightened owner to desire even more, until death claims his life.

The Rig Veda repeatedly mentions being "rich in cattle" (*RV* 1:8:8; 8:22:17; 9:92:6), "wealthy in cattle" (*RV* 1:9:7; cf. 1:33:1; 1:83:4), "wealth in cattle" (*RV* 3:1:23; 3:5:11; 3:6:11; 3:7:11; 3:15:7; 3:22:5; 3:23:5; 6:35:3; 7:94:9; 9:69:8; 10:42:7), and "winning cattle, winning wealth" (*RV* 8:64:11). Sometimes, the singer petitions one of the gods to "send . . . cattle in abundance" (*RV* 3:50:3), to "bring . . . [a] store of cattle" (*RV* 3:54:15; cf. 8:67:2; 10:42:10; 10:43:10: 10:44:10), to give cattle (cf. *RV* 4:22:10; 6:23:4), to "vouchsafe . . . cattle" (*RV* 5:42:4), or to grant treasures among which are cattle (cf. *RV* 7:27:5). In one hymn, the singer mentions "a hundred thousand" cattle (*RV* 10:102:9), "four thousand cattle" and "four thousand head of cattle" (*RV* 5:30:12, 15), "a thousand cattle" (*RV* 10:80:4, 5), "three hundred head of cattle" (*RV* 5:36:6), "hundreds of cattle" (*RV* 8:21:10; 10:95:3), and "wealth in . . . cattle [a] hundredfold" (*RV* 9:67:6). Maybe the best summary of *The Rig Veda's* understanding of cattle as wealth is found in hymn 42 of book 5:

"Wealth that brings bliss is found among the givers . . . of cattle . . ." (*RV* 5:42:8). This is why Agni, the god of fire, is petitioned to "guard . . . the life of all . . . cattle" (*RV* 1:72:6).

Cattle are so important in *The Rig Veda* that Indra is named Lord of Cattle. Indra wins cattle in combat (cf. *RV* 4:17:10). He is declared the "Lord of kine" (*RV* 6:45:21), the "Father of cattle" (*RV* 8:36:5), and the "Lord of cattle" (*RV* 7:18:4; 9:72:4; 10:47:1; 10:67:8; 10:121:3). In fact, Indra is "alone the Lord of cattle" (*RV* 7:98:6).

Because of their value, cattle are sacrificed. According to King Saul in the First Book of Samuel, the people spared the best of the cattle to sacrifice to the LORD (cf. 1 Sam 15:15), even though they were not supposed to do this. When Adonijah is claiming the throne of his father David, he sacrifices fatted cattle to God in order to cement his position before Solomon, David's designated heir, unseats him (cf. 1 Kgs 1:9, 19, 25). John's Gospel uniquely mentions people selling cattle to be sacrificed in the temple in Jerusalem (cf. John 2:14) which are driven out by Jesus (cf. John 2:15). Besides being used for sacrifice, cattle also could serve as a tithe (cf. 2 Chr 31:6; Tob 1:6).

Not to be forgotten is the fact that cattle serve as food for people. The Book of Ether in *Mormon* makes this clear (cf. Ether 9:18). The Bible presumes that people kill and eat cattle, but its concern is with regulations for sacrificing them to the LORD. In *The Rig Veda*, Indra is asked to provide "plenteous food" with the singers and to accompany them in their feast of "the foeman's cattle" (*RV* 1:121:15). Indra is also asked to "grant to the singer food with [a] store of cattle" (*RV* 6:35:4). Agni, too, is asked to give "food . . . and cattle" to the singer (*RV* 1:140:13) because "with might [he] gives much food in cattle even to the wicked wolf when he is hungry" (*RV* 6:13:5). And, finally, besides being edible, cattle provide milk. The singer asks Indra to answer his prayer for riches, like those desiring milk from cattle in goodly pasture (cf. *RV* 7:18:4).

Bulls

Zebu, a species of cattle, are, like all other cattle, divided by sex and named. Male cattle are called bulls. Biblically, bulls represent strength and fertility, and, as such, are sacrificed to Israel's God. The psalmist illustrates the bull's strength, stating, "Many bulls encircle me, strong bulls of Bashan surround me" (Ps 22:12). Because the area of Bashan in eastern Palestine was known for it rich pasture, Bashan bulls (cf. Deut 32:14) are known for their strength. The prophet Isaiah portrays the king of Assyria declaring that "like a bull [he has] brought down those who sat on thrones" (Isa 10:13). In a reflection on passion, the author of the OT (A) Book of Sirach advises the reader not to fall into the grip of passion, because he or she may be torn apart as by a bull (cf. Sir 6:2). The prophet Jeremiah mentions the bull-god of Egypt, Apis, in declaring that the LORD's strength is greater than his. "Why has Apis fled?" asks Jeremiah. "Why did your bull not stand?" Then, he answers, "Because the LORD thrust him down" (Jer 46:15). Later, in the same book, Jeremiah describes the destruction of the temple at the hands of the Babylonians, especially "the twelve bronze bulls that were under the sea, . . . which King Solomon had made for the house of the LORD" (Jer 52:20); the twelve bulls represented the twelve tribes of Israel united as one, strong nation. Jeremiah also describes the defeat of Babylon one day, stating that all the bulls should be slaughtered (cf. Jer 50:27); this is another way of saying that the strength of Babylon is defeated by God. The best illustration of the bull's strength is applied by Moses to the sons of Joseph, Ephraim and Manasseh, because of their military prowess; Moses uses the image of an aggressive bull. Moses states, "A firstborn bull—majesty is his! His horns are the horns of a wild ox; with them he gores the peoples, driving them to the ends of the earth" (Deut 33:17). Thus, the bull represents strength.

The bull is a sign of fertility. *The Rig Veda* mentions "the prolific bull" (*RV* 1:160:3). In one of his speeches Job reflects on the injustice of the wicked. He tells his friends that "[t]heir bull breeds without fail" (Job 21:10a). To sacrifice a bull to God is to give the LORD one's future prosperity, that is, the calves that the bull would have sired if he would have lived. Thus, bulls are slaughtered as an act of dependence upon God for the future.

The HB (OT) Book of Exodus narrates Moses' ordination of Aaron and his sons as priests. Moses takes a bull upon whose head Aaron and his sons lay their hands. Then, Moses slaughters the bull and puts some of its blood on the horns of the altar, pouring out the rest of the blood at the base of the altar. The fatty parts are burned on the altar, and the rest of the bull is burned outside the camp as a sin offering (cf. Exod 29:1–14; Lev 8:1–17). Because the ordination rite is to last seven days, a bull is offered every day as a sin offering (cf. Exod 29:36). Burnt offerings, as the Book of Leviticus states, consist of a bull upon which the offerer has laid his hand (cf. Lev 1:5–9). A bull of the herd without blemish serves as a sin offering to the LORD (cf. Lev 4:3). The sinner lays his hand on the head of the bull, and then it is slaughtered before the LORD. The priest takes some of the blood and sprinkles it seven times before the curtain of the sanctuary, puts blood on the horns of the altar, and pours the rest at the base of the altar. Then, he burns the fat on the altar and takes the rest of the bull outside the camp to be burned there (cf. Lev 4:3–12). If the whole congregation of Israel sins, then the elders lay their hands on the bull's head, and the rest of the ritual is followed as outlined above (cf. Lev 4:13–21).

The HB (OT) often mentions a young bull for a sin offering (cf. Lev 16:3) and the sprinkling of the bull's blood on the sanctuary curtain, the horns of the altar, the altar itself, or the mercy seat, that is, the place on the ark of the covenant where God was believed to sit (cf. Lev 16:14, 18). A young bull can also be a burnt offering (cf. Lev 23:18). As part of the dedication of the tabernacle, the Book of Numbers describes how for twelve consecutive days each tribe of Israel presented, among other items, one young bull for a burnt offering (cf. Num 7:15, 21, 27, 33, 39, 45, 51, 57, 63, 69, 75, 81). Thus, twelve bulls we prepared as burnt offerings (cf. Num 7:87). Also, for a sacrifice of well-being twenty-four bulls were offered (cf. Num 7:88).

When the Levites are cleansed, they, too, offer a young bull as a sin offering and another young bull as a burnt offering (cf. Num 8:5–13). A bull can be offered by any Israelite as "a burnt offering or a sacrifice, to fulfill a vow or as an offering of well-being" (Num 15:8; cf. 15:24).

In the narrative about Balaam called by Balak to curse the Israelites, Balaam instructs Balak to build seven altars and to prepare seven bulls to be offered, one on each altar as burnt offerings in order to divine the will of God. This ritual is done three times, and after each time the words God puts into Balaam's mouth bless the Israelites instead of curse them (cf. Num 23:1–30).

Later in the same book, the LORD instructs Moses that at the beginning of every month two young bulls are to be a burnt offering (cf. Num 28:11). Likewise, on the fourteenth day of the first month, two young bulls serve as a burnt offering (cf. Num 28:19), as they do on the day of the first fruits (cf. Num 28:27). On the first day of the seventh month, a single bull is offered (cf. Numbers 29:2), as is done of the tenth day (cf. Num 29:8). However, on the fifteenth day, thirteen young bulls are to be a burnt offering to the LORD (cf. Num 29:13). This begins a seven-day festival. On the second day twelve young bulls are offered (cf. Num 29:17); on the third day eleven bulls are offered (cf. Num 29:20); on the fourth day ten bulls are offered (cf. Num 29:23); on the fifth day nine bulls are offered (cf. Num 29:26); on the sixth day eight bulls are offered (cf. Num 29:29); on the seventh day seven bulls are offered (cf. Num 29:32), and on the eighth day one bull is offered (cf. Num 29:29:36).

In the HB (OT) Book of Judges, Gideon is called by God to eliminate idolatry from the land. In order to begin this process, he takes his father's bull to pull down Baal's altar. Then, he builds an altar for the LORD. Upon that altar, using the wood of the sacred pole representing the goddess Asherah, he prepares a burnt offering of a seven-year-old bull. The seven-year-old bull represents the sacred strength of God, who encompasses both heaven (signified by three) and earth (signified by four) (cf. Judg 6:25–28).

Using a three-year-old bull, representing a theophany, Hannah, wife of Elkanah, not only offers the bull to God, but presents her son, Samuel, to God at the shrine in Shiloh, where the ark of the covenant is located (cf. 1 Sam 1:21–28). Elijah needs only one bull for the theophany on Mount Carmel (cf. 1 Kgs 18:1–40). When bringing the ark of the covenant from Shiloh to Jerusalem, David sacrifices seven bulls, representing God's strength and pervading presence (cf. 1 Chr 15:26). Later, David will offer one thousand bulls as burnt offerings to the LORD after securing provisions for the building of the temple by his son, Solomon (cf. 1 Chr 29:21). The chronicler also records that the reforming King Hezekiah, after repairing the temple, slaughtered seven bulls among other animals as a sin offering to God for the people of his kingdom (cf. 2 Chr 29:20–24) while the members of the assembly brought burnt offerings of seventy bulls (cf. 2 Chr 29:32) and consecrated offerings of six hundred bulls (cf. 2 Chr 29:33). Later, the chronicler records that King Hezekiah of Judah gave those assembled for Passover one thousand bulls for offerings, and his officials gave another one thousand bulls (cf. 2 Chr 30:24). Likewise, King Josiah of Judah is reported to have given the people three thousand bulls, his officials gave another three hundred bulls (cf. 2 Chr 35:8), and the chiefs of the Levites gave five hundred bulls (cf. 2 Chr 35:9).

Once Ezra finishes rebuilding the temple in Jerusalem after the Babylonians had destroyed it in 587 BCE, part of the dedication ceremony consists of offering one hundred bulls (cf. Ezra 6:17). When some of the former captives return to Jerusalem, they offer twelve bulls as burnt offerings to God (cf. Ezra 8:35); the twelve bulls represent the strength of the twelve tribes of Israel. Job's three friends are told by the LORD to offer seven bulls as burnt offerings to quell God's anger at them (cf. Job 42:7–9).

Considering all the bulls that are sacrificed as sin offerings, well-being offerings, and burnt offerings, the psalmists present a paradox. The author of Psalm 50 portrays the LORD declaring to the house of Israel, "I will not accept a bull from your house" (Ps 50:9a). In the same Psalm, God asks, "Do I eat the flesh of bulls?" (Ps 50:13a) As the author of Psalm 51 states, God is interested in the contrite hearts of people. Then, bulls can be offered on his altar (cf. Ps 51:19). While one psalmist sings, "I will make an offering of bulls . . ." (Ps 66:15c), another psalmist declares that praise of God's name will please him more than "a bull with horns and hoofs" (Ps 69:30). The prophet Isaiah also emphasizes this point, portraying the LORD saying, "I do not delight in the blood of bulls . . ." (Isa 1:11c).

The prophet Ezekiel, while in Babylonian captivity, records God's words to him about the rebuilding of the temple in Jerusalem. Among those words is the directive that a bull be offered on the altar for sin (cf. Ezek 43:18–27). Furthermore, the directive concerning the putting of its blood on the four horns of the altar, the offering of a bull on the first day of the first month (cf. Ezek 45:18–20), the sacrifice of a bull as a sin offering, and the sacrifice of seven young bulls on each day of the seven-day festival (cf. Ezek 45:21–25) resemble those found in the HB (OT) books of Leviticus and Numbers. The offering of a bull on the day of a new moon (cf. Ezek 46:6) and on other festivals (cf. Ezek 46:11) also echo the same regulations found in Leviticus and Numbers.

In 70 CE, the second temple in Jerusalem was destroyed by the Romans. Thus, in the CB (NT) there is only one mention of bulls, and that is found in the Letter to the Hebrews. Most likely a sermon, rather than a letter, the author portrays Jesus as being a high priest who offered himself once for all. His how-much-more argument states that Jesus entered heaven not with the blood of unblemished bulls, but with his own blood (cf. Heb 9:11–14). Later the writer adds that "it is impossible for the blood of bulls . . . to take away sins" (Heb 10:4); only the blood of Christ can do that.

The Dhammapada uses the image of a bull's strength to describe a *brahmana*, that is, a person who has reached enlightenment or deep insight: "A bull, splendid, heroic, a great sage, a victor, passionless, who has bathed, awakened, that one I call a *brahmana*" (Dhp 26:422). In other words, the noble, enterprising, wise, powerful, passionless person, who has been cleansed of all desires, is awakened and is as strong as a bull. Aesop illustrates this same enlightened quality in his fable titled "The Gant and the Bull." After a gnat alights on one of the bull's horns and remains there for a while, the bug gets ready to fly away and asks the bull, "Do you mind if I go now?" The bull replies, "I didn't notice when you came, and I shan't know when you go away."[3]

Another of *Aesop's Fables* echoes the Bible by using the number three. In "The Lion and the Three Bulls," a lion, who thinks that he is no match for three powerful bulls, decides to foment jealousy among them. His plan works; the bulls, instead of grazing together, separate themselves from each other. This gives the lion the opportunity to kill them one by one.[4] In "The Lion and the Bull," the lion does not fare as well, even though the lion tricks the bull into coming to his den under the guise of sacrificing a sheep. When the bull gets there, he immediately recognizes what the lion is about to do—

---

3. Aesop, 30.
4. Cf. Ibid., 98.

kill him—and he leaves.⁵ In Aesop's third fable about a lion and a bull, titled "The Herdsman and the Lost Bull," a herder misses a young bull and goes in search of him. He makes a vow to Jupiter that if he should find the thief, he would sacrifice a calf. When he finds the bull being devoured by a lion, he prays to Jupiter, asking to escape from the lion, by offering the bull in place of a calf.⁶

While the bull represents strength, in "The Mouse and the Bull" the mouse illustrates that it is not always the strong who win. After a mouse bites a bull on the nose, the mouse runs into a hole in a wall to escape the angry bull, which charges the wall until it is exhausted. Thereupon the mouse emerges from his hole, bites the bull again, and runs back to his hole in the wall! The bull can do nothing except bellow and fume. From inside the wall, the bull hears the mouse say, "You big fellows don't always have it your own way, you see; sometimes we little ones come off best."⁷

Cows

Female cattle are called cows. In most cultures, cows are of lesser importance than bulls, except in Hindu culture. Their primary purpose in patriarchal cultures is to serve as receptacles for the bull's sperm, conceive calves, and give birth to calves. However, in Hindu culture "the cow is [the] sum of all things" (*RV* 1:173:8). While the god Indra is "like a bull," he is also "bounteous like a cow" (*RV* 8:1:2). Indra is "rich in kine," "lord of herds of kine," and "to worshippers, Indra is [like] a cow yielding in plenty kine" (*RV* 8:14:1, 2, 3). Even the earth is referred to as "a mother cow" (*RV* 10:176:1). Nelson explains that the cow for Hindus is mother because "human beings . . . depend upon the cow as upon their mother."⁸ Kemmerer says that cows "exemplify munificence and mother's love."⁹ Paper explains that people were dependent upon them "for animal protein (milk and milk products), edible oil (clarified butter), traction (draft animals), and fuel (dried dung)."¹⁰

Kemmerer narrates a Hindu tale about a famine in which a king searches the earth, looking for food for his people. According to Kemmerer, at some point in the story the "earth becomes a cow (a symbol of munificence) and begs for her life. The king grants the cow life in exchange for

5. Cf. Ibid., 113.
6. Cf. Ibid., 153.
7. Ibid., 111.
8. Nelson, "Cows," 180.
9. Kemmerer, *Animals*, 58.
10. Paper, "Humans and Animals," 328.

life-sustaining milk for his starving community."[11] She notes that "cows eat grass and produce milk; the people of India understood that living cows could carry them through famine much better than dead cows...."[12]

Nelson states that the cow "has undergone a gradual apotheosis, becoming over time a key symbol of all that is sacred to, and unifies, Hindus."[13] He adds that cows are "emblematic of all that is pure and holy."[14] According to Nelson, the story of Lakshmi, "a cow who was counted among the most faithful devotees"[15] of a twentieth-century saint, is noted for her spirituality. Bryant notes that cows "support everything in the world" and that eating beef "is like eating everything, and a person so doing will be reborn as a sinful being."[16]

Thus, it should come as no surprise that there are over 120 references to cows in *The Rig Veda*, and most of those concern the food the cow gives in terms of milk. *The Rig Veda* asks Indra to assist the singer like "a good cow [assists] him who milks" (*RV* 1:4:1). Another singer asks Indra to love the song he sings: "Milk may it yield us as, gone forth to pasture, the great cow pouring out her thousand rivers" (*RV* 4:41:5). "I call with hymns, as 'twere a cow to milk," states another hymn, "the friend who merits praise, the *brahman* who accepts the prayer," namely Indra (*RV* 6:45:7). Another sage "has poured forth his prayers [to Indra], desiring to milk [him] like a cow in goodly pasture" (*RV* 7:18:4). And another singer says to draw Indra to self "like a cow at milking" (*RV* 10:42:2). The following verse sums up best all the petitions made to Indra for milk: "Do you bestow upon us her, O Indra, who yields according to the singer's longing, that the great cow may, with exhaustless udder, pouring a thousand streams, give milk to feed us" (*RV* 10:133:7).

Agni is like "a cow who yields her milk" (*RV* 1:66:1); he "discerns like the cow's udder, the sweet taste of food" (*RV* 1:69:2). Agni is also the guardian of the homestead, and he is asked to give "sweet drink... of the milk the cow provides" (*RV* 1:153:4). Another hymn asks Agni to protect the singer from those who take what it not theirs: "The fiend... who steals the milch-cow's milk away, O Agni—tear off the heads of such with fiery fury. The cow gives milk each year; let not the [fiend] ever taste it" (*RV* 10:87:16–17a).

---

11. Kemmerer, *Animals*, 58.
12. Ibid., 59.
13. Nelson, "Cows," 180.
14. Ibid., 186.
15. Ibid., 187.
16. Bryant, "Vedic Subversion," 197.

The dawn is compared to "a cow [which] yields her udder" (*RV* 1:92:4). Morning and night are "like a cow good at milking" (*RV* 7:2:6). Even the sacred soma, the elixir of life, is said to impregnate the cow (cf. *RV* 9:99:6). Other phrases about milk include: "the milk shed from the cow" (*RV* 1:121:5), "a cow good to milk" (*RV* 1:186:4), "the cow's udder teems with milk" (*RV* 2:14:10), "the willing cow teeming with plenteous milk, full, inexhaustible" (*RV* 2:32:3), "the cow yields milk" (*RV* 4:57:2), and "milking the teeming cow for all-sustaining food" (*RV* 10:122:6a).

For Vayu, the god of the wind, "the nectar-yielding cow [Sabardugha] pours all rich treasures forth as milk" (*RV* 1:134:4). Likewise, "Aditi the milch-cow streams" milk (*RV* 1:153:4). In another hymn the singer turns to the holy gods, asking them to "pour milk for [him] even as a stately cow who, having sought the pasture, yields a thousand streams" (*RV* 10:101:9).

The Maruts, the storm gods, are petitioned to make the singer's prayers swell like a cow's udder (cf. *RV* 2:34:6). Another hymn devoted to the Maruts begins "Even to the wise let that be still a wonder to which the general name of cow is given." It continues, "The one has swelled among mankind for milking: Prsni has drained but once her fair bright udder" (*RV* 6:66:1). In other words, the Hindu goddess of the earth, Prsni, the mother of the Maruts, has given her milk but once when she brought forth her offspring. The cows of earth yield milk frequently and in abundance. "The cow, the famous mother of wealthy Maruts, pours her milk" (*RV* 8:83:1).

In *The Rig Veda*, the Asvins, divine twin horsemen representing the shining of sunrise and sunset, are repeatedly credited with making "the cow of Sayu stream refreshing milk" (*RV* 1:119:6). "[A]ncient Sayu [, a Hindu sage,] in his sore affliction [was helped by the Asvins, who] caused his cow to swell with milk" (*RV* 1:118:8), that is, they "made the barren cow give milk" (*RV* 1:112:3; cf. 1:116:22). "Bounteous, [they] filled the cow with milk for Sayu" (*RV* 6:62:7). In another hymn the Asvins are referred to as "wonder-workers, [who] filled with milk for Sayu the milkless cow" (*RV* 1:117:20). Also, they "have deposited . . . in the raw cow the first milk of the milch-cow" (*RV* 1:180:3). Again, the Asvins "listened when invoked to Sayu's calling. They made the cow pour forth her milk like water, and . . . strengthened with [their] strength the barren. May the cow nourish him with milk to feed him" (*RV* 7:68:8b, 9b). In book 10 of *The Rig Veda*, the singer of the hymn says: "Come, conquerors of the sundered mountain, to our home, Asvins, who made the cow stream milk for Sayu's sake" (*RV* 10:39:13a).

When all is said and done, "The cow [after] yielding milk goes her appointed way" (*RV* 10:65:6). Of course, the milk can be made into butter "pure, heated, of the cow, the milch-cow's bounty" (*RV* 4:1:6). It was Indra who "obtained the cow who feeds many" (*RV* 3:34:9), but the Asvins fill the "cow with food that never fails" (*RV* 6:63:8). In a very poetic way of writing, "Indra found meath collected in the milch-cow, by foot and hoof, in the cow's place of pasture" (*RV* 3:39:6). In other words, Indra found sweet rain turned into milk after tracking the cow by her footprints. A cow usually has a caretaker, otherwise it "wanders free without a herdsman" (*RV* 3:57:1). If the owner does not want the cow to wander, it must be tethered by the foot (cf. *RV* 4:12:6) or put in a stall (cf. *RV* 6:45:24), or "bound fast to every tree [where] the cow is lowing" (*RV* 10:27:22; cf. 2:34:15; 4:50:5).

Cows can be called. The singer of a hymn states that he calls Indra with songs "even as a cow to profit" him (*RV* 8:54:3), or "as the milkers call the cow who yields abundant milk" (*RV* 8:96:4 [4:4]), or one just "calling to his cow" (*RV* 10:146:4).

Not only are cows considered as sacred in Hinduism, but they are also a means for a person to count his wealth, unless there is "a thief lurking in [a] dark cave with a stolen cow" (*RV* 1:65:1). The singer asks to "be exceeding wealthy" and then declares, "[f]eed on the grass, O cow, at every season" (*RV* 1:164:40). Another singer declares, "Now let that wealthy cow of yours, O Indra, yield in return a boon to him who lauds you" (*RV* 2:11:21; 2:15:10; 2:16:9; 2:17:9; 2:18:9; 2:19:9; 2:20:9). Such wealthy cows come in all kinds of colors, such as "radiant-colored" (*RV* 1:137:3), "partly-colored" (*RV* 1:160:3), "of every hue" (*RV* 1:161:6), "black of hue" (*RV* 4:3:9), "white" (*RV* 4:33:1), "dark," and "red" (*RV* 10:61:4).

In other traditions, cows are considered wealth. For example, in the Bible when Jacob goes to meet his brother, Esau, he brings, among other things, a present of forty cows (cf. Gen 32:15). Also, the Bible considers the firstborn of a cow to belong to God (cf. Exod 34:19) and it needs to be redeemed because it is holy; if it is not redeemed, it is sacrificed to God (cf. Num 18:17). Several times the prophet Isaiah uses the image of a cow as a sign of prosperity and peace. For example, on the day that God defeats Israel's enemies, "one will keep alive a young cow . . . and will eat curds because of the abundance of milk" that it gives (Isa 7:21; cf. 2 Ne 17:21). According to Isaiah, the cow and the bear will graze together; their young will lie down together (cf. Isa 11:7; cf. 2 Ne 21:7; 30:13). As in Hindu culture, cow's dung was used as fuel (cf. Ezek 4:15). However, unlike Hindu culture, cows were considered as food in both the biblical world and in the Mormon world (cf. Ether 9:18; 1 Ne 18:25).

Steer

A steer is a male calf or a young bull in the cattle (bovine) family which has been castrated before reaching sexual maturity and is raised as food. However, the word "steer" can also designate a male calf under four years old. Thus, there exists some ambiguity as to the meaning of the word in literature. In general, the Bible does not use the word "steer," but *The New American Bible* translation does two times. When Abraham welcomed three visitors during the heat of the day, "[h]e ran to the herd, picked out a tender, choice steer, and gave it to a servant, who quickly prepared it" (Gen 18:7; cf. 18:8). *The Rig Veda* mentions that "a steer plows the barley" (*RV* 1:176:2), that "one who plows with steers brings corn" (*RV* 1:23:15), that the "steers ... plow [the] furrow happily" (*RV* 4:57:4) "as a plower [sings] to his steers" (*RV* 8:20:19). Also mentioned is "the vigorous steer who loves the kine" (*RV* 10:40:11) and "the vital vigor of the potent steer" (*RV* 10:43:11b). "Even the wild steer in his thirst is captured; the leather strap still holds his foot entangled" (*RV* 10:28:10).

In *The Rig Veda*, the god of fire, Agni, is repeatedly referred to as a "steer" (*RV* 10:4:5), a "bellowing steer" (*RV* 1:128:3; cf. 1:173:3b; 5:30:11), a "great steer" (*RV* 1:146:2), a "steer of men" (*RV* 1:149:2), as "the strong-necked steer, waxing in vigor" (*RV* 5:2:12), as "steer of eternal law" (*RV* 5:12:1), as "a steer of brilliant splendor" (*RV* 5:28:4), as "the steer with triple horn, the life-bestower" (*RV* 5:43:13), as "the swift red-hued steer" (*RV* 6:8:1a), as "[t]he foremost spotted steer [who] has made the mornings shine, and yearning after strength sustains all things that be" (*RV* 9:83:3), and as the "adorable steer" (*RV* 10:3:4). In a stanza of hymn 58 of book 4, Agni is described this way: "Four are his horns, three are the feet that bear him; his heads are two, his hands are seven in number. Bound with triple bond the steer roars loudly; the mighty god has entered in to mortals" (*RV* 4:58:3). Those who pay homage to Agni are said to keep "the red steer's law eternal" (*RV* 5:12:6a; cf. 5:12:2b), while others rejoice "for the steer's impregnating contact" (*RV* 5:47:6b).

However, Brhaspati, the Hindu god of prayer and devotion and the personification of piety and religion, the offerer of prayers and sacrifices to the gods, is called "the steer of all the gods" (*RV* 4:50:6). He "does sacrifice with steers, steers that have many an excellence" (*RV* 1:139:10). Furthermore, Parjanya, the god of rain and thunder clouds, is described as "the steer [who] roars loudly in far-reaching courses" (*RV* 4:56:1b); later, Parjanya is said to have nursed "the wild steer," that is, the soma plant nurtured by the god of rain (*RV* 9:113:3). "The steer ... risen above the sky" is the moon (*RV* 9:85:9a).

Indra is directly addressed as "steer" (*RV* 5:33:2a; 6:32:4b; 8:53:8; 9:109:20), "mighty steer" (*RV* 6:45:22; 9:106:1; 10:54:4), "ever-youthful steer" (*RV* 8:53:7), as "a steer to him who longs for steers" (*RV* 6:35:26)—that is, a giver of cattle—and compared to "a thirsty steer who roams the deserts" (*RV* 5:35:1b). Indu, who is Indra, is called a "tawny steer" (cf. *RV* 9:5:9b; 9:19:3a; 9:27:6), "a most splendid steer" (*RV* 9:2:2), "the steer [who] took notice of the people's songs of praise" (*RV* 10:43:6), and the "steer of conquering might, of real vigor" (*RV* 9:44:3b).

Indra is the "over-comer of all conquering forces with his great steer-like power that has no limit" (*RV* 10:44:1). Indeed, "Indra is [the] kind lord; his steers have vigor; his cows are many with abundant offspring" (*RV* 3:36:5). Indra is said to possess "two red steers, seeking goodly pasture" (*RV* 6:27:7); he is "a steer to him who longs for steers" (*RV* 6:45:26), that is a giver of cattle. And Indra-Varuna, the chief Hindu god combined with the water god, are "mighty and very rich . . . steers" in whom are combined "all power and might" (*RV* 7:82:2). In hymn 41 of book 4, Indra-Varuna are asked to be "the lovers of [the] song, as steers who love the milch-cow" (*RV* 4:41:5).

Dyaus, the Hindu sky god, is called "the red steer [which] sends his thunder downward" (*RV* 5:58:6b). Nahusa, a well-known king, is called "a strong young steer" (*RV* 7:95:3a). The storm deities, the Maruts, are "[l]ike steers in rapid motion" (*RV* 5:52:3). The Asvins, the gods of sunrise and sunset, are as "excellent as steers" (*RV* 5:74:1). In other hymns they are addressed as steers and asked to accept the singer's hymns with favor (cf. *RV* 7:70:7; 70:71:6; 7:73:3). And Varuna, the god of water, the celestial ocean, law, and the underworld, is called a steer (cf. *RV* 10:65:7b). However, hymn 69 of book 5 declares, "There stand the three steers, splendid in their brightness, who fill the three world-bowls with genial moisture" (*RV* 5:69:2b). The three steers are Agni, terrestrial fire on earth; Vayu, wind in the firmament; and Surya, the sun in heaven. Together they fill the world with fertilizing rain.

Even soma is referred to as a "steer" (*RV* 9:38:1; 9:65:10; 9:75:5; 9:86:3, 19, 38; 9:97:40, 41), an overflowing steer (cf. *RV* 8:52:9; 9:19:4; 9:27:3; 9:70:9), a shining steer (cf. *RV* 9:25:3), a steer who "bellowing on his way . . . runs onward to the wooden vats" (*RV* 9:28:4), a "steer effused" (*RV* 9:29:1a; 9:37:1, 5; cf. 9:51:4), a "loud bellowing . . . steer" (*RV* 9:63:20; cf. 9:76:5), an "active steer" (*RV* 9:63:21), "a steer by luster" (*RV* 9:65:4), a "steer [who] goes roaring on his way" (*RV* 9:70:6), a "steer enriched with sweets" (*RV* 9:80:5), a "steer made beautiful" (*RV* 9:86:11), a "well-armed steer" (*RV* 9:86:12), a "tawny steer [who] has bellowed in the wooden vats" (*RV* 9:86:31a; cf. 9:86:44; 9:101:16), a "steer enrobed in milk" (*RV* 9:86:40), a "flying steer" (*RV* 9:86:43), a "steer for the steer" (*RV* 9:87:4), "protector" (*RV* 9:89:3), "steer of the triple height" (*RV* 9:90:2), "steer roaring unto steer" (*RV* 9:91:3), the "steer who dwells on mountains" (*RV* 9:95:4), "a steer well-knowing" (*RV* 9:96:7), "a steer who strives to gain his third form" (*RV* 9:96:18), "a steer to herds" (*RV* 9:96:20), a "steer with [a] thousand streams" (*RV* 9:108:8), and "steer of heaven" (*RV* 9:108:11) . One drop of soma is "steer strong and omniform" (*RV* 6:41:3); it is a "steer-strong juice" (*RV* 9:6:6). Hymn 64 of book 9 seems to summarize this point of view: "Soma, you are a splendid steer, a steer of god, with steer-like sway; you are a steer ordaining laws. Steer-strong your might is as a steer's, steer-strong your wood, steer-like your drink; a steer indeed, O steer, you are" (*RV* 9:64:1–2). Therefore, those who have "drunk the steer act like a steer; drinking of this that finds the light" (*RV* 9:108:2).

Heifer

If the steer represents strength, power, and fertility, then the heifer, a young female cow which has never had a calf, represents purity, vulnerability, and shame. In the HB (OT) Book of Genesis, the LORD enters into a covenant with Abram using, among other animals, a heifer three years old (cf. Gen 15:9); the heifer is cut into two pieces, and the LORD, represented by a smoking fire pot and a flaming torch (cf. Gen 15:17) passes between them, thus entering into solemn agreement with Abram. The heifer represents God's purity.

The same type of purity is displayed when the prophet Samuel is commissioned by the LORD to go to Bethlehem and anoint David as king of Israel. Samuel is afraid that King Saul, whom God has rejected, will hear about his trip and kill him. The LORD tells Samuel, "Take a heifer with you, and say, 'I have come to sacrifice to the LORD'" (1 Sam 16:b). The heifer not only represents the purity of Samuel's sacrifice, but it also represents the purity of the one he anoints as the next king of Israel: David.

The Rig Veda, too, understands the heifer to be a sign of purity. One hymn states, "All sweetness is collected in the heifer, sweetness which Indra made for . . . enjoyment" (*RV* 3:30:14). And another hymn in honor of Agni, the god of fire, states that he receives the sacrifice of "a thousand heifers" (*RV* 10:69:7).

The HB (OT) Book of Numbers provides a detailed explanation of how the Israelites are to remove the impurity caused by contact with a human corpse. In order for the person to regain purity, the LORD instructs Moses and Aaron: "Tell the Israelites to bring you a red heifer without defect, in which there is no blemish and on which no yoke has been laid" (Num 19:2).

Zebu (Cattle, Bull, Cow, Steer, Heifer, Calf)

It is taken outside the camp where it is slaughtered. Its blood, represented by the red color of the heifer, is a very powerful purifying agent in biblical tradition, so the priest sprinkles it seven times towards the front of the tent of meeting. Then the heifer is to be burned in his sight (cf. Num 19:5) along with other items associated with purification, namely, cedar wood, hyssop, and crimson material (cf. Num 19:6). Once the heifer is burned, someone who is clean gathers the ashes of the heifer (cf. Num 19:9) and deposits them outside the camp to be kept to be mixed with water in order to remove the impurity of corpse contamination which lasts for seven days. A person who touches a corpse is sprinkled with the ashes and water mixture on the third and seventh days (cf. Num 19:12). The Letter to the Hebrews in the CB (NT) makes a direct reference to the ritual when the author states that if "the sprinkling of the ashes of a heifer" could sanctify "those who have been defiled so that their flesh is purified, how much more does "the blood of Christ . . . purify . . . conscience from dead works to worship the living God" (Heb 9:13–14). In other words, if a heifer's ashes mixed with water could purify those who had touched a corpse when sprinkled upon them, Jesus' blood purifies everyone for all time. McKenzie, commenting on the ritual described in the Book of Numbers, states, "The ashes are a kind of focus of uncleanness; they render unclean all persons involved in the slaying and burning of the animal and the gathering of the ashes and the sprinkling of the water of impurity, but they cleanse the objects and persons upon which the water is sprinkled."[17] Patton states: "Through sacrifice the animal becomes 'somebody'; it has religious and therefore social identity. In a sense, sacrifice makes the victim 'real.'"[18]

While not indicating that the ritual is designed to remove impurity because of contact with a corpse, *The Quran* mentions the sacrifice of a cow or heifer. Some translations use the word "cow" and some use the word "heifer." In chapter 2, named "The Cow" or "The Heifer," the author says:

> Remember, when Moses said to his people: "God demands that you sacrifice a cow [heifer]," they said: "Are you making fun of us?" And he said: "God forbid that I be of the ignorant." "Call on your Lord for us," they said, "that he might inform us what kind she should be." "Neither old nor young, says God, but of age in between," answered Moses. "So do as you are bid." "Call on your Lord," they said, "to tell us the color of the cow [heifer]." "God says," answered Moses, "a fawn colored cow [heifer], rich yellow, well pleasing to the eye." "Call on your Lord," they said,

---

17. McKenzie, *Dictionary*, 723.
18. Patton, "Animal Sacrifice," 398.

"to name its variety, as cows [heifers] be all alike to us. If God wills we shall be guided aright." And Moses said: "He says it's a cow [heifer] unyoked, nor worn out by plowing or watering the field, one in good shape with no mark or blemish." "Now have you brought us to the truth," they said; and then, after wavering, they sacrificed the cow [heifer]. (*Quran* 2:67–71)

The HB (OT) Book of Deuteronomy prescribes a similar ritual designed to remove the impurity of finding a body lying in the open country. The elders of the town nearest the body are to take a heifer that has never been yoked and bring her to a wadi with running water, where they break the heifer's neck. Then, all the elders of that town nearest the body wash their hands over the heifer, declaring that they did not shed the blood of the dead person (cf. Deut 21:3–4, 6–8).

Aesop narrates one fable about a heifer intended for sacrifice. Seeing an ox plowing, a heifer sympathizes with him in a patronizing way about the necessity of hard work. During a festival, the ox was turned loose into a pasture, but "the heifer was seized and led off to sacrifice."[19] The ox with a smile says to himself that he understands why the heifer enjoyed such an easy life, namely, that she was always intended for the altar.

In the HB (OT) Book of Judges, Samson tells the Philistines that if they "had not plowed with [his] heifer, [they] would not have found out [his] riddle" (Judg 14:18). Here, heifer is a synonym for wife; Samson's wife, a Philistine, betrayed him to his enemies by coaxing them to give her the answer to one of his riddles which she passed on to his enemies. Thus, the heifer represents the vulnerability of Samson's wife and her shame.

It is also found in the prophet Jeremiah, who couples it with the concept of shame. Jeremiah declares, "A beautiful heifer is Egypt; Egypt shall be put to shame" (Jer 46: 20a, 24a) because she did not come to Israel's help during the final siege of Jerusalem by the Babylonian King Nebuchadnezzar. The prophet adds that those who plunder Israel frisk about like a heifer on the grass (cf. Jer 50:11b); their "mother shall be utterly shamed, and she who bore you shall be disgraced" (Jer 50:12). In other words, Babylon's enemy, the Persians, will one day defeat her.

The prophet Hosea also uses a heifer to illustrate vulnerability and shame. He writes, "Like a stubborn heifer, Israel is stubborn" (Hos 4:16); the northern kingdom of Israel has become vulnerable to idolatry and is steeped in shame before God. Likewise, Hosea records God stating, "Ephraim was a trained heifer that loved to thresh, and I spared her fair neck; but I will make Ephraim break the ground" (Hos 10:11). Ephraim, another name for Israel,

---

19. Aesop, 144.

was once a docile people God chose and protected, but the nation turned to idols. Now, according to the LORD, the once-spared heifer will be yoked and made to furrow the earth. In other words, Israel will be punished for her vulnerability to idolatry, and she will be shamed.

In *The Rig Veda*, the heifer represents weakness when compared with the bull. In hymn 18 of book 4, the verse states: "The heifer has brought forth the strong, the mighty, the unconquerable bull, the furious Indra. The mother left her unlicked calf to wander, seeking himself, the path that he would follow" (*RV* 4:18:10). The weak heifer refers to Aditi, the young mother of the strong god Indra. Aditi is the celestial mother of every existing form, the synthesis of all things, primal substance. Using the image of a cow licking her calf clean after birth, the singer states that Aditi left Indra unlicked to make his own way to the greatness that is his. Using a similar metaphor, hymn 111 of book 10 states, "to the kine came the bull; the heifer's offspring with mighty bellowing has he arisen, and has pervaded even the spacious regions" (*RV* 10:111:2). The bull is Indra; the heifer is Aditi, Indra's mother. The heifer's offspring, Indra, is stronger than his goddess mother; thus heifer represents weakness when compared to bull.

Calf

All that remains in this zebu entry of cattle, bull, cow, steer, and heifer is calf. Calf can refer either to a young bull or cow; thus, it is a generic word describing the offspring of a bull and a cow. The calf is often romanticized in culture to represent child-like innocence. For example, the psalmist sings about God's voice using the image of thunder: "The voice of the LORD . . . breaks the cedars of Lebanon. He makes Lebanon skip like a calf . . . "(Ps 29:5–6a). The prophet Isaiah, too, views world peace as a time when "the calf and the lion and the fatling [would lie down] together" (Isa 11:6). This same idea is echoed two times in *Mormon* (cf. 2 Ne 21:6; 30:12).

The Rig Veda also loves the image of "a cow beside her calf" (*RV* 1:32:9), "the mother close unto her calf" (*RV* 1:110:8; cf. 1:111:1), the "cow full of pasture turn[ing] . . . to her calf" (*RV* 2:16:18), united "as a calf with mother kine" (*RV* 9:104:2) or "as a calf with mother cows" (*RV* 9:105:2), and "a cow hasten[ing] to her calf" (*RV* 10:145:6). *The Rig Veda* also employs the image of a mother cow strengthening her calf (cf. *RV* 9:61:14; 3:41:5) "like milch-kine who seek their calf with milk" (*RV* 9:86:2). "A young calf [rushes] to the udder of its dam" (*RV* 9:69:1), while "the mother stands, the youngling, loosed, is feeding" (*RV* 10:27:14a).

The other image used by the *Rig Veda* to portray the innocence of the calf is the mother licking her offspring (cf. *RV* 3:55:14). In hymn 33 of book 3, two rivers are "like two bright mother cows who lick their youngling" (*RV* 3:33:1). "Licking as 'twere their calf the pair of mothers flow onward . . ." continues the hymn (*RV* 3:33:3). In a similar vein another hymn sings of "two full mother cows [which] lick their youngling" (*RV* 7:2:5). "[I]n the morning of its life, the mothers lick the new-born calf" (*RV* 9:100:1) and "as cows . . . lick the new-born calf" (*RV* 9:100:7) are used in the same hymn.

Other tender images of the calf include the cow's pregnancy. The cow calves and never miscarries, states Job (cf. Job 21:10). The hymns in *The Rig Veda* tell about "barren cows, [which] with bullocks" result in "kine in calf" (*RV* 2:7:5), "here one and here another calf" (*RV* 8:59:14), and "the cow's offspring" (*RV* 7:35:14).

Another tender image is the loud lowing (cf. *RV* 10:27:14b) made by calves. In hymn 38 of book 1, the lightning is compared to "a cow . . . [which] lows and follows, mother-like, her youngling, when [the] rain-flood has been loosened" (*RV* 1:38:8). In hymn 164 of the same book, the stanza states that "the calf lowed, and looked upon the mother, the cow" (*RV* 1:164:9). The mother cow comes "yearning in spirit for her calf and lowing" (*RV* 1:164:27). *The Rig Veda* also states "the cows seek the stall to meet the lowing calf that longs for milk" (*RV* 8:43:17). Hymn 119 of book 10 portrays Indra declaring, "The hymn has reached me, like a cow [which] lows to meet her darling calf" (*RV* 10:119:4). The beauty of the pregnant cow giving birth to her calf and lowing is summarized in hymn 164 of book 1: "The cow has lowed after her blinking youngling; she licks his forehead, as she lows, to form it. His mouth she fondly calls to her warm udder, and suckles him with milk while gently lowing" (*RV* 1:164:28).

Of the god Agni in the form of lightning, one hymn states, "Wandering here the radiant calf finds none to fetter him" (*RV* 8:61:5). However, a calf needs to be trained, as the Hebrew prophet Jeremiah portrays the LORD rehearsing Ephraim's (Israel's) line: "You disciplined me, and I took the discipline; I was like a calf untrained" (Jer 31:18). Calves are trained with cords (cf. *RV* 2:28:6; 7:86:5) and stalls where "the milch-cow feeds her calf" (*RV* 2:34:8). They are "led by the ear" (*RV* 8:59:15).

In biblical literature, a calf can be eaten as veal. Abraham chooses a calf, tender and good, and gives it to his servant to prepare for his three visitors (cf. Gen 18:7). After King Saul consults a medium, "the woman had a fatted calf in the house [which] she quickly slaughtered" and prepared for the king and his men (1 Sam 28:24). However, the most famous account of a fatted calf is found in the CB (NT) Gospel According to Luke. In the parable commonly known as the prodigal son, when the son returns to his father, the father kills the fatted calf for the feast celebrating his son's return (cf. Luke 15:23, 27, 31). In the ancient world, the fatted calf could be kept on the first floor of the house because people lived on the second floor, or it was raised in a stall (cf. 1 Ne 22:24; 3 Ne 25:2). It was an animal kept for a special occasion, when it was killed and eaten.

On the eighth day of the consecration of Aaron and his sons as priests, the LORD instructs Moses to take a bull calf for a sin offering without blemish and offer it to God for Aaron, his sons, and the elders of the people (cf. Lev 9:2). The people of Israel are instructed to take a calf, a yearling without blemish, for a burnt offering (cf. Lev 9:3). After slaughtering the calf, Aaron takes its blood and puts some on the horns of the altar and pours out the rest at the base of the altar. Then, he does the same with the people's burnt offering (cf. Lev 9:8–17). The prophet Jeremiah alludes to the fact that calves were often used in covenant-making ceremonies where they were cut in two and the parties pass between their parts indicating that if either breaks the covenant, what happened to the sacrificed calves would happen to the person who breaks the covenant (cf. Jer 34:18–19).

Patton narrates a tale from the Talmud about a rabbi who encounters "a calf on its way to kosher slaughter."[20] It broke away and attempted to hide under the rabbi's clothes, lowing in terror, but the rabbi was unmoved and directed that it proceed to slaughter. Patton states:

> The calf's breaking away from restraint and seeking refuge under the skirts of a great religious authority transforms it from an anonymous food source into an individual. The calf becomes a religious "person," specifically, a supplicant in relationship with another religious person—an arbiter, a potential source of mercy.[21]

She continues, stating that "the principle of sacrifice is one of elevation and individuation of the victim."[22] Ritual killing looks like the negation of life, but this is a way "of mimicking the gods' undying, unchanging state," states Patton.[23] "Sacrifice changes the animal not into a state of death, but into a state of deathlessness."[24] A metamorphosis takes place; the sacrificed calf becomes like the gods, not perishable, eternal. This is why baby cattle, calves, were used in Israelite rituals.

20. Patton, "Animal Sacrifice," 398.
21. Ibid., 399.
22. Ibid.
23. Ibid.
24. Ibid.

However, in all of biblical literature it is the golden calf story that is narrated over and over again and alluded to many times. The story begins in the HB (OT) Book of Exodus. Moses is delayed on Mount Sinai (Horeb), and the Israelites begin to panic. So, Aaron collects their objects of gold, melts the gold, pours it into a mold, "and cast an image of a calf" (Exod 32:4); the people declare the calf to be their god and begin to worship it. Before Moses leaves the mountain to return to the people, the LORD tells him that the people have cast for themselves an image of a calf, and have worshiped it and sacrificed to it (cf. Exod 32:8). God is ready to destroy the people, but Moses pleads with and convinces him not to do it. When he gets back to the camp and sees the calf and the dancing (cf. Exod 32:19), he throws down the tablets of the law, takes "the calf that they had made, burned it with fire, ground it to powder, scattered it on the water, and made the Israelites drink it" (Exod 32:20). Next, Moses questions Aaron, who tells him that he collected the gold and threw it into the fire and out came the calf (cf. Exod 32:24). Later, the LORD sends a plague on the people, because they made the calf (cf. Exod 32:35).

In the HB (OT) Book of Deuteronomy, Moses recounts how the people had cast for themselves an image of a calf (cf. Deut 9:16) and how he took "the calf, and burned it with fire and crushed it, grinding it thoroughly, until it was reduced to dust; and [he] threw the dust of it into the stream that [ran] down the mountain" (Deut 9:21). On a day of communal penance, Nehemiah remembers the story of how the people had cast an image of a calf for themselves (cf. Neh 9:18). Even Psalm 106 recounts how the people "made a calf at Horeb and worshiped a cast image" (Ps 106:19). In the CB (NT), Stephen, one of those men chosen by the apostles to wait on tables, remembers the Israelites' unwillingness to obey the God who had brought them out of Egypt. He says, "At that time they made a calf, offered a sacrifice to the idol, and reveled in the works of their hands" (Acts 7:41).

After the kingdom of Israel separated from the kingdom of Judah in 930 BCE, the first king of Israel, Jeroboam I, established the worship of the golden calf at Bethel and Dan which brought about a religious schism between the two Israelite realms. This provokes the prophet Hosea, referring to Samaria, the capital of the northern kingdom of Israel, to state, "Your calf is rejected, O Samaria. The calf of Samaria shall be broken to pieces" (Hos 8:5a, 6b). "The inhabitants of Samaria tremble for the calf . . . . Israel shall be ashamed of his idol" (Hos 10:5a, 6b). Later, Hosea adds that the people of Israel "keep on sinning and make a cast image for themselves, idols of silver made according to their understanding, all of them the work of artisans. 'Sacrifice to these,' they say. People are kissing calves!" (Hos 13:2)

The OT (A) Book of Tobit begins with Tobit recounting his youth in the land of Israel and how his whole tribe deserted the house of David and Jerusalem. He writes: "All my kindred and our ancestral house of Naphtali sacrificed to the calf that King Jeroboam of Israel had erected in Dan and on all the mountains of Galilee" (Tob 1:5).

The worship of a golden calf also made its way into the Mormon Church. In a revelation he received on January 19, 1841, Joseph Smith writes that a certain Almon Babbitt has set up "a golden calf for the worship of [God's] people" (D&C 107:27). However, nothing else is said or written about it.

Aesop narrates one short fable about "The Bull and the Calf." As a fully grown bull is struggling to get through the barn door and into his stall, a young calf offers to show him how to get in. The bull, amused, says to the calf, "I knew that way before you were born."[25] The fable demonstrates the wisdom of age over the folly of youth.

Grimm's Complete Fairy Tales contains a story titled "The Little Farmer" which illustrates trickery, on the part of the farmer and his wife, and idiocy, on the part of the herder. In a certain village, there lived many rich farmers, but only one poor one, who did not even have a cow. However, the little farmer has the idea to have his wife's godfather make "a calf of wood and paint it brown, so as to look just like any other; and then in time perhaps it [would] grow big and become a cow."[26] The farmer's wife's godfather was a joiner, so he made a calf "with its head down and neck stretched out as if it were grazing."[27] The next morning, as the herder was driving all the other cows of the village to pasture, the farmer presented his calf and told the drover that he would have to carry it to the pasture. So, the drover "tucked it under his arm, carried it into the meadows, and stood it in the grass [, where it] stayed where it was put, and seemed to be eating all the time."[28]

When evening came, the drover told the calf either to walk back to the farmer or to remain where it was standing. However, the farmer saw the cow herder returning without his calf and asked him about it. The drover told the farmer that he had called it, but it had decided to remain where it was. Both went looking for it in the fields, but they could not find it; the farmer concluded that someone had stolen it, while the drover concluded that it had run away! The farmer brought the cow herder before the bailiff,

---

25. Aesop, 147.
26. Grimm, 13.
27. Ibid.
28. Ibid.

"who ordered him for his carelessness to give the Little Farmer a cow for the missing calf."[29]

Now that the farmer and his wife have a cow, they need fodder, but they are too poor to buy any, and they must kill the cow, sell the meat and skin, and, hopefully, make enough money to buy another cow. While trying to sell the hide, the farmer rescues a raven with a broken wing and, after it begins to storm, seeks shelter in the miller's house, where he tricks the miller's wife into feeding him and the miller into giving him three hundred dollars which he uses to his benefit. As he prospered, the other farmers wondered how he had done so well; he told them that he had sold his calf skin for three hundred dollars. "When the other farmers heard this, they wished to share such good luck, and ran home, killed all their cows, [and] skinned them in order to sell them also for the same high price . . . ."[30] However, the farmer had tricked them, and they were only offered three dollars per skin. When they tried to kill him, he tricked a shepherd into taking his place. Thus, the farmer ended up with a flock a sheep. When the villagers wanted sheep, too, he directed them to jump into the lake to fetch the sheep that were merely reflections of the clouds in the blue sky. All were drowned in the water, and the Little Farmer became a rich man as a trickster.

Thus, zebu have been explored as cattle, bulls, cows, steers, heifers, and calves. The importance of the zebu—or any bovine—can be seen in the many words used to describe its various forms. Cattle form a herd led by a herder, who may take them to and from pasture. They can be used to count one's wealth, and, of course, are frequently offered as sacrifice to God. The male cow, the bull, represents strength and fertility; sacrificing a bull demonstrates a person's dependence on God. Except in Hinduism where the cow is considered the sum of all things, in most cultures the cow is revered as a sacred mother which feeds her young and others with milk. Many Hindu gods are compared to cows. The young bull, known as a steer, represents strength, power, and fertility. Many Hindu gods are called steers; even the sacred soma drink, because of its strength, is identified frequently as a steer. The young cow, known as a heifer, represents purity, vulnerability, and shame. Finally, the calf, the generic name for either a young steer or heifer or both, stands for innocence, peace, and tenderness. A calf can also be used in sacrifice. The zebu understood as cattle, bull, steer, heifer, and calf is, indeed, a sacred animal offering a variety of spiritual characteristics worthy of imitation.

29. Ibid.
30. Ibid., 16.

Zebu (Cattle, Bull, Cow, Steer, Heifer, Calf)

Journal/Meditation: What does a herd of cattle seen along the road mean to you? Do you recognize strength in the bull, mothering in the cow, power in the steer, purity in the heifer, and innocence in the calf? What spiritual virtue of cattle is easiest for you to imitate?

Prayer: Ever-living LORD, God of Israel, you decreed that the cattle you created be offered in sacred sacrifice to you to demonstrate that everything belongs to you and is dependent upon you for life. Give me the strength of the bull, the gentleness of the cow, the power of the steer, the purity of the heifer, and the innocence of the calf so that I may never cease to praise you for your wisdom. Hear my prayer in the name of Jesus Christ, your Son, who lives and reigns with you and the Holy Spirit, one God, forever and ever. Amen.

Bibliography

Aesop's Fables. Translated by V.S. Vernon Jones. New York: Avenel, 1912.

Anderson, E.N., and Lisa Raphals. "Daoism and Animals." In *A Communion of Subjects: Animals in Religion, Science, and Ethics*, edited by Paul Waldau and Kimberley Patton, 275–90. New York: Columbia University Press, 2006.

Apostolos-Cappadona, Diane. "On the *Dynamis* of Animals, or How *Animalium* Became *Anthropos*." In *A Communion of Subjects: Animals in Religion, Science, and Ethics*, edited by Paul Waldau and Kimberley Patton, 439–57. New York: Columbia University Press, 2006.

Berry, Thomas. "Prologue: Loneliness and Presence." In *A Communion of Subjects: Animals in Religion, Science, and Ethics*, edited by Paul Waldau and Kimberley Patton, 5–10. New York: Columbia University Press, 2006.

Blenkinsopp, Joseph. "Deuteronomy." In *The New Jerome Biblical Commentary*, edited by Raymond E. Brown, Joseph A. Fitzmyer, and Roland E. Murphy, 94–109. Englewood Cliffs, NJ: Prentice Hall, 1990.

Book of Doctrine and Covenants, The. Independence, MO: Reorganized Church of Jesus Christ of Latter Day Saints, 1947.

Book of Mormon, The. Translated by Joseph Smith. Salt Lake City, UT: The Church of Jesus Christ of Latter-Day Saints, 1976.

Bradley, Sculley, Richmond Croom Beatty, and E. Hudson Long, eds. "Edgar Allen Poe." In *The American Tradition in Literature: Volume 1*. New York: W.W. Norton, 1967.

Bryant, Edwin. "Strategies of Vedic Subversion: The Emergence of Vegetarianism in Post-Vedic India." In *A Communion of Subjects: Animals in Religion, Science, and Ethics*, edited by Paul Waldau and Kimberley Patton, 194–203. New York: Columbia University Press, 2006.

Bulfinch, Thomas. *Bulfinch's Mythology*. New York: Crown, 1979.

Carola, Robert. "Paul Bunyan." In *American Folktales, Myths, Legends*, edited by Leslie Conron, 184–87. New York: Madison Park, 2009.

Cavendish, Richard, ed. *Legends of the World*. New York: Barnes & Noble, 1994.

Chapple, Christopher. "Inherent Value without Nostalgia: Animals and the Jaina Tradition." In *A Communion of Subjects: Animals in Religion, Science, and Ethics*, edited by Paul Waldau and Kimberley Patton, 241–49. New York: Columbia University Press, 2006.

Conron, Leslie, ed. *American Folktales, Myths, Legends*. New York: Madison Park, 2009.

Consolmagno, Guy. "Sci-fi Guy." *U. S. Catholic* 80:3 (2015) 35–38.

Doniger, Wendy. "A Symbol in Search of an Object: The Mythology of Horses in India." In *A Communion of Subjects: Animals in Religion, Science, and Ethics*, edited by Paul Waldau and Kimberley Patton, 335-50. New York: Columbia University Press, 2006.

Doctrine and Covenants of The Church of Jesus Christ of Latter-day Saints Containing Revelations Given to Joseph Smith, the Prophet, with Some Additions by His Successors in the Presidency of the Church, The. www.lds.org.

"Easter Proclamation (*Exsultet*), The." In *The Roman Missal*. Collegeville, MN: Liturgical, 2011.

Eicher-Catt, Deborah. "Signs of Sacred Play: Musings on the Semiotics of Rainbows." *Listening: Journal of Communication Ethics, Religion, and Culture* 48:3 (2013) 224-39.

Foltz, Richard. "'This She-camel of God is a Sign to You': Dimensions of Animals in Islamic Tradition and Muslim Culture." In *A Communion of Subjects: Animals in Religion, Science, and Ethics*, edited by Paul Waldau and Kimberley Patton, 149-59. New York: Columbia University Press, 2006.

Francke, A.H. *Antiquities of Indian Tibet*. New Delhi, India: S. Chand, 1972.

Griffin, Donald. "From Cognition to Consciousness." In *A Communion of Subjects: Animals in Religion, Science, and Ethics*, edited by Paul Waldau and Kimberley Patton, 481-504. New York: Columbia University Press, 2006.

Grim, John. "Knowing and Being Known by Animals: Indigenous Perspectives on Personhood." In *A Communion of Subjects: Animals in Religion, Science, and Ethics*, edited by Paul Waldau and Kimberley Patton, 373-90. New York: Columbia University Press, 2006.

Grimm's Complete Fairy Tales. Garden City, NY: Nelson Doubleday, not dated.

Harris, Ian. "'A Vast Unsupervised Recycling Plant': Animals and the Buddhist Cosmos." In *A Communion of Subjects: Animals in Religion, Science, and Ethics*, edited by Paul Waldau and Kimberley Patton, 207-17. New York: Columbia University Press, 2006.

Harris, Joel Chandler, "How Mr. Rabbit was Too Sharp for Mr. Fox." In *American Folktales, Myths, Legends*, edited by Leslie Conron, 175-78. New York: Madison Park, 2009.

"Heron and the Turtle, The." www.mesopotamiangods.com/the-heron-and-the-turtle-translation/.

Holy Bible, The, Translated from The Latin Vulgate: Diligently Compared with The Hebrew, Greek, and Other Editions in Divers Languages. Philadelphia: John E. Potter, 1748.

"How the Indians Obtained Dogs." www.calverley.ca.

Jacobs, Joseph. "The Story of the Three Little Pigs." In *The Annotated Classic Fairy Tales*, edited by Maria Tatar, 206-11. New York: W.W. Norton, 2002.

Kassam, Zayn. "The Case of the Animals Versus Man: Toward An Ecology of Being." In *A Communion of Subjects: Animals in Religion, Science, and Ethics*, edited by Paul Waldau and Kimberley Patton, 160-69. New York: Columbia University Press, 2006.

Kemmerer, Lisa. *Animals and World Religions*. New York: Oxford University Press, 2012.

Kienzle, Beverly. "The Bestiary of Heretics: Imaging Medieval Christianity Heresy with Insects and Animals." In *A Communion of Subjects: Animals in Religion, Science, and Ethics*, edited by Paul Waldau and Kimberley Patton, 103–16. New York: Columbia University Press, 2006.

Kleber, Albert. *History of St. Meinrad Archabbey 1854–1954*. St. Meinrad, IN: Grail, 1954.

Lawrence, Elizabeth. "Hunting the Wren: A Sacred Bird in Ritual." In *A Communion of Subjects: Animals in Religion, Science, and Ethics*, edited by Paul Waldau and Kimberley Patton, 406–12. New York: Columbia University Press, 2006.

Littleton, C. Scott, ed. *Mythology: The Illustrated Anthology of World Myth and Storytelling*. London: Duncan Baird, 2002.

Mackenzie, R.A.F., and Roland E. Murphy. "Job." In *The New Jerome Biblical Commentary*, edited by Raymond E. Brown, Joseph A. Fitzmyer, and Roland E. Murphy, 466–88. Englewood Cliffs, NY: Prentice Hall, 1990.

McGinnis, Claire Mathews. "Job's Dialogue with God: Coming to Terms with an Untamed World." *The Bible Today* 53:2 (2015) 87–92.

McKenzie, John L. *Dictionary of the Bible*. Milwaukee: Bruce, 1965.

Mortensen, Eric. "Raven Augury from Tibet to Alaska: Dialects, Divine Agency, and the Bird's-Eye View." In *A Communion of Subjects: Animals in Religion, Science, and Ethics*, edited by Paul Waldau and Kimberley Patton, 421–36. New York: Columbia University Press, 2006.

"Native American Culture." www.cultureofnativeamericans.weebly.com.

"Native American Legends: Two Wolves." www.firstpeople.us.

Nelson, Lance. "Cows, Elephants, Dogs, and Other Lesser Embodiments of Atman: Reflections on Hindu Attitudes Toward Nonhuman Animals." In *A Communion of Subjects: Animals in Religion, Science, and Ethics*, edited by Paul Waldau and Kimberley Patton, 179–93. New York: Columbia University Press, 2006.

New American Bible, The. Washington, DC: Confraternity of Christian Doctrine, 1970.

New American Bible Revised Edition, The. Washington, DC: Confraternity of Christian Doctrine, 2010.

O'Day, Gail R., and David Peterson, eds. *The Access Bible: New Revised Standard Version with the Apocryphal/Deuterocanonical Books*. New York: Oxford University Press, 1999.

Official King James Bible Online, The. www.kingjamesbiblieonline.org.

Opoku, Kofi. "Animals in African Mythology." In *A Communion of Subjects: Animals in Religion, Science, and Ethics*, edited by Paul Waldau and Kimberley Patton, 351–59. New York: Columbia University Press, 2006.

Paper, Jordan. "Humans and Animals: The History from a Religio-Ecological Perspective." In *A Communion of Subjects: Animals in Religion, Science, and Ethics*, edited by Paul Waldau and Kimberley Patton, 325–32. New York: Columbia University Press, 2006.

Patton, Kimberley. "'Caught with Ourselves in the Net of Life and Time': Traditional Views of Animals in Religion." In *A Communion of Subjects: Animals in Religion, Science, and Ethics*, edited by Paul Waldau and Kimberley Patton, 27–39. New York: Columbia University Press, 2006.

———. "Animal Sacrifice: Metaphysics of the Sublimated Victim." In *A Communion of Subjects: Animals in Religion, Science, and Ethics*, edited by Paul Waldau and Kimberley Patton, 391–405. New York: Columbia University Press, 2006.

Pelikan, Jaroslav, ed. *Sacred Writings, Volume 3, Islam: The Quran*. Translated by Ahmed Ali. New York: Book-of-the-Month Club, 1992.

———. *Sacred Writings, Volume 4, Confucianism: The Analects of Confucius*. Translated by Arthur Waley. New York: Book-of-the-Month Club, 1992.

———. *Sacred Writings, Volume 5, Hinduism: The Rig Veda*. Translated by Ralph T.H. Griffith. New York: Book-of-the-Month Club, 1992.

———. *Sacred Writings, Volume 6, Buddhism: The Dhammapada*. Translated by John Ross Carter, Mahinda Palihawadana. New York: Book-of-the-Month Club, 1992.

Roman Missal, The. Collegeville, MN: Liturgical, 2011.

Rounds, Glen. "Babe the Mighty Blue Ox." In *American Folktales, Myths, Legends*, edited by Leslie Conron, 188–89. New York: Madison Park, 2009.

Schimmel, Anemarie. *Rumi*. New Delhi, India: Oxford University Press, 2014.

Sheldrake, Philip. *Spirituality: A Very Short Introduction*. Oxford: Oxford University Press, 2012.

Skinner, Charles M. "The Enchanted Horse." In *American Folktales, Myths, Legends*, edited by Leslie Conron, 18–22. New York: Madison Park, 2009.

———. "How the Black Horse Was Beaten." In *American Folktales, Myths, Legends*, edited by Leslie Conron, 134–36. New York: Madison Park, 2009.

Smith, Bertha H. "Yosemite: Large Grizzly Bear." In *American Folktales, Myths, Legends*, edited by Leslie Conron, 23–28. New York: Madison Park, 2009.

Sterckx, Roel. "'Of a Tawny Bull We Make Offering:' Animals in Early Chinese Religion." In *A Communion of Subjects: Animals in Religion, Science, and Ethics*, edited by Paul Waldau and Kimberley Patton, 259–72. New York: Columbia University Press, 2006.

"Story of the Three Bears, The." In *The Annotated Classic Fairy Tales*, edited by Maria Tatar, 245–52. New York: W.W. Norton, 2002.

Tatar, Maria, ed. *The Annotated Classic Fairy Tales*. New York: W.W. Norton, 2002.

Taylor, Rodney. "Of Animals and Humans: The Confucian Perspective." In *A Communion of Subjects: Animals in Religion, Science, and Ethics*, edited by Paul Waldau and Kimberley Patton, 293–307. New York: Columbia University Press, 2006.

Twain, Mark. "The Notorious Jumping Frog of Calaveras County." In *American Folktales, Myths, Legends*, edited by Leslie Conron, 156–65. New York: Madison Park, 2009.

"Twelve Days of Christmas, The." www.carols.org.uk/the_twelve_days_of_christmas.htm.

Vargas, Ivette. "Snake-Kings, Boars' Heads, Deer Parks, Monkey Talk: Animals as Transmitters and Transformers in Indian and Tibetan Buddhist Narratives." In *A Communion of Subjects: Animals in Religion, Science, and Ethics*, edited by Paul Waldau and Kimberley Patton, 218–37. New York: Columbia University Press, 2006.

"Which One Do You Feed?" www.nativeamericanembassy.net.

Other Books by Mark G. Boyer

History of St. Joachim Parish: 1822—1972; 1723—1973

Day by Day through the Easter Season

Following the Star: Daily Reflections for Advent and Christmas

Mystagogy: Liturgical Paschal Spirituality for Lent and Easter

Return to the Lord: A Lenten Journey of Daily Reflections

The Liturgical Environment: What the Documents Say

Breathing Deeply of God's New Life: Preparing Spiritually for the Sacraments of Initiation

Mary's Day—Saturday: Meditations for Marian Celebrations

Why Suffer?: The Answer of Jesus

A Month-by-Month Guide to Entertaining Angels

Biblical Reflections on Male Spirituality

"Seeking Grace with Every Step": The Spirituality of John Denver

Home Is a Holy Place

Day by Ordinary Day with Mark

Day by Ordinary Day with Matthew

Day by Ordinary Day with Luke

Baptized into Christ's Death and Resurrection: Preparing to Celebrate a Christian Funeral: Vol. 1: Adults

Baptized into Christ's Death and Resurrection: Preparing to Celebrate a Christian Funeral: Vol. 2: Children

The Greatest Gift of All: Reflections and Prayers for the Christmas Season

Meditations for Ministers

Waiting in Joyful Hope: Reflections for Advent 2001

Filled with New Light: Reflections for Christmas 2001–2002

Lent and Easter Prayer at Home

Using Film to Teach New Testament

Other Books by Mark G. Boyer

Waiting in Joyful Hope: Daily Reflections for Advent and Christmas 2002–2003

Waiting in Joyful Hope: Daily Reflections for Advent and Christmas 2003–2004

The Liturgical Environment: What the Documents Say (second edition)

Reflections on the Rosary

When Day Is Done: Nighttime Prayers through the Church Year

Take Up Your Cross and Follow: Daily Lenten Reflections

These Thy Gifts: A Collection of Simple Meal Prayers

Day by Ordinary Day: Daily Reflections on the First Readings, Year One

Day by Ordinary Day: Daily Reflections on the First Readings, Year Two

Mountain Reflections: A Collection of Photos and Meditations

Nature Spirituality: Praying with Wind, Water, Earth, Fire

A Spirituality of Ageing

Caroling through Advent and Christmas

Weekday Saints: Reflections on Their Scriptures

Human Wholeness: A Spirituality of Relationship

The Liturgical Environment: What the Documents Say (third edition)

A Simple Systematic Mariology

Praying Your Way through Luke's Gospel and the Acts of the Apostles

www.ingramcontent.com/pod-product-compliance
Lightning Source LLC
Chambersburg PA
CBHW050342230426
43663CB00010B/1954